D0083403

FRANKLIN AND BACHE

In 1798, Federalists ridiculed editor Benjamin Franklin Bache and his fellow Jeffersonian Republicans for objecting to Adams administration policies in the undeclared naval war with France. George Washington, who was brought out of retirement to command American forces, is shown with his soldiers in this detail from *The Times: A Political Portrait*. James Madison obstructs the former president's carriage with his pen while Albert Gallatin and Thomas Jefferson (far right) attempt to stop the wheels of government. Bache is being trampled while a dog expresses the Federalist opinion of his newspaper, *The Aurora and General Advertiser*. (Reproduced with the permission of the New York Historical Society, New York City)

FRANKLIN
AND BACHE

Envisioning the
Enlightened Republic

JEFFERY A. SMITH

New York   Oxford
OXFORD UNIVERSITY PRESS
1990

Oxford University Press

Oxford New York Toronto
Delhi Bombay Calcutta Madras Karachi
Petaling Jaya Singapore Hong Kong Tokyo
Nairobi Dar es Salaam Cape Town
Melbourne Auckland

and associated companies in
Berlin Ibadan

Published by Oxford University Press, Inc.,
200 Madison Avenue, New York, New York 10016

Oxford is a registered trademark of Oxford University Press

Library of Congress Cataloging-in-Publication Data
Smith, Jeffery Alan.
Franklin and Bache: envisioning the enlightened republic/
Jeffery A. Smith.
p. cm.
ISBN 0-19-505676-0
1. Bache, Benjamin Franklin, 1769–1798. 2. Journalists—
United States—Biography. 3. Franklin, Benjamin, 1706–1790—
Family. 4. United States—Politics and government—
1783–1809. 5. Journalism—United States—History—
18th century. I. Title.
E302.6.B14S65 1990
973.3'092'2—dc20
[B]   89-26610   CIP

9 8 7 6 5 4 3 2 1

Printed in the United States of America
on acid-free paper

For Vincent and Claire

Acknowledgments

I WOULD LIKE TO ACKNOWLEDGE JOHN F. MURRAY RESEARCH FUNDS FROM the School of Journalism and Mass Communication at the University of Iowa, a developmental assignment from the University of Iowa, and the persistent efforts of my research assistants: Ralph Frasca, Kathie Hoxsie, Haeryon Kim, Joanna Werch, and Daniel Zinkand. I am particularly grateful to the staffs of the American Philosophical Society Library, the Franklin Papers at Yale University, and the University of Iowa Library where most of the research for this book was completed. I wish to thank the *Pennsylvania Magazine of History and Biography* for permission to incorporate portions of my October 1988 article, "The Enlightenment Education of Benjamin Franklin Bache," into this book. I sincerely appreciate the superb editing and production work of Valerie Aubry, Ellen Barrie, Marcia Carlson, Ellen Fuchs, Susan Meigs, Marion Osmun, and Niko Pfund at Oxford University Press. I thank my wife, Geneviève, for her translations of materials in French, and hope that my children, Vincent and Claire, will someday have the same pleasure in reading this book that I did in writing it. It is to both of them that this book is dedicated.

Contents

FRANKLIN
AND BACHE

Introduction

MUCH OF THE IMPETUS FOR CHANGE IN MODERN HISTORY CAN BE TRACED to a form of social consciousness which matured and unfolded in the Enlightenment. A common characteristic of the American and French Revolutions was the professed objective of humanity's liberation from oppression and deprivation. In the Declaration of Independence, the people were said to have a right to establish governments that seemed to them "most likely to effect their safety and happiness." The first of the king's "repeated injuries and usurpations" listed in that document was his refusal to "assent to laws the most wholesome and necessary for the public good."

Having found at least some degree of material well-being and self-determination before their rebellion, Americans saw less need for the kind of fierce change that characterized some later revolutions than for liberal alterations in societal structure and behavior, adjustments they believed would at once allow for individual autonomy, political equilibrium, and human progress. Doubts about the truth of divine revelation had not yet extended so far as to undermine moral idealism, and the resentment of economic differences did not produce plans for collectivist structures. Being created equal and having an inalienable right to pursue happiness could be considered simply natural, "self-evident" truths. Political equality did not have to mean exact economic equality, and personal happiness might not ever be achieved, but the opportunity to seek fulfillment as freely as possible was to be preserved.

The American Revolution did not promise a new, smoothly managed utopia so much as a new age in which citizens could work for their own benefit and the benefit of their communities. The appeal of Thomas Paine's phenomenally popular *Common Sense* lay in its spirited rejection of outworn hierarchies and its emotional evocation of beginning the world again. In recent decades, however, studies of eighteenth-century America have given increased attention to the more formal intellectual history of the nation's founding. Historians of early America have examined public and private discourse and have argued that the country's revolutionary republicanism was profoundly influenced by English Oppositionist ideology with its distrust of power and luxury and its stress on the importance of political independence and honest, industrious conduct. This set of principles in turn had its roots in antecedent versions of republican ideology.[1]

Yet, while usually deployed in standard political declamation by those out of power, classical republican ideology was abstract and elastic enough to be used by virtually any group.[2] Its doctrines included press freedom as a check on government,[3] as well as the notion that societies could avoid the dangers of party strife and corruption by cultivating civic virtue and selecting wise, independent leaders. In its emphasis on vigilance to preserve liberty, the ideology was largely preventative in nature and by itself cannot account for the revolutionary exhilaration of the final decades of the eighteenth century.[4]

Many Americans were both more opportunistic and more hopeful of overall human advancement than a focus on the suspicions and self-sacrifice of classical republicanism reveals.[5] Although there was a stress on selfless civic virtue not only in classical republicanism but also in religious thought and natural rights liberalism, Americans were seeking personal economic rewards through self-government and self-improvement in the late eighteenth century.[6] Also pulsating within the American experiment, particularly for the laboring classes striving to protect their interests,[7] was the belief that a more mutually supportive and egalitarian society could be created by the country at large. "The language of early American politics reflected the absorption of Enlightenment ideas as well as Oppositionist ones," Linda Kerber has observed, "and was reshaped by real people, who had to make real judgments, as they moved toward the liberal, individualist, capitalist compromise which we have come to know."[8]

The "real judgments" of a phenomenon as complex, wrenching,

and unpredictable as a rebellion should not be depicted as merely the outcome of systematic thought or the bloodless calculation of interests. Revolution is not so cool and predetermined, but rather is comprised, at its most fundamental level, of many decisions about what is tolerable and what is possible. As writings such as the Declaration of Independence and *Common Sense* suggested, the boundaries of what was tolerable had been crossed by 1776, and Americans now believed that their future lives and fortunes relied upon their virtuous resolve and what the Declaration of Independence called "the protection of Divine Providence." After winning the war, citizens of the United States felt they had entered a wonderfully promising new era in human affairs. In 1783, George Washington composed a letter to the state governors in which he expressed elation over the awareness that Americans were becoming the free, independent, and ultimately responsible possessors of a vast tract of land "abounding with all the necessaries and conveniencies of life." Using imagery customary to the patriot cause,[9] he wrote of Americans:

> They are, from this period, to be considered as the Actors on a most conspicuous Theatre, which seems to be peculiarly designated by Providence for the display of human greatness and felicity. . . . The foundation of our Empire was not laid in the gloomy age of Ignorance and Superstition, but at an Epocha when the rights of mankind were better understood and more clearly defined, than at any former period, the researches of the human mind, after social happiness, have been carried to a great extent. . . . At this auspicious period, the United States came into existence as a Nation, and if their Citizens should not be completely free and happy, the fault will be intirely their own.[10]

The constitutional design for the country's departure from authoritarian tradition did not emanate from a naive creed of human reason and perfectibility, but instead was founded on more empirical conceptions about the nature of individuals and institutions. The political science of Hume, Montesquieu, and Madison, relying on analysis of historical experience, taught that no one could be entirely trusted with authority, that not only did the people have to control government, but also that the government had to be constructed to control the individuals and factions seeking power for self-serving purposes.[11] The Constitution's limits on political participation and on government action thus can be interpreted both as a manifestation of the mistrust inherent in republican ideology and as an endorsement of liberal and egalitarian hopes. Property was to be protected and popular sovereignty was to be achieved, but political decision making was cushioned from the pressures of private ambition and majority will by the various branches, levels, and procedural mechanisms of government.

Although a considerable amount of recent scholarship examines the demonology of Anglo-American republicanism,[12] much work remains to be done on the more affirmative aspects of eighteenth-century thought. The word "Enlightenment" may be too nebulous for historians,[13] and the concept itself may seem too remote in the present era, but, like "republican" and "liberal," "enlightened" has the advantage of being a term that was actually part of eighteenth-century rhetoric. Enlightened thought can be defined broadly as those conceptions of the world which recognized the imperfect state of human affairs and advocated libertarian remedies. The categories of early American libertarianism that historians use and often disagree about— "republican," "liberal," and "egalitarian," for example[14]—were each concerned with improving the general condition of humanity and can be said to fit within the "Enlightenment."

The problem was then seen as the dismal condition of the majority of the world's people, and the solutions were believed to be knowledge, rights, and the more or less controlled release of human energy. To apply an analogy of Sir Lewis Namier's, the realities of this revolutionary age provided the underlying emotions, the music, while the mélange of opinions was mere libretto.[15] Ideas can certainly flow from history as much as history can emerge from ideas. An understanding of past mentalities requires a knowledge of common frustrations and aspirations.

Perhaps the most satisfactory method of recovering how Enlightenment perceptions influenced the political culture of early America is to study how such feelings affected "real people" making real decisions. While far from ordinary, two such people were Philadelphia printers, Benjamin Franklin and his grandson, Benjamin Franklin Bache. As journalists, Franklin and Bache were in the occupation of enlightenment. To them and to like-minded contemporaries, the press broke bonds of ignorance for lower orders of society and educated them in ways to prosper and to assert their rights. Facing growing economic inequality and social tensions in the eighteenth century,[16] however, such proponents of popular causes as Franklin and Bache could become incensed with the defenders of privilege and resort to caustic satire, personal invective, and propagandistic exaggeration.

Enlightenment sentiment—if understood as the celebration of a growth of knowledge and support for a wide range of societal reforms—was present in much of the journalism of eighteenth-century America.[17] Newspapers and pamphlets, after all, were the primary means of presenting ideas for public approval.[18] In addition to their own efforts to produce edifying reading material for public consumption, printers published European[19] and American writers who advocated concepts associated with human progress. Like many journalists in early America, Benjamin Franklin and Benjamin Franklin Bache incorporated multiple Enlightenment visions of society into their work. Franklin promoted republicanism, egalitarianism, and economic liberalism at a stately pace for nearly seventy years, while Bache presented a similar combination of libertarian views in the course of an intense, eight-year newspaper career.

For Franklin, of course, ideals were bound to clash with political demands as well as social and economic realities. A self-educated pragmatist,[20] Franklin found humor and patience useful as he pursued his Enlightenment goals as a writer and statesman. Throughout his life, he displayed caution about many of the major issues he faced. He preached tolerance and a respect for the common good and was distressed by the contentious style of journalism practiced in the new nation.

Bache, on the other hand, received strict training from his grandfather who supervised his education and guided him into the printing trade. Raised according to his grandfather's Enlightenment precepts, he was prepared to champion Franklinian causes and analyses whatever the cost. While Franklin's political communication was often conciliatory, Bache's lofty editorials grew increasingly strident as he took a leading role in the violent emergence of the party press in the 1790s. Old journalistic norms of classical republican impartiality and decency were withering as the course of the new, participatory government was debated and partisan fervor surged in the United States.

Both Franklin and Bache were among the press harbingers of the "Revolution of 1800"—the triumph of the Jeffersonian Republican coalition that espoused the combined Enlightenment ideals of self-

discipline, free trade, political equality, and benign, popular government. If the desire for change can arise as much from the heart as the
head, then some of the intangible influences of political culture and
more visceral responses of those who sought a transformation of their
society should be examined. This book is a dual biography of two
journalists who were among the Americans charting a vibrant moral
trajectory for the future of the republic.

CHAPTER 1

The Pursuit of the Common Good

Life in eighteenth-century America was radically reordered by new wealth and by a new, more participatory kind of politics. By the eve of the Revolution, white colonists had what was evidently the highest average income in the world and a rising gross economic output that was already approximately 40 percent of Britain's.[1] The gains were not evenly distributed, however. Gaps between the social classes were widening, particularly in northern cities where mansions were being built for the rich while almshouses and workhouses were being constructed for a growing population of the poor. In the early 1770s, the top 5 percent of taxpayers in Boston and Philadelphia held about half of the taxable assets in their communities. The lower half of society had approximately 3 to 5 percent of the total wealth.[2]

Such disparities—along with periodic unemployment and losses in real wages—spurred the middle and lower ranks of society to abandon traditional deference politics and to take an increasing role in governmental affairs.[3] In the decades prior to the Stamp Act, contending coalitions, seeking public support in forms ranging from voter turnout to mob actions, undermined respect for authority by publishing defamatory attacks on government officials and political adversaries.[4] Much of the rhetoric played on the economic frustrations of the majority of colonists.[5]

The inflaming of mass resentment against British policies eventually aided the cause of independence,[6] but by 1787 the "violence of faction," as James Madison described the competition of interests in

9

The Federalist No. 10, appeared to some to be endangering the stability of the country's popular governments. Madison noted complaints "that the public good is disregarded in the conflicts of rival parties; and that measures are too often decided, not according to the rules of justice, and the rights of the minor party; but by the superior force of an interested and over-bearing majority." Madison wrote that "the most common and durable source of factions, has been the various and unequal distribution of property" and that the "regulation of these various and interfering interests forms the principal task of modern Legislation, and involves the spirit of party and faction in the necessary and ordinary operations of Government."[7]

If a more just, stable, and widely prosperous political order was thought necessary in early America, then the role of the people was crucial. Libertarian writings were published to persuade the public not only to defend freedoms in line with classical republican fears, but also to support the notions of the common good associated with revolutionary egalitarianism as well as the incentives of private interest recognized by economic liberalism. Pamphlets or newspaper essays like the *Federalist* could sometimes be ambitious efforts to advocate a workable amalgamation of such principles. More often, eighteenth-century journalists used these schools of libertarian thought in a fragmented fashion, appearing more concerned with immediate issues than with building one all-encompassing philosophy.[8]

Not until the emergence of the Jeffersonian Republicans, it seems, did a truly comprehensive, integrated, and dynamic Enlightenment ideology become available to most Americans. Although traditional libertarian thought had advanced democratic principles, it was not firmly grounded in trust of the masses. Classical republicans might argue, as did the English journalists John Trenchard and Thomas Gordon in the 1720s, that individuals needed to place "the general Welfare" above personal happiness and that laws could be required to prevent some people from becoming "too rich" and thereby endangering equality and liberty. Yet at the same time the classical republicans might also have grave doubts about the judgment of the common person and the benefits of educating the populace. "Who are greater Rogues than Scholars, as they are called?" asked Trenchard and Gordon in *Cato's Letters*, a newspaper series highly esteemed in the colonies. "Nothing keeps the Herd of Mankind so honest, as breeding

them up to Industry, and keeping them always employed in Hard-
Labour."[9]

In the Jeffersonian view, however, the American people at large
would advance politically, economically, and socially with the proper
education, incentives, and environment. They could achieve a peaceful, comfortable, and intellectually satisfying life through their own
careful effort and compassionate conduct. The ideologies of Enlightenment libertarianism—which coalesced in the writings of the Jeffersonian Republicans—were aimed at improving the general well-being
of society in their own particular ways and at condemning the abuse
of power and privilege. Writers appealed to the minds of a new reading public, opposing both the oppression of the many by the few and
the few by the many. With its spirit of liberation and investigation,
the Enlightenment challenged the status quo by encouraging individuals to think for themselves and to be open to new understandings.
Thus the "Age of Reason" was more precisely both what Kant called
the "age of criticism"[10] and what Franklin termed "the Age of Experiments."[11] The Enlightenment republicanism of the Jeffersonians, a
product of frustrations with the past and of visions of a freer and more
equitable future, upheld the fundamental American belief that a people's good will and good deeds can alter the course of history.

I

Early American journalists often spoke of being committed to open
inquiry and of serving the common good with publications that were
decent, impartial, informative, and entertaining.[12] Newspapers, wrote
editor Samuel Hall in 1768, were an inexpensive and efficient means
of providing "the most useful Knowledge to Mankind, tending to preserve and promote the Liberty, Happiness and Welfare of Civil Society."[13] In reality, however, eighteenth-century newspaper writing was
frequently partisan, vituperative, and pedantic.[14] Introducing his
avowedly Republican *American and Daily Advertiser* in 1799, Alexander Martin decried the "hacknied, hypocritical protestations of those
editors, who *at first*, avow a rigid *impartiality*, and as soon as their
papers have gained a circulation, prostitute themselves to the service
of any party which will dispense the 'lo[a]ves and *fishes*' with the greatest liberality."[15]

Although much publishing was in fact devoted to political dia-
tribe rather than the dispassionate search for truth, thoughtful, high-
minded journalism did exist. One of the practitioners with an unfeigned attachment to the Enlightenment ideals of free investigation
and human happiness was also the best-known journalist of early
America, Benjamin Franklin. Franklin's reasonableness and wit were
well suited for a public career in an age of extremes in wealth, politics, and social status. To a large extent, Franklin achieved renown
through his ability to connect the highest values of libertarianism,
humanitarianism, and religion to the realities of the time without being
dry, impractical, or overly antagonistic. Like George Washington, the
other full-fledged American icon of the revolutionary era, Franklin
usually managed to appear above the fray and concerned with the
common good. "Washington and Franklin could never do any thing
but what was imputed to pure, disinterested patriotism," John Adams
complained in 1811, "I never could do anything but what was ascribed to sinister motives."[16] Unlike Washington and Adams, Franklin devoted much of his public career to improving the lives of those
least likely to have their share of society's benefits, the laboring poor
and middle classes.

As his autobiography demonstrates in detail, Franklin himself
emerged from the lower echelons of colonial society. Having ascended
to the top of the social pyramid as a self-made man, he could thus
speak as a journalist and memoirist from a background that relatively
few eighteenth-century Americans had.[17] Lacking wealth and education, he acquired both through shrewdness and determination. Seeing
a need for public institutions of health and learning in Philadelphia,
he used his organizational and writing skills to establish a library, a
hospital, and a college. Franklin was in a virtually unique position to
assess the difficulties of the majority of Americans and to propose
solutions.

Other journalists—such as Samuel Adams, Thomas Paine, and
Matthew Lyon—were attuned to both the thought of Enlightenment
libertarianism and the exigencies of the mass citizenry,[18] but lacked
the prestige, experience, and broad outlook Franklin had gained as
a philanthropist, scientist, and public official. Franklin took satisfaction from his accomplishments, but guarded against letting his self-
confidence and self-interest become self-absorption or selfishness. Raised
in a Puritan home, Franklin took the habits of self-examination and

benevolence and, at an early age, composed a list of thirteen virtues to follow in life, including order, frugality, industry, sincerity, justice, moderation, and humility.[19]

Placing the list in his memoirs decades later, Franklin attributed the success of his private and public careers to the degree to which he had been able to practice the virtues. "Nothing so likely to make a Man's Fortune as Virtue," he remarked, observing that he had long planned to comment on the advantages of each attribute in a book to be called *The Art of Virtue*. The unwritten book, he said, "would have shown the *Means & Manner* of obtaining Virtue; which would have distinguish'd it from the mere Exhortation to be good, that does not instruct." Then quoting from the second chapter of the Book of James, which spoke of the need to combine faith with actions and the evil of favoring the rich and exploiting the poor, Franklin pointed to the folly of "the Apostle's Man of verbal Charity" who merely exhorted the poor to be fed and clothed "without showing to the Naked & the Hungry *how* or where they might get Cloaths or Victuals."[20]

Although compatible with tenets of republicanism and capitalism, the list was not merely a prescription for upright materialism. Franklin believed, as he related in his autobiography, that "the most acceptable Service of God was the doing Good to Man; that our Souls are immortal; and that all Crime will be punished & Virtue rewarded either here or hereafter."[21] Virtue was to be cultivated, in his view, not merely because it was rational in terms of benefits, but also because it was moral. Having emerged from "the Poverty & Obscurity" of his birth, he said at the beginning of his memoirs, he thought others might wish to imitate "the conducting Means I made use of, which, with the Blessing of God, so well succeeded."[22]

Accepting the Puritan concept of "preparation" for grace through hard work and kindness, Franklin sought earthly happiness as well as eventual salvation through good conduct.[23] Among the repeated references to divine approval in his autobiography is the inscription he chose for his parents' gravestone: "Without an Estate or any gainful employment, By constant Labour and Industry, With God's Blessing, They maintained a large Family Comfortably." Then Franklin added: "From this Instance, Reader, Be encouraged to Diligence in thy Calling, And Distrust not Providence."[24] In the earliest portion of his memoirs, composed in 1771, he acknowledged God's "kind Providence" in his own life. "This, induces me to *hope*, tho' I must not

presume," Franklin wrote, "that the same Goodness will still be exer-
cis'd towards me in continuing that Happiness, or in enabling me to
bear a fatal Reverso, which I may experience as others have done,
the Complexion of my future Fortune being known to him only: and
in whose Power it is to bless to us even our Afflictions."[25]

Franklin's stated belief in the role of God in human affairs evidently rested on more than literary custom. At a tense point in the
deliberations of the Constitutional Convention, he made an unsuccessful motion that each day's session begin with prayers "imploring
the Assistance of Heaven and its Blessings on our Deliberations." He
reminded the delegates that in the same room at the start of the Revolution Americans had prayed for divine protection and said he hoped
they would again think of "humbly applying to the Father of Lights
to illuminate our Understandings." The country had "frequent Instances of a superintending Providence" in its favor during the war,
Franklin said, and if they failed now "Mankind may hereafter, from
this unfortunate Instance, despair of establishing Government by human Wisdom, and leave it to Chance, War, and Conquest."[26]

Some of the delegates familiar with Franklin's reputation in worldly
matters may have been surprised to hear him say that the longer he
lived the more convinced he became *"that GOD governs in the Affairs
of Men,"* but his speech on the motion left room for "human Wisdom."[27] Human wisdom produced virtuous conduct which, with divine help, made a better world. The starting point, however, was
wisdom, and Franklin's speech advocating prayer pointed to the disputes of the Convention as "melancholy Proof of the Imperfection of
the Human Understanding."[28] In his speech at the closing of the
Convention, he said he agreed to the Constitution despite what he
perceived to be its faults because he had learned in the course of a
long life that he was not always right and that he might change his
mind. He doubted "whether any other Convention we can obtain,
may be able to make a better constitution; for, when you assemble a
number of men, to have the advantage of their joint wisdom, you
inevitably assemble with those men all their prejudices, their passions,
their errors of opinion, their local interests, and their selfish views."[29]

Franklin, in fact, could be as doubtful about the efficacy of human reason and as devoted to the cause of a wise tolerance as Montaigne and Voltaire. "Men I find to be a Sort of Beings very badly
constructed," he wrote to Joseph Priestley in 1782, "as they are gen-

erally more easily provok'd than reconcil'd, more disposed to do Mischief to each other than to make Reparation, much more easily deceiv'd than undeceiv'd, and having more Pride and even Pleasure in killing than in begetting one another." After describing a naval battle of the revolutionary war, he added, "Devils never treat one another in this cruel manner; they have more Sense, and more of what Men (vainly) call *Humanity.*"[30]

After the hostilities with Britain, Franklin, the Enlightenment philosopher, continued to express outrage at the senselessness of war. "I hope . . . that Mankind will at length, as they call themselves reasonable Creatures, have Reason and Sense enough to settle their Differences without cutting Throats; for, in my opinion, *there never was a good War, or a bad Peace,*" he wrote to a correspondent. "What vast additions to the Conveniences and Comforts of Living might Mankind have acquired, if the Money spent in Wars had been employed in Works of public utility!" England, he said, might have been made "a compleat Paradise" if the millions had been spent "in doing good, which in the last War have been spent in doing Mischief; in bringing Misery into thousands of Families, and destroying the Lives of so many thousands of working people, who might have performed the useful labour!"[31]

Franklin did not usually display emotion in his public life, but he was moved by the needless human suffering of ordinary people. Many of the civic improvements he sought, such as street paving for Philadelphia and better postal service for the colonies, as well as his inventions, including the Pennsylvania Fireplace and lightning rods, were attempts to improve the quality and safety of everyday life. In the middle of his autobiography's discussion of hiring the poor to clean streets, Franklin commented, "The Happiness of Man consists in small Advantages occurring every Day."[32] Explaining why he wrote a pamphlet to promote his more efficient stove but refused to patent the device, he said he followed the principle "*That as we enjoy great Advantages from the Inventions of others, we should be glad of an Opportunity to serve others by any Invention of ours, and this we should do freely and generously.*"[33]

In private moments, Franklin did show the intensity of his feelings about the exploited and oppressed. Companions reported that slavery infuriated him and he wept at reading the public addresses on the closing of Boston harbor. On a factory tour in England, he was proudly shown clothing to be shipped to the continent and America. Noticing how shabbily the workers themselves were dressed, he asked the manufacturer, "Have you none for the Factory-Workers of Norwich?"[34] In a lighter anecdote, preserved in his memoirs, Franklin described his resolve not to contribute any of the coins in his pocket to an orphanage being proposed by the revivalist George Whitefield because he disapproved of the location. Listening to Whitefield's eloquent sermon, however, he changed his mind. "As he proceeded I began to soften, and concluded to give the Coppers," Franklin wrote. "Another Stroke of his Oratory made me asham'd of that, and determin'd me to give the Silver; & he finish'd so admirably, that I empty'd my Pocket wholly into the Collector's Dish, Gold and all."[35]

To Franklin, then, human wisdom consisted of a practical and compassionate sense of morality. Through moral wisdom, human beings could progress, with God's blessing, to a state of happiness and eventual salvation. The undependable nature of mere reason was illustrated in another story in his autobiography. In his youth, he noted, he practiced vegetarianism, believing that killing animals was "a kind of unprovok'd Murder." On a sea voyage, however, he was tempted by the smell of fish being fried. Having seen small fish in the stomachs of fish being prepared, he decided he could eat them if they ate each other. "So convenient a thing it is to be a *reasonable Creature*," Franklin remarked wryly, "since it enables one to find or make a Reason for every thing one has a mind to do."[36]

II

Doubting human reason and yet desiring improvement of the human condition, Franklin faced the problem of how to encourage more enlightened thought and behavior. The way to satisfy God, help others, and find personal contentment, he believed, was to live a life of personal rectitude and good works. "Strive to be the *greatest* Man in your Country, and you may be disappointed," Poor Richard said, "Strive to be the *best*, and you may succeed: He may well win the race that runs by himself."[37] Private morality and public virtue were already goals of both religion and republican political theory, but Franklin recognized that few met these objectives. People, he thought, had not really learned the benefits of living properly. "If villains understood the advantages of being virtuous," he told companions in France, "they would turn honest out of villainy."[38]

In Franklin's mind, churches failed to improve the world because they emphasized doctrine at the expense of action. He thought that public worship had some influence on behavior, but that the religions he knew went beyond fundamental points and into "other Articles which without any Tendency to inspire, promote or confirm Morality, serv'd principally to divide us & make us unfriendly to one another." Finding some of the dogma of his own religious training "unintelligible" or "doubtful" and hearing his Philadelphia minister preach theological polemics rather than the morals of "good Citizens," Franklin chose to create his own prayers and liturgies rather than attend church services.[39]

Republics and republicanism failed, Franklin as well as others thought, because personal ambition and avarice produced destructive factions[40] which in turn invited tyranny. He believed that "only a virtuous people are capable of freedom. As nations become corrupt and vicious, they have more need of masters."[41] In his "Observations on my Reading History in Library," composed in 1731 and inserted in his memoirs more than fifty years later, he wrote that parties were responsible for the world's confusion and that few in public life "act from a meer View of the Good of their Country" and fewer still "with a View to the Good of Mankind."[42] He twice told the Constitutional Convention that he feared the country would eventually revert to despotism, despite their efforts, once the leaders and eventually the people themselves were corrupted. The difficulty was that "the Love of Power and the Love of Money" which led to factions were "two Passions which have a powerful Influence in the Affairs of men."[43]

Franklin brought to the Convention of 1787 a classical republican's fear of strong leaders and financial power. One of his proposals to foster democracy and avoid corruption was that officers in the executive branch not receive salaries. "Place before the eyes of Men a Post of *Honour,* that shall at the same time be a Place of *Profit,*" he said, "and they will move Heaven and Earth to obtain it." He hoped "that the Pleasure of doing Good and serving their Country, and the Respect such Conduct entitles them to, are sufficient Motives with some Minds, to give up a great Portion of their Time to the Public, without the mean Inducement of pecuniary Satisfaction."[44] Franklin was not, however, in favor of the federal government being dominated by the wealthy who could afford to give time to public office. According to notes taken at the convention, when Charles Pinckney moved that there be property qualifications for members of Congress "to make them independent & respectable," he objected:

> Doctr Franklin expressed his dislike of every thing that tended to debase the spirit of the common people. If honesty was often the companion of wealth, and if poverty was exposed to peculiar temptation, it was not less true that the possession of property increased the desire of more property—Some of the greatest rogues he was ever acquainted with, were the richest rogues. We should remember the character which the Scripture requires in Rulers, that they should be men hating covetousness—This Constitution will be much read and attended to in Europe, and if it should betray a great partiality to the rich—will not only hurt us in the esteem of the most liberal and enlightened men there, but discourage the common people from removing to this Country. [45]

Franklin also spoke in favor of the "common people" when the delegates considered whether property qualifications should be set for voters in Congressional elections. Neither limitation passed. [46] Franklin—and evidently his fellow delegates—did not accept the classical republican supposition that landless laborers could not be trusted with a role in government. [47] At the convention and in his later defense of Pennsylvania's radically democratic 1776 constitution, Franklin was a forceful advocate of egalitarianism. Writing in support of the state constitution, with its broad franchise, plural executive, and unicameral legislature, he insisted "the important ends of Civil Society, and the personal Securities of Life and Liberty, these remain the same in every Member of the society; and the poorest continues to have an equal Claim to them with the most opulent, whatever Difference Time, Chance, or Industry may occasion in their Circumstances." [48]

Fearing the behavior of factions and distrusting the wealthy and powerful, however, Franklin was not particularly optimistic about the federal Constitution. After the convention, according to an often-repeated tale, he was asked if the country was to have a republic or a monarchy. "A republic, if you can keep it," was Franklin's reported reply. [49] He thought political systems, including experiments such as the United States Constitution, could not be counted upon to work properly by themselves and, in fact, were not even very important as such. Any form of government, Franklin maintained in his closing speech at the convention, could be "a blessing to the people, if well administered." He predicted the country would be well administered for a time, but then could "only end in despotism, as other forms have done before it, when the people shall become so corrupted as to need despotic government." He suggested that the delegates sign the document, despite any objections, and that they turn their "future thoughts and endeavours to the means of having it *well adminis-tered.*"[50]

Like other political theorists of early America, Franklin was a student of what made societies flourish and fail and was distressed by the prospects of luxury and party warfare. His conclusion that only a virtuous people concerned with the common good were capable of freedom was a standard position of classical republicanism.[51] The Constitution, however, reflected a bleak Madisonian belief that, as the tenth *Federalist* put it, "the *causes* of faction cannot be removed; and that relief is only to be sought in the means of controlling its *effects.*"[52] Madison wrote:

> It is in vain to say, that enlightened statesmen will be able to adjust these clashing interests, and render them all subservient to the public good. Enlightened statesmen will not always be at the helm: Nor, in many cases, can such an adjustment be made at all, without taking into view indirect and remote considerations, which will rarely prevail over the immediate interest which one party may find in disregarding the rights of another, or the good of the whole.[53]

Rather than rely very much on virtue in politics, Madison sought a complicated mechanism of checks and balances designed to defeat unjust measures.[54] He told the readers of the *Federalist* they could "behold a Republican remedy for the diseases most incident to Republican Government" in the Constitution.[55] Franklin, on the other hand, was inclined to think structure was less important than democratic sentiment and admired the simple, participatory character of Pennsylvania's constitution with its provisions for rotation in office, open meetings, and freedom of the press.[56] He was less comfortable with the spirit behind the federal Constitution. Franklin observed, in his widely circulated closing speech, that the document was not enough. In urging the delegates to abandon their differences and work together for ratification and proper administration, he said, "Much of the strength and efficiency of any government, in procuring and securing happiness to the people, depends on *opinion*, on the general opinion of the goodness of that government, as well as of the wisdom and integrity of its governors."[57]

To Franklin, then, the success of the new political system would still be contingent upon correct conduct in offices of public trust, conduct the public had to be prepared to judge on the principles of liberty, political equality, and public welfare. Even Madison, speaking at the Virginia ratifying convention, admitted that no "theoretical checks" would render the country secure if the people lacked the necessary wisdom to chose proper leaders. "To suppose that any form of government will secure liberty or happiness without any virtue in the people, is a chimerical idea," Madison said. "If there be sufficient virtue and intelligence in the community, it will be exercised in the selection of these men. So that we do not depend on their virtue, or put confidence in our rulers, but in the people who are to choose them."[58] He later remarked, "A popular Government, without popular information, or the means of acquiring it, is but a Prologue to a Farce or a Tragedy; or, perhaps, both."[59]

III

Free from Britain's rule in economic and political matters, the Americans of the early republic had new opportunities to exercise personal initiative. Recognizing the importance of public awareness in civic and private affairs, Enlightenment statesmen, including Franklin, Madison, and Jefferson, used their rhetorical and political skills to support education and journalism.[60] Franklin, in particular, had a lifelong interest in reading and schooling. He credited America's libraries, including the one he founded in Philadelphia, with making "common Tradesmen & Farmers as intelligent as most Gentlemen from other Countries" and with perhaps therefore contributing to "the Stand so generally made throughout the Colonies in Defence of their Privileges."[61] Much late eighteenth-century discourse, however, did not directly concern the people's defense of their liberties, but rather the dangers seen in the private arrangements of capitalism and in the citizen participation of a republican government. How, Americans wondered, could decline be avoided in a society in which people are free to pursue their happiness and yet must be governed with their consent?

Although articulated in varying ways, a prevalent eighteenth-century concept of history was that nations rose and fell in cyclical patterns, that young, virtuous, equitable societies gradually became enfeebled with luxury, inequality, and tyranny and, like Rome, decayed and collapsed.[62] It was in this sense that Jefferson could suggest that "a little rebellion now and then is a good thing" because it prevented the degeneracy of government.[63] Americans of the revolutionary generation assumed that their country, in contrast to an old and corrupt Britain, was in an early phase of the process and was justified in breaking away from social misery and authoritarian rule to form a vigorous new republic dedicated to individual liberty and the public good.[64] The maintenance of such principles, they continually asserted, required the discipline of civic and private virtue.[65]

With the rise of the Jeffersonian Republicans, however, came altered perceptions of how freedom and the public welfare could be achieved. Virtue became less a matter of classical republican self-control and more a matter of Enlightenment natural rights and self-fulfillment. The Jeffersonians saw a moral significance in developing a particular version of capitalism, a Lockean one in which the ordinary person was to enjoy the liberty, equality, and property that governments were established to protect. Attaining this new order, they believed, would be possible mainly through commercial farming, which would help preserve individual honesty, independence, and prosperity as the United States produced food and fibers for growing world markets. Large-scale manufacturing, on the other hand, was seen as a corrupting force which drove nations into conflict, created an erratic economy based on artificial needs, forced workers to accept low wages, and concentrated wealth and power in the hands of a few.[66]

The Republicans, therefore, sought a future in which Americans would deal in the necessities and simple comforts of life through free trade and not follow the example of British mercantilism with its wars, national debt, poverty, market coercion, and oligarchy. The Republican future was to be a largely self-regulating one. Government would be small and taxes low because the country would be peacefully pursuing agriculture rather than manipulating financial and manufacturing ventures and entering international conflicts. Farmers could be self-sufficient when necessary and could export surpluses when possible. When factory wages were too low or the population grew, Americans could move westward into new territories. Aristocratic values would have no place, and self-interest, by stimulating industriousness and therefore virtue, would be in the national interest.[67] A people satisfied with their material comforts, unlike the lower classes of Europe, could be relied upon to govern themselves intelligently and to maintain respect for the law.[68] Insurrections would be moderate and self-extinguishing where citizens were free and able to elect their governors.[69]

Variations on themes certainly occurred,[70] but in 1800, Americans elected a president who, rejecting the Hamiltonian policies of the previous decade, found John Locke's work on government "perfect as far as it goes" and admired Adam Smith's *The Wealth of Nations* as "the best book extant" on political economy.[71] In his own *Notes on the State of Virginia*, Thomas Jefferson had written, "Those who labour in the earth are the chosen people of God, if ever he had a chosen people, whose breasts he has made his peculiar deposit for substantial and genuine virtue."[72] At his first inauguration, Jefferson spoke of equal justice, peace and trade with all nations, land for thousands of generations, encouragement of agriculture and its "handmaid" commerce, and "wise and frugal government, which shall restrain men from injuring one another, shall leave them otherwise free to regulate their own pursuits of industry & improvement, and shall not take from the mouth of labor the bread it has earned." Republican government, he said, was at "the full tide of successful experiment."[73]

Jefferson viewed his election with a sense of satisfaction and hope. During the campaign he had been viciously attacked in the Federalist press as an atheist, radical, fool, coward, libertine, and thief,[74] but he defeated an incumbent president in what he regarded as a revolution of republican principles overturning monarchical ones.[75] His inaugural address suggested that political intolerance might be eliminated, that it might be possible for citizens to "unite with one heart & one mind" because every difference of opinion between parties did not have to mean a difference of principle. The country could undertake "common efforts for the common good."[76] Finally, it seemed at the beginning of a new century that America could expect the development of the society Jefferson described to Madison in 1787 after seeing the Constitution for the first time:

I think our governments will remain virtuous for many centuries; as long as they are chiefly agricultural; and this will be as long as there shall be vacant lands in any part of America. When they get piled upon one another in large cities, as in Europe, they will become corrupt as in Europe. Above all things I hope the education of the common people will be attended to; convinced that on their good sense we may rely with the most security for the preservation of a due degree of liberty.[77]

Modern agriculture and open markets were to be merely the economic foundation of a reordered society. The Republican program rejected domination by a privileged elite in favor of a broadly enfranchised, independent, well-educated electorate that would keep the country free and content. A broad franchise was important, Jefferson believed, "because the corrupting the whole mass of people will exceed any private resources of wealth: and public ones cannot be provided but by levies on the people." Dependence, he maintained, "begets subservience and venality, suffocates the germ of virtue, and prepares fit tools for the designs of ambition." Education, he said, enabled citizens "to know ambition under every disguise it may assume."[78] If there was to be a class of citizens involved in leadership, it would be what Jefferson termed the "natural aristocracy" of "virtue and talents" rather than the "artificial aristocracy, founded on birth and wealth." The role of voters would be to distinguish between the two as they would separate "the wheat from the chaff."[79]

The Jeffersonian solution to the political, economic, and social issues of the early republic rested on the assumption of Jefferson's *Notes* that it is "the manners and spirit of a people which preserve a republic in vigour" and that the moral corruption of "the mass of cultivators is a phenomenon of which no age nor nation has furnished an example."[80] In seeing the citizenry as naturally virtuous when free, comfortable, and independent, Jeffersonian thought offered a dramatic contrast to Hamiltonian contempt for free-trade theory, democratic participation, and the status of common people.

Although the Republican program was enacted to a large extent,[81] advances in farming, science, and technology, which so intrigued Jefferson, made agriculture an occupation for a small portion of the population by the twentieth century. The Jeffersonians nevertheless managed to meld the classical republican suspicion of power, the egalitarian reliance on the public, and the liberal belief in natural laws into a formidable political ideology which still provides emotional undercurrents in American politics. "Morality listens to this," President Jefferson said of his political economy, "and so invariably do the laws of nature create our duties and interests, that when they seem to be at variance, we ought to suspect some fallacy in our reasonings."[82]

Jefferson, like Franklin, came to believe that virtue and happiness were interdependent, that political equality and mass education were necessary in a republic, and that commercial farming and westward expansion would offer security for the foreseeable future. Accepting the stress on agriculture and free trade in French physiocratic thought as well as the classical republican abhorrence of financial corruption, Franklin had views on political economy that were remarkably similar to those of Thomas Jefferson.[83] Franklin's career, in fact, suggests that a Jeffersonian combination of Enlightenment libertarian schools of thought can be found in American journalism in the decades before the Republicans' ascendancy at the beginning of the nineteenth century.[84] The fervent publications of his grandson, Benjamin Franklin Bache, are indicative of how impassioned such sentiments became during the administrations of Washington and Adams. Indeed, Jefferson's first inaugural address identified his party's principles as "the bright constellation which has gone before us, & guided our steps, thro' an age of Revolution and Reformation."[85]

ONE

Benjamin Franklin and the Foundations of Enlightenment Republicanism

CHAPTER

2

The Science of Doing Good

BENJAMIN FRANKLIN COMBINED IDEAS AND ACCOMPLISHMENTS AS EF-fective revolutionaries customarily have, but he adopted a distinctively American ideal of active individuals and passive government. "From a Child I was fond of Reading," he wrote in his memoirs, "and all the little Money that came into my Hands was ever laid out in Books." In his father's library he found "a Book of Defoe's called an Essay on Projects and another of Dr. Mather's call'd Essays to do Good, which perhaps gave me a Turn of Thinking that had an Influence on some of the principal future Events of my Life." Franklin was impressed by the community-minded approaches to injustice and suffering the two books described. Both works pointed to practical ways altruistic individuals could organize themselves to assist the poor, uneducated, and unprotected. Recalling the impact of Rev. Cotton Mather's essay more than sixty years after reading it, Franklin said of himself that he had "always set a greater value on the character of a *doer of good,* than on any other kind of reputation."[1]

Although he was a printer's apprentice who had spent only two years in school, Benjamin Franklin read widely on his own, acquiring an impressive knowledge of Western thought, from the religion of Mather and the humanism of Defoe to the philosophy of Locke and the libertarian ideology of *Cato's Letters.*[2] What Franklin distilled from the writings he knew was the importance of civic virtue and the need for a more politically and economically just society. Literature of his age suggested that improvement was possible through democratic discussion and personal initiative. Ordinary citizens could voluntarily associate for their own benefit and that of others. Through his reading and his experience, Franklin was able to grasp the degree to which traditional hierarchical authority was disintegrating, and responsibility for the public welfare was shifting toward those politicians and private individuals who were prepared to accept it. With less control coming from above, more would have to come from within the community itself. As a leader and a journalist, Franklin acted on his Enlightenment belief, one also embraced by Jefferson, that people would be rational and public-spirited if given freedom, education, and the proper environment.

I

Believing, as he said in his memoirs, that parties only selfishly fomented divisions in society and that it was "every ones Interest to be virtuous, who wish'd to be happy even in this World," Benjamin Franklin usually sought results through personal, often symbolic acts and through community organizations rather than public institutions. As well as any eighteenth-century American did, he embodied the Enlightenment spirit of enterprising and equitable behavior and guarded that image carefully. Remembering his early days in the printing business, he wrote:

> In order to secure my Credit and Character as a Tradesman, I took care not only to be in *Reality* Industrious & frugal, but to avoid all *Appearances* of the Contrary. I drest plainly; I was seen at no Places of idle Diversion; I never went out a-fishing or shooting; a Book, indeed, sometimes debauch'd me from my Work; but that was seldom, snug, & gave no Scandal; and to show that I was not above my Business, I sometimes brought home the Paper I purchas'd at the Stores, thro' the Streets on a Wheelbarrow.[3]

Yet he carried out his public duties with a genial informality that exasperated the punctilious John Adams and amused the usually serious Thomas Jefferson and the equally humorless James Madison, both of whom enjoyed recounting anecdotes of Franklin's wit and nonchalance. "He has the most affectionate and insinuating Way of charming the Woman or the Man that he fixes on," John Adams complained while observing Franklin in France. "It is the most silly and ridiculous Way imaginable, in the Sight of an American, but it succeeds, to admiration, fullsome and sickish as it is, in Europe." Adams was disgusted to find "Painters, Statuaries, Sculptors, China Potters" and others busy reproducing the likeness of his fellow diplomat,[4] who was being lionized as nature's nobleman, the amiable genius of an uncorrupted and unfettered new world. Franklin, he sputtered, was being given undeserved credit for the American Revolution and was not even responsible for "the Constitution of Pensylvania, bad as it is."[5]

Not a believer in simple democracy or egalitarian society, John Adams was unable to fathom Franklin's seemingly vain willingness to forgo diplomatic work in order to receive the admiration of crowds of French well-wishers "come to have the honour to see the great Franklin, and to have the pleasure of telling Stories about his Simplicity, his bald head and scattering strait hairs, among their Acquaintances." In France, Adams was an austere classical republican made irascible by facing extravagant, absolute monarchy on the one hand and cheerful, democratic insouciance on the other.[6] An admirer of the balancing of social orders in the English Constitution, Adams was uncomfortable with both the dazzling display of French aristocracy and the freedom, informality, and national unity emblematized by Franklin— a man of plain manners and attire even at Versailles—and eventually by Jefferson, who sometimes wore working clothes and slippers when greeting White House visitors.

Adams's dignified, pugnacious, institutional mentality, which may have been well suited to the period when he, Franklin, and Jefferson were assigned to write the Declaration of Independence, was increasingly outmoded toward the end of the eighteenth century. Americans may have retained much of their revolutionary zeal for life and liberty, but they were beginning to give more attention to their pursuit of happiness and creation as equals. An open and classless political style appealed to citizens who had fought a revolution, achieved popular sovereignty, and saw no particular need to salute their nominal superiors.[7] The federal Constitution had given ultimate power to the people, had prohibited titles of nobility, and had created a framework its chief author and defender, James Madison, said would protect everyone, the weak as well as the powerful. "In the extended republic of the United States, and among the great variety of interests, parties and sects which it embraces," he wrote in the *Federalist*, "a coalition of a majority of the whole society could seldom take place on any other principles than those of justice and the general good."[8]

If Madison made a seminal contribution to the theory of the new order, and Jefferson was in the vanguard of political practice, Franklin brought to the Enlightenment science of societal management a profound sense of how private happiness and the general welfare could be promoted by individual behavior that might appear only self-centered. Franklin, for instance, recognized the role of ego fulfillment in encouraging people to do good work and good works. In his memoirs, he admitted being vain himself, but excused the vice as "often productive of Good" and remarked that "in many Cases it would not be quite absurd if a Man were to thank God for his Vanity among the other Comforts of Life." Pride, though a sin and an apparent affront to Enlightenment egalitarianism, could be a basis for worthy actions. Franklin observed that being chosen for public offices would not only "enlarge my Power of doing Good," but would also flatter his ambition, especially "considering my low Beginning." Recalling that his father had frequently repeated a proverb of Solomon, "*Seest thou a Man diligent in his Calling, he shall stand before Kings,*" Franklin noted that he himself had met five kings. He wrote that pride was in fact so difficult to subdue that if he thought he had done so, then he would probably be proud of his humility. Aware of how healthy pride could become self-defeating arrogance, however, Franklin took precautions to avoid uttering any "dogmatical Expression" or monopolizing the recognition for his projects.[9]

Besides self-esteem, another potentially useful incentive, one which was denounced by the clergy and classical republicans, was the desire for costly goods. Americans of the revolutionary era, including Franklin, had expressed endless fears that European luxuries and vices were corrupting the country by exacerbating social inequalities and subverting the sober and benevolent spirit thought essential for a republic.[10] Remembering how he and his wife Deborah gradually acquired a large collection of silver and china, Franklin wrote in his autobiography in 1784 that "Luxury will enter Families, and make a Progress, in Spite of Principle." At the same time he was beginning to wonder if the evil was as serious as it was thought to be. "Is not the Hope of one day being able to purchase and enjoy Luxuries a great Spur to

Labour and Industry?" he asked a correspondent. "May not Luxury, therefore, produce more than it consumes, if without such a Spur People would be, as they are naturally enough inclined to be, lazy and indolent?" In any case, he concluded that too much time was spent in the pursuit of "Superfluities."[11]

Franklin did not see commerce as the naturally beneficial force and foundation of national greatness that Hume and Hamilton did,[12] but rather as a complicated reality that did harm or good depending on the circumstances. Franklin took a position later held by Jeffersonians which approved of the capitalism of the small, independent producer who made comforts and necessities, but not that of the wealthy landlord and large manufacturer who kept their dependent workers impoverished.[13] After touring Scotland, Ireland, and England in 1771, Franklin gave American friends cautionary accounts of barefoot makers of shoes and stockings, spinners and weavers dressed in rags, and tenants "poor, tattered, dirty, and abject in Spirit." This was in contrast to "the Happiness of New England, where every Man is a Freeholder, has a Vote in publick Affairs, lives in a tidy warm House, has plenty of good Food and Fewel, with whole Cloaths from Head to Foot, the Manufactury perhaps of his own Family." Britain's mercantilist system, he concluded, was "depressing Multitudes below the Savage State that a few may be rais'd above it."[14]

In addition to seeing the possible beneficial effects of the pursuit of personal desires, Franklin perceived that the enlightened citizen of a more laissez-faire society would need the kind of voluntary associations that Cotton Mather had envisioned and that in the next century so impressed Tocqueville with their number and diversity.[15] Franklin demonstrated what he called "an early projecting public Spirit" when, as a leader of the boys he played with, he organized a group of friends to build a stone wharf on the edge of a salt marsh. Later, as a young printer, he established his Junto, a club Franklin characterized as "the best School of Philosophy, Morals & Politics that then existed in the Province." The members included tradesmen, novice intellectuals, and "Robert Grace, a young Gentleman of some Fortune" who saved Franklin's business with a timely loan.[16] Franklin composed for the group a list of "Standing Queries" to be discussed at each meeting. The questions, an inventory of Enlightenment concerns, were designed to prompt discussion of authors, virtue, liberty, justice, and successes and failures in business. Members took turns choosing topics for debate. On one such occasion, Franklin not only wrote the questions, but also his answers:

> *Quest.* Wherein consists the Happiness of a rational Creature?
> *Ans.* In having a Sound Mind and a healthy Body, a Sufficiency of the Necessaries and Conveniencies of Life, together with the Favour of God, and the Love of Mankind.
> *Qu.* What do you mean by a sound Mind?
> *A.* A Faculty of reasoning justly and truly in searching after [and] discovering such Truths as relate to my Happiness. Which Faculty is the Gift of God, capable of being improv'd by Experience and Instruction, into Wisdom.
> *Q.* What is Wisdom?
> *A.* The Knowledge of what will be best for us on all Occasions and of the best Ways of attaining it.[17]

Members of the Junto were expected to help each other achieve virtue and well-being. They were required to avow that they loved "mankind in general," believed in tolerating "mere speculative opinions," and impartially sought "truth for truth's sake." As well as being "serviceable to *mankind*," they were also supposed to defend each other's reputations and advise one another in making decisions. The Junto helped Franklin obtain additional printing jobs, backed him in his civic projects, including the Library Company and the University of Pennsylvania, and provided him with an opportunity to test ideas ranging from a city watch and fire protection to the philosophy of his essay "On the Providence of God in the Government of the World."[18]

Other eighteenth-century clubs in Britain and America offered opportunities to discuss politics, business, and intellectual issues, but a group such as Franklin's displayed the level of ritual, commitment, and sophistication later found in revolutionary committees and the "self-created societies" of Democratic-Republicans that angered Washington and advanced Jeffersonian ideals. The Junto, however, was designed more for what Franklin called "mutual Improvement" than for direct involvement in politics. The Junto member was expected to exhibit the traits Franklin associated with an individual's success—to be flexible, well-informed, persistent, calculating, autonomous, confident, and socially adept. Franklin detested "Croakers" who merely complained about societal conditions. He hoped to found one day a model group that would practice his list of thirteen virtues and eventually lead to the creation of a "united Party for Virtue" formed by gathering "the Virtuous and good Men of all Nations into a regular Body, to be govern'd by suitable good and wise Rules." The forerunner group would operate on the principles

> That the Members should engage to afford their Advice Assistance and Support to each other in promoting one another's Interest Business and Advancement in Life: That for Distinction we should be call'd the Society of the *Free and Easy*; Free, as being by the general Practice and Habit of Virtues, free from the Domination of Vice, and particularly by the Practice of Industry & Frugality, free from Debt, which exposes a Man to Confinement and a Species of Slavery to his Creditors.[19]

Franklin's feelings about debt, cooperation, and self-improvement were similar to sentiments Jefferson and other Americans expressed, but he was perhaps more specific about how to become independent, prosperous, and public-spirited. He thought, as he said in his autobiography, that "one Man of tolerable Abilities may work great Changes, & accomplish great Affairs among Mankind, if he first forms a good Plan, and, cutting off all Amusements or other Employments that would divert his Attention, makes the Execution of that same Plan his sole Study and Business." Franklin self-consciously cultivated the virtues and traits he believed prepared individuals to do good work and good works. By writing his memoirs, which he hoped would show others the usefulness of virtue, and by providing an example as a leader in areas as diverse as the post office, militia, and the American Philosophical Society, Franklin was demonstrating what citizens could carry out on their own in a freer and yet more complex and demanding world.[20]

II

Of all Franklin's occupations, none continued longer than that of journalist. Over the course of seven decades, in America, England, and France, he continually wrote newspaper essays and pamphlets. As a young printer and publisher, Franklin had a natural opportunity to communicate his thoughts to the public, but he was, as he remembered in his memoirs, "extreamly ambitious" to become "a tolerable

English Writer." In his *Poor Richard* almanac, he observed that "The Hope of acquiring lasting FAME, is, with many Authors, a most powerful Motive to Writing."[21] Franklin's skill as a writer, which he described as "of great Use to me in the Course of my Life" and as "a principal Means of my Advancement," made him a celebrity and helped him succeed as a scientist, politician, and philanthropist. Franklin's purpose, however, was not merely to become well known. In an essay on literary style for his *Pennsylvania Gazette*, Franklin proffered a maxim, *"That no Piece can properly be called good, and well written, which is void of any Tendency to benefit the Reader, either by improving his Virtue or his Knowledge."*[22]

He nevertheless believed that most people did not want plain, pedantic tutelage and therefore wished that "well meaning sensible Men would not lessen their Power of doing Good by a Positive assuming Manner that seldom fails to disgust." Discussing techniques of persuasion in his autobiography, Franklin recommended expressing oneself "in Terms of modest Diffidence" and remembering Alexander Pope's advice that *"Men should be taught as if you taught them not."* Accordingly, when his brother James was in hiding in 1723 after refusing to submit his combative *New-England Courant* to government censorship, seventeen-year-old Benjamin became the ostensible editor of the paper and announced that the new approach would be "to entertain the Town with the most comical and diverting Incidents of Humane Life" as well as "the most ludicrous and odd Parts of Life." The purpose would be to provide useful examples and "serious Morals," but the method would not be dull and dry. "Pieces of Pleasancy and Mirth have a secret Charm in them to allay the Heats and Tumors of our Spirits, and to make a Man forget his restless Resentments," he told his readers. "They have a strange Power to tune the harsh Disorders of the Soul, and reduce us to a serene and placid State of Mind."[23]

Franklin had already practiced his pedagogy of moral education through disarming journalistic entertainment with a series of fourteen essays he had written for the *Courant* in 1722 under the pseudonym "Silence Dogood." The mostly local topics ranged from the "extravagant Foolery" of hoop petticoats to a recipe for a New England funeral elegy. Dogood's wry chronicles of life in Boston may have been fanciful, but they conveyed earnest messages about religious hypocrisy and zealotry, the expense of education, the pecuniary interests of leaders, the costs of drunkenness, the poverty of widows, and other individual and societal problems. At the outset, Dogood explained that she had made use of a private library with books chosen "to inform the Understanding rightly, and enable the Mind to frame great and noble Ideas." Her aim, she said, was to serve her country and to be "an Enemy to Vice, and a Friend of Vertue," as well as "a mortal Enemy to arbitrary Government and unlimited Power."[24]

The style and approach of the Silence Dogood series owed much to Joseph Addison's *Spectator,* the greatly admired periodical Franklin had used as a model in teaching himself literary technique. Mr. Spectator was a "Silent Man" who took to newspaper writing to counter the "Vice and Folly into which the Age is Fallen." He pledged to make his readers' "Instruction agreeable, and their Diversion useful" and "to enliven Morality with Wit, and to temper Wit with Morality." In a *Spectator* explication of "the Exercise of Virtue," Addison advanced precisely the sort of Enlightenment creed Franklin would embrace for himself and impart to others:

> To advise the Ignorant, relieve the Needy, comfort the Afflicted, are Duties that fall in our way almost every Day of our Lives. A Man has frequent Opportunities of mitigating the Fierceness of a Party; of doing Justice to the Character of a deserving Man; of softning the Envious, quieting the Angry, and rectifying the Prejudiced, which are all of them Employments suited to a reasonable Nature, and bring great Satisfaction to the Person who can busy himself in them with Discretion.[25]

The soothing, patronizing brand of Enlightenment journalism in the *Spectator* was not what Franklin found in his brother's newspaper, however. The *Courant* writers, named the "Hell-Fire Club" by their enemies, attacked religious and secular authorities with vitriolic satire. Setting itself up as an advocate for the people, the paper routinely insulted Boston's theocrats and oligarchs and voiced the libertarian sentiments of England's radical Whigs, particularly the newspaper essayists John Trenchard and Thomas Gordon, the authors of *Cato's Letters*. When the Massachusetts legislature took offense at a satirical news item and imprisoned James Franklin for a month in 1722, Benjamin "resented a good deal" his brother's confinement and, when

questioned by the Council, "did not give them any Satisfaction."
Writing as Silence Dogood, he quoted Trenchard and Gordon's *Cato*
at length, saying that government officials were merely *"Trustees of
the People"* and that "Only the *wicked Governours* of Men dread what
is said of them." In a parody of the legislative proceedings against
James Franklin, a sarcastic *Courant* writer observed:

> And truly 'tis a fatal Omen,
> When Knowledge, which belongs to no Men
> But to the Clergy and the Judges,
> Gets in the Heads of common Drudges.[26]

The subscribers, who the *Courant* asserted were "far greater" in
number than those of Boston's two competing papers, may have been
ready to seek a more participatory kind of politics, but the role of
newspapers in such contests was not yet taken for granted. "I remember his being dissuaded by some of his Friends from the Undertaking,
as not likely to succeed," Franklin said of his brother, "one Newspaper being in their Judgment enough for America." The *Courant* was a
foretaste of journalism later in the century and gave Benjamin Franklin an education in assertive writing and antiauthoritarian thought.
He had, as he noted in his memoirs, "made bold to give our Rulers
some Rubs" and had come to be regarded "as a young Genius that
had a Turn for Libelling & Satyr." James appreciated his apprentice's
talents but argued with him on other matters and occasionally beat
him. "I fancy his harsh & tyrannical Treatment of me, might be a
means of impressing me with that Aversion to arbitrary Power that
has stuck to me thro' my whole Life," Franklin wrote in the autobiography, admitting that his own "saucy & provoking" behavior might
have occasioned the fights.[27]

In the autumn of 1723, angry at his brother and recognizing he
had made himself "a little obnoxious" to the government, Benjamin
ran away to New York and then Philadelphia, looking for a job as a
printer. He took with him a knowledge of two of the most striking
forms of Enlightenment journalism, the benevolent, mannerly, politically neutral Addisonian essay, and the strident, suspicious, sometimes caustic style of classical republicanism, both of which could make
use of the penetrating wit which Franklin had in abundance. Franklin, however, was irenic enough to prefer the role of friend of virtue

to that of enemy of arbitrary power. Silence Dogood, after all, was able to say of herself that she was "courteous and affable" and "good humour'd (unless I am first provok'd)."[28] Like many early American printers, Franklin began publishing with the express goal of benignly enlightening the public rather than airing personal or partisan animosities. He generally adhered to his journalistic principles but was in some cases angry or ambitious enough to enter the fray when his philosophies or pocketbook were in jeopardy.

III

In Pennsylvania, Franklin was able to test his philosophies for a new age in the practice of politics, philanthropy, and writing for the public. The journalism began with his eight "Busy-Body" essays for Andrew Bradford's *American Weekly Mercury* in 1729. Busy-Body, like Silence Dogood, described himself as devoted to "the Publick Good" and "the noble Principles of Virtue," but, in contrast to his Boston predecessor, more readily accepted the need to "sometimes talk Politicks." Franklin ended his contributions when a spirited Busy-Body piece on a paper currency controversy in the province was removed from the paper. The essay said a lack of currency had placed the people in economic misery and hinted that public disturbances would occur if legislation was not passed. Franklin then published his own pamphlet arguing that printing money would benefit the majority of citizens. "It was well receiv'd by the common People in general," he later said, "but the Rich Men dislik'd it."[29]

Franklin's pamphlet, *A Modest Enquiry into the Nature and Necessity of a Paper-Currency*, was remarkable for its use of the labor theory of value in a way which Karl Marx would later admire.[30] In contrast to the standard mercantilist position that emphasized the importance of commerce and the inflow of precious metals, Franklin took up the seventeenth-century arguments of Sir William Petty that the labor necessary for production was the proper measure of value. Money, the pamphlet said, was what it purchased, and what it purchased was the labor it took to produce a commodity. Values were therefore best judged by labor, and trade was merely "the Exchange of Labour for Labour."[31] Such a perspective ascribed to the producing classes, long regarded as urban rabble or rustic peasants, a status and consequence rarely recognized in the wealthier and more conservative levels of society. In an increasingly modern economy, one no longer dominated by presumptions of servitude, individuals like Franklin could begin to see the significance of their contributions and well-being to society.

The "Cry among the People for more Paper-Money," as Franklin called it in his memoirs, had been a central issue in the economically depressed 1720s and had revealed conflicts between the interests of creditors and debtors, between the wealthy few who had profited from trade and land speculation and the rest of the province. Opposition to the proprietary-mercantile elite came from a coalition of farmers and city dwellers headed by Assembly Speaker David Lloyd and Governor Sir William Keith. Countering the stand of the provincial oligarchy's leader, James Logan, that disparities in wealth were merely the result of sobriety, industry, and frugality, members of the Keith-Lloyd alliance were strident proponents of egalitarianism and government protection of majority interests. "We all know it is neither the Great, the Rich, nor the Learned, that compose the Body of any People," Keith said in a speech at the opening of the Assembly in 1722, "and that Civil Government ought carefully to protect the poor laborious and industrious Part of Mankind, in the Enjoyment of their just Rights, and equal Liberties and Privileges, with the rest of their Fellow Creatures."[32]

Keith, as ambitious as he was impecunious, apparently hoped to topple the proprietors and become royal governor. Removed from office by the Penns in 1726, he was chosen for the Assembly in an election accompanied by mob violence, but he failed in an attempt to unseat Lloyd in a vote for the speakership and returned to England where he was imprisoned for debt. Keith had felt that Benjamin Franklin had promise as a writer and printer and so had taken pains to cultivate the young man with visits, dinners, and offers of financial help which he proved unable to provide. Franklin thought of him as "one of the best Men in the World" and later in life concluded that he had been "a pretty good Writer, & a good Governor for the People, tho' not for his Constituents the Proprietaries, whose Instructions he sometimes disregarded."[33]

Franklin himself eventually became a popular leader seeking a more responsive form of government in prerevolutionary Pennsylvania, but he had not yet established himself in journalism, the occupation that would propel his rise in politics. An opportunity came in 1729 when he was able to take over the foundering *Universal Instruc-*

tor *in all Arts and Sciences; and Pennsylvania Gazette,* a newspaper published by Samuel Keimer, a religious enthusiast who had once employed Franklin. The *Instructor,* which Keimer had started when he learned that Franklin had plans to begin his own newspaper, tried to enlighten readers with encyclopedia excerpts and other stale material that Franklin ridiculed in Bradford's *Mercury.* As Busy-Body, he told Keimer to let his books "moulder on their proper Shelves" and to apply himself to "a Study much more profitable, The Knowledge of Mankind, and of thy Self."[34]

Franklin's views on mankind and himself made popular politics and journalism a natural choice. While Keimer had only been able to attract ninety subscribers, Franklin made the paper "extreamly profitable." He shortened the name of the paper to the *Pennsylvania Gazette,* announced that he would abandon the "abstruse and insignificant" material Keimer was printing, and promised to make the paper "as agreeable and useful an Entertainment" as he could. Franklin immediately revealed his editorial sentiments in an analysis of a heated debate in Massachusetts over legislative control of the governor's income. The people of that colony had found his demand for a fixed salary a violation of their charter, Franklin wrote, and "judg'd that by the Dictates of Reason there should be a mutual Dependence between the *Governor* and the *Governed,* and that to make any Governour independent on his People, would be dangerous, and destructive of their Liberties, and the ready Way to establish Tyranny."[35]

The young journalist's writings, which displayed an assortment of libertarian predilections, quickly brought him an ample number of subscribers, the encouragement of the "leading Men," and political patronage in the form of public printing including currency and legislative proceedings. The business expanded prodigiously and even reached into other provinces. In 1736, for instance, Franklin had to apologize for the irregular publication of his paper because he was in New Jersey with his press "labouring for the publick Good, to make Money more plentiful." As early as 1731, Franklin was able to undertake a partnership to set up one of his journeymen in South Carolina, the first of a number of such arrangements in the colonies. As a prosperous businessman, who was able to retire from active involvement in his shop at the age of forty-one, he was successful and self-confident enough to compose essays such as his "Advice to a Young Tradesman" in which he observed that "TIME is Money" and that the

"Way to Wealth" was "INDUSTRY and FRUGALITY" as long as the "Being who governs the World" did not determine otherwise.[36]

To his advantage, Franklin's own career appeared to confirm his belief that the public good and private interest could be compatible. The person who exercised self-control and served the people, it seemed, could have both money and esteem. In his autobiography, Franklin pointed to two of his *Pennsylvania Gazette* essays, discussed in the Junto and then published in February of 1735, that outlined what they called a reasonable "Science of Virtue." The first, a Socratic dialogue assailing wrong, rapacious conduct, has Socrates and Crito discussing a "well-dress'd" but dishonest "Gentleman of this City." Arguing that improper behavior offends both God and man and brings "many Inconveniences," the piece concluded that since virtue was really the true interest and happiness of everyone, "the Vicious Man however learned, cannot be *a Man of Sense*, but is a Fool, a Dunce, and a Blockhead." The second *Gazette* essay maintained that public spirit and personal virtues, such as temperance, justice, and charity, did not have to be seen as self-denying, but could rather be the positive result of "a natural benevolent Inclination."[37]

Franklin, as he said in his memoirs, regarded his newspaper as a "Means of Instruction, & in that View frequently reprinted in it Extracts from the Spectator and other moral Writers." He also used the *Gazette* "to prepare the Minds of the People" for his civic projects. Occasionally, however, his desire to teach the populace led to more objectionable pieces. His distaste for religious doctrine and intolerance was evident from time to time, as in his humorous but irreverent "Witch Trial at Mount Holly" hoax. He felt obliged to write his "Apology for Printers" for the paper after publishing an advertisement which ridiculed the Anglican clergy. The "Apology" contended that if printers "sometimes print vicious or silly things not worth reading, it may not be because they approve such things themselves, but because the People are so viciously and corruptly educated that good things are not encouraged." Franklin said that he printed the advertisement without any malice and had made a practice of not printing "Party or Personal Reflections."[38]

IV

In his autobiography, Franklin advised young printers to follow his example in avoiding scurrilous political commentary and the defamation of individuals, saying that his experience had shown "such a Course of Conduct will not on the whole be injurious to their Interests." Nevertheless, having seen how his brother's *New-England Courant* had used popular politics and personal attacks to build circulation, Franklin knew how to attract attention when starting a publication. As Busy-Body, he said he wished to inculcate virtue and depreciate vice:

> But as I know the Mob hate Instruction, and the Generality would never read beyond the first Line of my Lectures, if they were usually fill'd with nothing but wholesome Precepts and Advice; I must therefore sometimes humour them in their own Way. There are a Set of Great Names in the Province, who are the common Objects of Popular Dislike. If I can now and then overcome my Reluctance, and prevail with my self to Satyrize a little, one of these Gentlemen, the Expectation of meeting with such a Gratification, will induce many to read me through, who would otherwise proceed immediately to the Foreign News.

When he was anxious to establish himself as a printer, he taunted Keimer as a "sowre Philosopher" in the *Mercury* and raised the libertarian banner in his discussion of paper money and the Massachusetts salary dispute. In starting his almanac, he mocked his philomath rival "Titan Leeds" and established his credentials as "Poor Richard" by commenting in the first of his almanacs, "A rich rogue, is like a fat hog, who never does good til as dead as a log." In launching his short-lived *General Magazine* in 1740, he accused his competitors, John Webbe and Andrew Bradford, of stealing his idea and promised "Essays, controversial, humourous, philosophical, religious, moral or political."[39]

Once established, however, Franklin's periodicals neither courted nor entirely avoided controversy. The magazine, which lasted only for six issues, consisted mostly of poems, prices, and government proceedings but did include significant documents pertaining to colonial affairs and the Great Awakening. The newspaper, which continued long after Franklin's death, usually reflected the serene, reasonable, high-minded public image he had cultivated. When his patron Andrew Hamilton, the popular leader of the 1730s, was portrayed as a devious politician in Bradford's *Mercury*, Franklin published an interview in which Hamilton calmly answered the charges by deftly depicting them as an example of the way the powerful attacked the just liberties of the innocent. "He steadily maintained the Cause of Liberty," Franklin wrote in a stirring obituary of Hamilton in 1741, "and the Laws made, during the time he was Speaker of the Assembly, which was many Years, will be a lasting Monument of his Affection to the People, and of his Concern for the welfare of this Province."[40]

A hallmark of the *Pennsylvania Gazette's* enlightened equanimity was the longer essay upholding the rights and dignity of the people. One was James Alexander's eloquent four-part defense of Andrew Hamilton's arguments at the seditious libel trial of John Peter Zenger in 1735.[41] Another was John Webbe's egalitarian "Z" essays which appeared in April and May of 1736. "We are all born naturally equal," he stated flatly, adding that obedience was owed to magistrates, but to ones of "our own Choice." The "Z" essays were generously sprinkled with the terms "good of the Whole," "the Publick Good," and "general Welfare." Webbe, a lawyer who had dealings with Franklin, wrote that virtuous actions could be defined as those "which have a Tendency to promote the Happiness of Mankind." The public had to know, he said, that the rights of mankind were "not a Gift bestowed upon us by other Men, *but a Right that belongs to us by the Laws of God and Nature.*" Webbe asserted that in a popular government the judgment of the people could be seen as infallible as long as it was not biased by faction or deluded by designing leaders.[42]

Feeling that his newspaper should be more of a moral preceptor than a party mechanism, Franklin sought to give his readers a sense of the world in which vice led to ruin, particularly the vice of drunkenness, which was repeatedly depicted in his autobiography as the downfall of laborers and others. Concluding a rueful news account of a woman's death from drink, for instance, the *Gazette* observed, "People cannot be too cautious of the first Steps that may lead them to be engaged in a Habit the most invincible and the most pernicious of all others." Yet, believing that plain moralizing was ineffective, Franklin could treat even the serious topic of alcohol with some humor. Both as Silence Dogood and as the editor of the *Gazette*, he made his point about the subject while offering readers a "drinker's dictionary," his list of synonyms for intoxication ranging from "boozy" to "tipsey." To Franklin, those who overindulged were robbed of their wealth and dignity. In one of his countless maxims as Poor Richard, he simply stated, "Nothing more like a Fool, than a drunken Man."[43]

The importance Franklin ascribed to his almanac is best captured in his autobiography, where he noted that he sold ten thousand copies a year and made a considerable profit. "And observing that it was generally read, scarce any Neighbourhood in the Province being without it," Franklin said, "I consider'd it as a proper Vehicle for conveying Instruction among the common People, who bought scarce any other Books." The instruction consisted of "Proverbial Sentences, chiefly such as inculcated Industry and Frugality, as the Means of procuring Wealth and thereby securing Virtue, it being more difficult for a Man in Want to act always honestly, as (to use here one of those Proverbs) *it is hard for an empty Sack to stand upright.*" In Franklin's mind, the practice of virtue was connected to economic status. The duty of the prosperous was to do more good for the sake of society, and the duty of the needy was to do more work for their own benefit. Franklin was delighted that "great Numbers" of a compilation of the almanac's sayings were "bought by the Clergy & Gentry to distribute gratis among their poor Parishioners and Tenants."[44]

Whatever Franklin said about making his periodicals benign vehicles of instruction, however, did not necessarily apply to his pamphlet publishing. The acrimonious material he did not think appropriate for his newspaper could, as he said in his memoirs, be printed "separately if desired, and the Author might have as many Copies as he pleased to distribute himself." This way, he reasoned, he was both preserving "Liberty of the Press" and maintaining his promise to furnish subscribers "with what might be either useful or entertaining." He did not wish to fill his newspaper with "private Altercation" that did not concern the general readership. Thus, when Franklin took controversial stands in religious or political debates, such as his defense of Rev. Samuel Hemphill in 1735, his insistence on military preparations in 1747, and his partisanship in Pennsylvania's politics during the 1750s and 1760s, he was inclined to use pamphlets rather than the *Pennsylvania Gazette.*[45]

Like many other printers, including the partners he took, Franklin espoused nonpartisanship in newspaper journalism. Factions and the personal libels they spawned were, after all, often condemned in colonial America. The existence of parties suggested that members of society were failing to work together for the general welfare, and volleys of defamation not only aggravated hostilities but also degraded the participants. "If Animosities arise, and that we should be obliged to take Party, let each of us range himself on the Side that unfurls *the Ensigns of publick Good,*" John Webbe argued in his first "Z" essay for the *Gazette.* "Factions will then vanish, which, if not timely suppressed, may overturn the *Ballance,* the Palladium of Liberty, and crush us under it's Ruins."[46] In his periodicals, Benjamin Franklin attempted to show ordinary Americans how to live according to their best interests and the best interests of others. His colonial journalism was intended to be a guide to a new, more enlightened order in which human sufferings were eased and liberties enjoyed.

CHAPTER

3

Educating the Enlightened Child

HAVING RETIRED FROM ACTIVE PARTICIPATION IN HIS PRINTING BUSI-
ness in 1748, Benjamin Franklin entered a profitable eighteen-year
partnership with David Hall thinking that his fortune would allow
him to devote the rest of his life to scientific "Studies and Amusements." As he related in his autobiography, however, "the Publick
now considering me as a Man of Leisure, laid hold of me for their
Purposes; every Part of our Civil Government, and almost at the same
time, imposing some Duty upon me."[1] Within a decade of quitting
his trade, Franklin was elected to city offices and to the Assembly,
was appointed joint deputy postmaster general for North America,
and was occupied in military and political affairs at the outbreak of
the French and Indian War. He also took the lead in establishing the
University of Pennsylvania, the Pennsylvania Hospital, and the Philadelphia Contributorship, a fire insurance company.

Franklin was pleased at having "so many spontaneous Testimon-
ies of the public's good Opinion" of him and the opportunity to practice what he had so long preached. His unrealized plan to withdraw
from business and public affairs, he had said to his fellow scientist
Cadwallader Colden in 1748, was intended to allow him "to enjoy
Life and my Friends" and to pursue his research on subjects that "may
produce something for the common Benefit of Mankind." Two years
later, however, Franklin was succumbing to the lure of public service
and advising the same correspondent not to let his studies have more
than their due weight. "Had Newton been Pilot but of a single com-

mon Ship," Franklin reasoned, "the finest of his Discoveries would
scarce have excus'd, or atton'd for his abandoning the Helm one Hour
in Time of Danger; how much less if she had carried the Fate of the
Commonwealth."[2] In the remaining four decades of his life, Franklin
worked to secure the fate of Pennsylvania and the United States as a
politician, diplomat, and statesman.

Public service, however, had its frustrations. Pennsylvania may
have been founded with William Penn's hopes of toleration, simplicity, peace, and egalitarianism, but Quaker influence and ideals had
declined by mid-century with the immigration of other groups and
generally increasing attention to worldly matters.[3] At the same time,
colonial America's political situation was reaching a critical stage and
becoming hard for someone of Franklin's interests to ignore, in spite
of personal costs. The sharp disappointments he experienced in prerevolutionary provincial affairs included the collapse of the Albany
Plan of Union he helped to develop, the defeat of General Edward
Braddock, who rejected his admonitions about fighting Indians, his
removal as president of the college's board of trustees in the wake of
partisan feuding, public quarrels with the proprietors' governors, and
a host of painful episodes in England trying to settle the Assembly's
differences with the Penns over the taxation of their proprietary estates and to resolve the controversies between the colonies and the
British government. Political enemies meanwhile used the press to
condemn him variously as a leveling incendiary, an immoral, ambitious swindler, and a betrayer of the patriot cause.[4]

In print and in private, Franklin sometimes reacted to these events
with weary resignation. In his autobiography, which provides some of
the dispiriting details and then ends not far into this part of his life,
he commented on the "incredible Meanness" of the proprietors and
the failure of Parliament to preserve colonial liberties.[5] He regretted
that Governor Robert Hunter Morris was the kind of person who loved
disputing. "They get Victory sometimes," Franklin observed of argu-
mentative people, "but they never get Good Will, which would be of
more use to them." Franklin enjoyed his personal relations with Morris and his successor, William Denny, but fought them politically. His
desire, he told Governor Denny who attempted to ply him with wine
and promises of reward, was merely measures "for the Good of the
People." To his London correspondent, Peter Collinson, he wrote, "I
may be mistaken in what is that Publick Good; but at least I mean
well."[6]

Franklin regarded as clear-cut wrongs the Penn's apparent greed in resisting taxation and Parliament's evident injustice in approving impositions on the colonies. Yet he was initially reluctant to take truly belligerent stands against either. He may have had some of the personal ambition opponents attributed to him, ambition to be either a popular leader or a royal official, but he was at least able to turn down the offers Denny made, saying, "my Circumstances, Thanks to God, were such as to make Proprietary Favours unnecessary to me; and that being a Member of the Assembly, I could not possibly accept of any." [7] Franklin was deeply disturbed by a world "full of the Errors of States & Princes" in which few *"Know their own Good, or knowing it pursue."* Leaders, in particular, were not insightful enough to prevent problems from arising. "Those who govern, having much Business on their Hands, do not generally like to take the Trouble of considering and carrying into Execution new Projects," he concluded in his memoirs. "The best public Measures are therefore seldom *adopted* from *previous Wisdom,* but *forc'd by the Occasion."* [8]

In Franklin's analysis, then, the public good was difficult to achieve because individuals were too preoccupied or too unwilling to seek it. The task of those who would enlighten others therefore was to stimulate a sense of human folly and injustice while still advancing the idea that people were capable of managing themselves better. Franklin's approach to living was thus much like the method he described in his widely published essay "The Morals of Chess." Like life, he observed, chess taught foresight, circumspection, caution, and the importance of not being discouraged by present appearances. The game also offered opportunities to obtain the affection and good will of others through playing with "generous civility." [9]

Accordingly, Franklin believed that education should instill a sense of obligation to live not only for oneself, but also for others. He articulated and practiced the emerging libertarian precept that learning could be a weapon against human misery, that the primary purpose of reading and schooling should not be to impart abstruse, arcane knowledge, but rather to implant the skills and values of capable, public-spirited citizens.

I

Benjamin Franklin Bache entered his celebrated grandfather's life at a distance. Benjamin Franklin was in the middle of a ten-year stay in

England when, in 1769, his daughter Sarah gave birth to the boy in Philadelphia. Two years earlier, Franklin had disapproved of Sarah's wish to wed a heavily indebted merchant whom he had not met, Richard Bache, and had since maintained an icy displeasure with the marriage.[10] Franklin's wife, Deborah, and Sally, as his daughter was called, were pitifully anxious to repair relations with the disappointed family patriarch. Deborah sent her husband pleasing descriptions of their grandson's even temper and resemblance to him. Franklin responded with presents and, having lost his own son Francis to small-pox at the age of four, forwarded expert medical advice on inocula-tion. "All who have seen my Grandson, agree with you in their Accounts of his being an uncommonly fine Boy," Franklin wrote to his sister Jane Mecom, "which brings often afresh to my Mind the Idea of my Son Franky, tho' now dead 36 Years, whom I have seldom since seen equal'd in every thing, and whom to this Day I cannot think of without a Sigh."[11]

The appearance of the baby helped reconcile Franklin to his only daughter's decision, as letter after letter from Deborah described the happiness she had from the boy she referred to as her little "King-bird." Benny, she wrote with a good deal of imagination, was sending his repects at the age of four months and was soon admiring house-hold portraits of his long-absent grandfather and long-dead Uncle Francis.[12] No event in the Kingbird's life was too insignificant for the correspondence. The child could be moved to tears by music and had been once by the thought of his distant grandfather dying.[13] He pro-ceeded carefully in learning to walk and announced at the age of two that he wanted to go to school. At four, he decided to use money he had received as a gift to buy a present for his newborn brother Wil-liam.[14] Benny was thus presented as promising material for the kind of cautious, compassionate, knowledgeable adult Franklin idealized, and the grandfather grew increasingly euphoric over the child. One tale of Benny's kindness and generosity toward his brother made Franklin exclaim: "'Tis a precious little Fellow! How much I long to see him!"[15]

The subject of his little "Benny Boy" lifted the grandfather's spir-its in an often grim period of his life. Between 1765 and 1775, Frank-lin was engaged in a series of propaganda battles for American causes. Using pseudonyms, he was a regular contributor to the London press and a thoroughly frustrated critic of what he regarded as the folly of Britain's colonial policies. Attempting to serve as a spokesman for reason and moderation, Franklin began to sense that his efforts to please or at least calm everyone were not working. "It is remarkable that soldiers by profession, men truly and unquestionably brave, seldom advise war but in cases of extream necessity," he wrote in a *London Chronicle* essay condemning journalists and "coffee-house talkers" for advocating the use of force against the colonies. "While mere rhetoricians, tongue-pads and scribes . . . are ever bawling for war on the most trifling occasions, and seem the most blood-thirsty of mankind." [16]

In the summer of 1771, a particularly low point in his lengthy stay in England, he retreated to the Twyford home of Jonathan Shipley, the Bishop of St. Asaph, where he wrote the first part of his memoirs over a period of two weeks. When he prepared to depart, the bishop's wife, Anna, convinced him to stay an additional day to celebrate Benny's second birthday. A "Floating Island," the customary birthday dessert for the Shipley children, was eaten, and the as yet unseen toddler was toasted by a guest who had already passed her one-hundredth year. "The Bishop's Lady politely added, *and that he may be* as good *a Man as his Grandfather,* I said I hop'd he would be *much better,*" Franklin reported to Deborah. "The Bishop, still more complaisant than his Lady, said, We will compound the Matter; and be contented if he should not prove *quite so good.*" [17]

Americans like Franklin were beginning to believe that good citizens were produced by a strict, philosophically sound upbringing. During the last decades of the eighteenth century, they were concluding that republics could only thrive where the young acquired liberal educations that impressed on them the importance of moral duties and political rights. [18] In a pamphlet on public schools that was written after the Revolution, Franklin's friend Dr. Benjamin Rush insisted, "Let our pupil be taught that he does not belong to himself, but that he is public property. Let him be taught to love his family, but let him be taught, at the same time, that he must forsake and even forget them, when the welfare of his country requires it." Rush thought it should be possible to thus "convert men into republican machines" so that they might have the fortitude to perform their parts in the "great machine" of society. [19] As Poor Richard, Franklin wrote that public spirit made myriads happy by being the "Parent of Trade, Wealth, Liberty and Peace." The almanac also advised, "Let thy Child's first Lesson be Obedience, and the second may be what thou wilt." [20]

Accordingly, Franklin congratulated his wife on one occasion for not interfering when Benny was spanked, "as I feared, from your Fondness of him, that he would be too much humoured, and perhaps spoiled." Sally assured her father of the boy's "manly behaviour," but made it clear that Benny and the family were anxious to see him return to Philadelphia.[21] Hopes that Franklin would come back were routinely dashed, but there were no doubts about his rigorous and sometimes overbearing involvement in family affairs from the other side of the Atlantic. Although he might admit that he would "long to be at home to play with Ben"[22] and would send him useful presents such as a hat or even five guineas to invest,[23] Franklin expected his grandson to measure up to his standards. Indeed, Franklin could go so far as to seem to preempt the parents entirely. "I am glad the little Fellow continues well, and that Sally is so careful to be with him out of Town during the Hot Weather," he wrote to Deborah in the summer of 1771. "I consider her as nursing him for me, and shall pay her handsomely for her Trouble when I return."[24]

II

For all of his public affability, Franklin was exacting and even severe in his private life. The new American he envisaged would be liberal and gracious in community affairs and yet exercise rigorous control in personal matters. To contribute to society, the individual needed not only to have properly enlightened ideas, but also the discipline to see them realized. As he demonstrated in his long absence from Deborah, in his reaction to Sally's marriage, and later in his unforgiving treatment of his son William, the royal governor of New Jersey, for taking the loyalist side in the Revolution, Franklin could have higher priorities than the immediate rewards of family affection. In fact, for all his attention to the intellect of various women in the course of his life, he would sometimes admonish his wife and daughter as if they were foolish children. Exasperated with Deborah's inability to manage money, he told Sally, a daughter he periodically accused of having too much taste for luxury, that she should keep exact accountings of the household expenses and send them to London for his perusal. "Study Poor Richard a little," he added, "and you may find some Benefit from his Instructions."[25] His "dear little Benjamin," on the other hand, was to be treated as a little adult and expected to go "into the Cold Bath like a Man."[26]

Franklin may have been slow to take the kinds of impassioned political stands which led to wasteful and often irrational societal conflicts, but he was a self-assured and unrelenting judge of individual behavior. Citizens were to acquire wealth for the security of their family and benefit of the community and, as his autobiography conveyed, were to do justice to their parents and benefactors. When his son William violated these principles by, as Franklin put it, deserting him in his old age and "taking up Arms against me, in a Cause, wherein my good Fame, Fortune and Life were all at Stake," no reconciliation was seriously considered. After the Revolution he wrote to William:

> You conceived, you say, that your Duty to your King and Regard for your Country requir'd this. I ought not to blame you for differing in sentiment with me in Public Affairs. We are Men, all subject to Errors. Our Opinions are not in our own Power; they are form'd and govern'd much by Circumstances, that are often as inexplicable as they are irresistible. Your Situation was such that few would have censured your remaining Neuter, *tho' there are Natural Duties which precede political ones, and cannot be extinguish'd by them.*[27]

Having once been eager to make William his confidant and to oversee his rise to a governorship, Franklin effectively disinherited his only living son in his will, saying, "The part he acted against me in the late war, which is of public notoriety, will account for my leaving him no more of an estate he endeavoured to deprive me of."[28] Filial devotion, economic security, and working for the welfare of society were bedrock principles for a man who deeply respected his own father and acquired a fortune which allowed him to give time and money to philanthropic causes. Franklin bequeathed a substantial sum for a fund "to assist young married artificers in setting up their business" in Boston and Philadelphia, money which was to be used eventually in public works to benefit all citizens. He hoped that the cities would "accept the offer of these donations as a mark of my good will, a token of my gratitude, and a testimony of my earnest desire to be useful to them after my departure."[29]

Franklin discussed the respect due to parents in a letter to Sally in which he joined the chorus of Americans denouncing the formation of the Society of Cincinnati after the war. Saying that the former officers were trying to establish "an Order of *hereditary Knights*," contrary to the democratic spirit of the country, he maintained that honor did not *descend* through posterity, but rather *ascended*, as the Chinese believed, from an individual to his mother and father "on the supposition that it must have been owing to the Education, Instruction, and good Example afforded him by his Parents, that he was rendered capable of serving the Publick." Franklin suggested that the badges of the society be worn by parents instead of passed down to children as "a kind of Obedience to the Fourth Commandment, in which God enjoins us to *honour* our Father and Mother, but has nowhere directed us to honour our Children."[30]

The Fourth Commandment was evidently not so important to Franklin's son and daughter. William in 1762 had spurned Franklin's choice for a bride, deciding to wed a fragile aristocrat, Elizabeth Downes, rather than Franklin's beloved English "daughter," Polly Stevenson. William's refusal to succumb to Franklin's entreaties to resign his post at the outbreak of the war brought about an irreversible estrangement between father and son. William haughtily declared that if his father intended to set the colonies on fire, he hoped Benjamin "would take care to run away by the light of it." Sally had the right politics but her own ideas about marriage and other matters. (Although her father's will had requested that she not use them for what he said was "the expensive, vain, and useless fashion" of wearing jewelry, Sally financed a trip to Europe after his death by selling some of the 408 diamonds surrounding a miniature portrait of Louis XVI which Franklin had received from the monarch himself.)[31]

Late in life, Franklin consequently was left with a heartfelt wish for a descendant who could honor him and conform to what he, in his public career and writings, had so long represented. William had fathered an illegitimate son in 1760 while in England but had no offspring with his wife. During the revolutionary period, Franklin's affections were thus increasingly drawn to his grandson and namesake Benjamin Franklin Bache. Near the end of his residence in London, he told his family he was exceedingly pleased to have their "Kingbird" stories and was longing to return to be with the child.[32] "If I hear that he continues a good Boy," he wrote of Benny, "I shall love him very much."[33]

III

In his criticism of the Society of Cincinnati, Benjamin Franklin noted that its bald eagle emblem had been thought by some to look more like a turkey, a resemblance he said was not to be regretted. He playfully asserted that since the eagle was "of bad moral Character," stealing food from other creatures and therefore existing "like those among Men who live by Sharping and Robbing," the turkey was "a much more respectable Bird." The turkey was in fact first found in North America, he said, and was courageous in defending its farmyard, though it was, admittedly, "a little vain and silly." The eagle, he observed, was "a rank Coward; the little *KingBird,* not bigger than a Sparrow, attacks him boldly and drives him out the District."[34] Franklin wanted his own little Kingbird to be bold enough to fight for Enlightenment libertarian causes, and Americans to live by their labor and mutual concern and to protect themselves from outside encroachment.

Franklin's method for inculcating such commitments was based on the growing sense during the eighteenth century that people were not naturally wicked beings, debilitated by original sin, and that given the right environment and instruction they could live moral lives and flourish in the world.[35] Enlightenment writers contended that if humans were not inherently evil, then they could be kindly but firmly guided to develop the traits of self-control and goodwill which would improve society by improving its members. Virtue would conquer vice in individuals, educational theorists such as Locke argued, if rewards and punishments consisted of esteem and disgrace rather than bribes and beatings, at least for children old enough to reason. Because they were expected to embark on a course of self-improvement and eventually to reap the personal benefits of success, children were expected to submit to the standards of wise adults as they would eventually sacrifice some private desires to the public good.[36] The republican child, Benjamin Rush wrote, "must be taught to amass wealth, but it must be only to encrease his power of contributing to the wants and demands of the state"; the way students learned the subordination of good citizenship was to have the authority of their masters "be as *absolute* as possible."[37]

Franklin practiced strong discipline, but a discipline based on the Lockean notion of esteem and disgrace. Like other Americans, however, he did not concur with Locke's belief that education was best conducted for the sons of gentlemen by private tutors in the home. Franklin thought, as the Jeffersonians would later maintain,[38] that a widespread diffusion of knowledge was necessary not only to expand opportunities for success, but also to preserve republican morality and government. In a letter to Samuel Johnson, the clergyman and educator he unsuccessfully sought to head the new Academy of Philadelphia in 1750 and 1751, Franklin wrote:

> I think with you, that nothing is of more importance for the public weal, than to form and train up youth in wisdom and virtue. Wise and good men are, in my opinion, the *strength* of a state: much more so than riches or arms, which, under the management of Ignorance and Wickedness, often draw on destruction, instead of providing for the safety of a people. And though the culture bestowed on *many* should be successful only with a *few*, yet the influence of those few and the service in their power, may be very great.[39]

Franklin believed, along with many Enlightenment writers, that instruction made the greatest impact in childhood. He told Johnson that "general virtue is more probably to be expected and obtained from the *education* of youth, than from the *exhortation* of adult persons; bad habits and vices of the mind, being, like diseases of the body, more easily prevented than cured."[40] Franklin's views were similar to those later published by his correspondent Lord Kames, who stressed the role of parents in producing good citizens and the importance of their "sweetening the temper of their children and improving their benevolence" at an early age. Adults could not be held accountable for their opinions, Kames observed in an essay on education, because as children their minds were like blank paper and received opinions which could not be eradicated. "Therefore, neglect no opportunity of setting virtue and vice before your child in their proper colours," he advised, "repeat to it often that if it be good, every person will love it; if naughty, that every person will hate it; and, in a word, that happiness is the result of virtue; misery of vice."[41]

Franklin's philosophy was spelled out in his 1749 pamphlet *Proposals Relating to the Education of Youth in Pennsylvania*, which relied on Milton, Locke, and other English writers in advocating exercise for the body and a broad curriculum for the mind.[42] Because time was limited, Franklin wrote, students should study subjects that were the "*most useful* and *most ornamental.*" Courses should therefore range from drawing, which he regarded as "a kind of Universal Language," and farming, the "Improvement of Agriculture being useful to all, and Skill in it no Disparagement to any," to history, which would teach the advantages of morality and liberty, and science, which provided both beneficial improvements and "new Proofs of Divine Providence." Writing should be taught with *Cato's Letters,* Algernon Sidney, and other "Classicks" as models. A good education, Franklin said, was "the surest Foundation of the Happiness both of private Families and of Common-wealths" and should be supported by governments to produce people "qualified to serve the Publick with Honour to themselves, and to their Country." The pamphlet concluded:

> With the whole should be constantly inculcated and cultivated, that *Benignity of Mind,* which shows itself in *searching for* and *seizing* every Opportunity *to serve* and *to oblige;* and is the Foundation of what is called GOOD BREEDING; highly useful to the Possessor, and most agreeable to all.
>
> The Idea of what is *true Merit,* should also be often presented to Youth, explain'd and impress'd on their Minds, as consisting in an *Inclination* join'd with an *Ability* to serve Mankind, one's Country, Friends and Family; which *Ability* is (with the Blessing of God) to be acquir'd or greatly encreas'd by *true Learning;* and should indeed be the great *Aim* and *End* of all Learning.[43]

The academy and college established in Philadelphia soon after Franklin's pamphlet appeared was quickly beset by religious and political altercations, and in 1756 he was removed as president of the trustees. The provost, Rev. William Smith, was suspected of favoring his own Anglican church at the expense of other denominations that supported the undertaking and was known to be exerting himself in the proprietary cause with articles and pamphlets attacking Franklin. Although his memoirs said "a Number" of the students were "distinguish'd by their improv'd Abilities, servicable in public Stations, and Ornaments to their Country," Franklin could not be entirely satisfied. In requesting financial support from the City Council in 1750, he had observed that most of the contributions had come from the trustees themselves, "many of whom have no Children of their own to educate, but act from a View to the Public Good, without Regard to Sect or Party." Annoyed with the direction the institution had taken, and particularly by its neglect of the English language, he expressed regret to the final days of his life that he had been too often absent from the country to exert his influence in school affairs.[44]

IV

While in London before the Revolution, Franklin did oversee the education of William Franklin's son William Temple Franklin, whose illegitimate birth and existence in England were kept quiet and perhaps were even unknown to Deborah. Benjamin had wanted Temple educated at Eton and Oxford but was wary of the "Relaxation of all Discipline, the viciousness of the Youth, and Extravagance of the Expence" in the country's prestigious schools. He told William that he considered good sense, "the Knowledge of Men," as important as the liberal arts and thought that it was best learned "by a Boy in a Croud of Boys."[45] Temple was accordingly educated in James Elphinston's boarding school in Kent, a modest institution with a reputation for good morals and practical training. Finally, after Deborah's death in 1774 and after fifteen years of being raised by guardians and schoolmasters, Temple was brought to America by his grandfather in 1775 and acknowledged as the son of the otherwise childless royal governor.[46]

The country Franklin returned to in that year had entered the hostilities he had long worked to avoid. Arriving in Philadelphia with Temple, he learned of the battles of Lexington and Concord and for the first time saw his five-year-old grandson, Benjamin Franklin Bache. As the months passed, news came of battles, burnings, and blockades. By midyear, Washington was appointed commander-in-chief and America was in full rebellion. At Franklin's home, the new addition to the Bache family, two-year-old William, was imitating the drilling soldiers by marching with a toy gun and whistling as if playing a fife.[47] In January of 1776, Thomas Paine, who had arrived in Philadelphia at the end of 1774 with a letter of introduction from Franklin to Richard Bache,[48] published his *Common Sense* pamphlet denouncing hereditary power and welcoming an independent American republic that would begin the world anew and be a refuge for mankind.

Franklin, one of the Americans who retained affection for Paine as the writer's reputation declined,[49] had also taken up the martial spirit of the Revolution. As a member of the Second Continental Congress, he, at the age of seventy, plunged into the exhausting details of running a country at war. With the help of Richard Bache, he reorganized the postal system and arranged for the printing of paper currency which bore encouraging, egalitarian messages in its designs.[50] Franklin was also involved in military preparations and creating a seal for the United States. The seal he and a committee proposed used the motto "E PLURIBUS UNUM" and the "Eye of Providence in a radiant Triangle."[51] He had never been more busy, he wrote Joseph Priestly, adding, "It will scarce be credited in Britain that men can be as diligent with us from zeal for the public good, as with you for thousands per annum. Such is the difference between uncorrupted new states, and corrupted old ones."[52]

When contacted by Lord Howe, one of England's peace commissioners, in the summer of 1776 to discuss the possibility of negotiating a resolution to the conflict, Franklin maintained that a reconciliation would be impossible on any terms that a country as rapacious as Britain would be willing to accept, and that warfare in America would be as ruinous to the mother country as the Crusades had been to Europe. "I have not the Vanity, my Lord, to think of intimidating by thus predicting the Effects of this War," he wrote, "for I know it will in England have the Fate of all my former Predictions, not to be believed till the Event shall verify it." Franklin said that he had long worked to preserve "that fine and noble China Vase the British Empire," but that once it was broken, reuniting the parts was scarcely possible.[53]

At the same time that Franklin was handling his Congressional duties and overseeing defense measures, he and his son were engaged in a delicate battle of wills over Temple's future. William, while struggling to maintain some semblance of British rule in New Jersey, was also attempting to exert some authority over the son he had hardly known. He had hoped to send Temple to King's College in New York, a loyalist stronghold, but the boy was instead sent to the College of Philadelphia, presumably at his grandfather's insistence.[54] Temple did spend time at Perth Amboy with his parents, however, and, when in Philadelphia to attend classes, was sternly admonished by William to devote himself to his studies.

Franklin, wary of his English-bred grandson falling under loyalist influence and embarrassed by William's efforts to obstruct the progress of the Revolution, expressed no regret when the governor of New

Jersey was finally arrested by patriot troops in June of 1776 and taken to Connecticut for confinement. Temple went to New Jersey to comfort his stepmother and was slow to return, worrying his grandfather that he was reluctant to go back to school. Franklin wrote to warn him that it was "the Time of Life in which you are to lay the Foundations of your future Improvement, and of your Importance among Men." He added that his cousin Benny had written Temple but that the letter was so unintelligible that it might have raised the suspicions of a revolutionary committee if it were intercepted, especially since it was "directed to a Tory House."[55] Franklin was not alone among patriot leaders in having loyalist relatives, but, he later said of William's political stand, "nothing has ever hurt me so much and affected me with such keen Sensations."[56]

Remaining at Perth Amboy into September, Temple asked for his grandfather's permission to go to Connecticut to see his father. Franklin refused, "for many reasons which I have not time to write." In response, Temple said his father had left the decision to Elizabeth of when he should return to Philadelphia and that she seemed inclined to keep him longer. Temple speculated that his grandfather thought he would carry improper "intelligence" to William and insisted that he was "entirely ignorant of every thing relating to Publick Affairs, except the petty News, which is talk'd of by every body, and is in all the Publick Prints." Franklin replied that he had no such fear, but instead was concerned about both his studies and his welfare on the long journey while the roads were being traveled by men with "infectious Camp Distemper." Indeed, it was an anxious time; British soldiers had just won the Battle of Long Island and moved into New York City, not far from Perth Amboy where patriot troops had been stationed over the summer. Franklin's next letter to Temple came six days later. "I hope you will return hither immediately, and that your Mother will make no Objection to it," he wrote in haste, "something offering here that will be much to your Advantage if you are not out of the way."[57]

When he reached Philadelphia, Temple learned that his grandfather had accepted a mission to France to negotiate treaties and obtain aid. The old revolutionary's preparations for the voyage included giving Congress a loan of all of his own money he could raise, "between three and four thousand pounds," and turning over his responsibilities as postmaster general to Richard Bache. Franklin planned to have the sixteen-year-old Temple serve as his secretary and decided to take his other grandson as well. His "special good Boy" Benny, Franklin wrote to his English friend Polly Stevenson Hewson, would obtain "a little French Language and Address" and then be sent over "to pay his Respects" to Polly's then two-year-old daughter Elizabeth. Shortly after returning to Philadelphia, Franklin, playing matchmaker, had discussed the English baby with Benny and found that his only objection was that she was too young, a problem the grandfather thought would "lessen every day." He only hoped, he told Polly, that he would live long enough to dance at the wedding.[58]

V

Franklin was unable to be so lighthearted about his ocean journey which, he later said, "almost demolish'd me." He and his grandsons departed on October 26 aboard the American warship *Reprisal* and, although they evaded British navy vessels and made good time, the crossing was so rough and the food so difficult to chew that Franklin arrived with "scarce strength to stand." Winds prevented the ship from entering the Loire, and the three were taken ashore at Auray in a fishing boat on December 3. They had difficulty understanding the boatman, who spoke the Breton language, but were able to make out the word for "devil." The village proved to be "a wretched place" with no carriages to be hired. A driver sent for from a nearby village arrived the next evening and took them in the dark through a forest where a gang of robbers had killed travelers only two weeks before.[59]

On the way to Paris, the adulation of the French for the old philosopher was lavishly displayed. Franklin was greeted by enthusiastic crowds of well-wishers at the first city they stopped in, Nantes. There he wrote to his sister Jane Mecom, "You can have no Conception of the Respect with which I am receiv'd and treated here by the first People, in my private Character: for as yet I have assum'd no public One."[60] With the news of his arrival preceding him, Franklin and the two boys stopped at Versailles, where the rupture in Anglo-American relations had been long awaited. They reached Paris on December 21, and a week later negotiations began with the French foreign minister, Comte de Vergennes.

While Franklin and his grandsons were on the road to Paris, his daughter Sally and sister Jane were fleeing an advancing British army

that threatened Philadelphia. From Goshen, twenty-four miles outside
the city, Jane Mecom wrote, "I was distresd at yr leveing us but as
affairs have turned out I have blesd God you were absent."[61] Franklin, in fact, found comfortable accommodations at the Hôtel de Valentinois in Passy, a small village on the Seine. "I enjoy here an ex-
ceeding good State of Health.—I live in a fine airy House on a Hill,
which has a large Garden with fine Walks in it, about 1/2 an hours
Drive from the City of Paris," he wrote cheerfully to Jane in 1777. "I
walk a little every Day in the Garden, have a good Appetite & sleep
well." Having his grandchildren with him, he added, was "a Comfort
and Pleasure to me."[62]

Before enrolling Benny in the nearby Le Coeur boarding school,
Franklin took his seven-year-old grandson to Paris to visit Voltaire,
who was so old and infirm that stories in the press had already said he
was dead. The reports were true, Voltaire had remarked in some witty
verse, only somewhat premature. In the presence of some twenty wit-
nesses, Voltaire was asked to give a blessing to the boy. He put his
hand on Benny's head and said in English, "God and Liberty."[63]
Hearing an account of the meeting in England, where he was in exile,
Thomas Hutchinson, former royal governor of Massachusetts, remarked to Lord Mansfield that it was "difficult to say which of those
words had been most used to bad purposes."[64]

Adults did not hesitate to express their wishes for Benny Bache
or to exert their authority over him. His mother wrote to Franklin
that she hoped the boy would behave well enough to earn his love.
"We used to think he gave little trouble at home," Sally told her
father, "but that was perhaps a mothers partiality."[65] Richard Bache
later instructed Benny to "pay strict attention to everything your
Grandfather says."[66] The parents had little reason to worry, however.
At once the supreme authority, oracle of enlightenment, and closest
source of affection in his grandson's life, Franklin took over the duties
of a parent with ease. Benny, wearing a wig and dressed in silk breeches
and stockings, accepted life in a boarding school and took dancing
lessons. "He dines with me every Sunday and some Holidays," Franklin informed his son-in-law in the spring of 1777. "He begins to speak
French readily, and reads it pretty well, for the time."[67]

Their parental anxieties were further allayed by the events of
that year. After returning to Philadelphia in the summer, the Bache

family was driven into the countryside by British troops, who occupied the city in the fall. "We are happy to hear that Ben likes his School and that he improves fast," Richard Bache said to Franklin at the beginning of 1778. "We esteem it a happy circumstance his going with you, for as things have turned out, had he remained here, he would have lost a deal of precious time, which is now usefully, I hope, employed."[68]

With his schoolmaster's supervision and his grandfather's regular attention, Benny Bache was able to cope with a new culture and a new language. In addition to French, the school offered Latin, Greek, fencing, music, and drawing. M. Le Coeur offered rewards to the best students as "an Encouragement."[69] After a year, Benny was joined by Jesse Deane and John Quincy Adams, the sons of Franklin's fellow diplomats Silas Deane and John Adams. John Adams brought the boys, both about Benny's age, from America in the spring of 1778.

What Benny gained in companionship, however, Franklin lost in the sour note Adams' presence introduced into the pleasurable life of Passy. Adams saw Franklin in "a Scene of continual discipation," usually spending his afternoons in the company of women in the neighborhood and coming home "at all hours from Nine to twelve O Clock at night." Franklin's offenses were apparently nothing more than playing chess, listening to music, and flirting with French friends, particularly Madame Brillon de Jouy, a composer and respected musician, and Madame Helvétius, widow of the philosopher. Still, Adams found the kind of social life Franklin enjoyed thoroughly insidious. "I often asked myself how this rage for Amusements of every kind, and this disinclination to serious Business, would answer in our republican Governments in America," he later reflected. "It seemed to me that every Thing must run to ruin."[70]

Adams, who had arrived too late to play a role in the treaties of commerce and alliance signed in 1778, was Franklin's equal as a commissioner, but was dejected at having to take over the mundane task of untangling the finances of the American mission. More than a little jealous of Franklin, Adams disparaged his abilities to others and eventually harbored enough suspicions of Franklin and the French to make Franklin conclude that he was "sometimes, and in some things, absolutely out of his senses."[71] The criticisms he received from Adams and other Americans were not resented, Franklin said, because those who "are unhappy because others are happy, must meet daily with so many Causes of Torment, that I conceive them to be already in a State of Damnation."[72]

Yet, neither the republicanism of Poor Richard nor the future of Benny Bache could be far from his thoughts. Franklin felt a humorous sort of guilt over his own eating habits and lack of exercise,[73] and the aristocratic surroundings were anything but a model of hard work and virtuous living. At the Hôtel de Valentinois itself, Captain John Paul Jones was carrying on a romance with Madame Thérèse Chaumont, the wife of Franklin's host.[74] After two years of school at Passy, the boy was sent to Geneva. "As he is destined to live in a Protestant Country, and a Republic," Franklin explained, "I thought it best to finish his Education where the proper Principles prevail."[75] Franklin assured Richard Bache that Benny "went very cheerfully." He told others that the French nobility sent their sons to Geneva, despite the religious difference, because the education and morals were better than in Paris.[76]

Making the Republican Citizen

DURING THE REVOLUTIONARY ERA, AMERICANS WERE SELF-consciously moving toward a national political system they called a republic. The federal Constitution, moreover, guaranteed each state a "Republican form of government." The term "republic" could be defined negatively as a government without monarchical rule, and positively as a political system in which voters would, as Madison expressed it, select wise representatives to "refine and enlarge the public views" with a voice which may be "more consonant to the public good, than if pronounced by the people themselves convened for the purpose."[1] The "first object" of such a government, Madison said in the *Federalist,* should be "the protection of different and unequal faculties of acquiring property."[2]

The concept of a republic could also be a more communitarian ideal in which the citizens would expect legislators to reflect their constituents' interests and yet would have a joint concern with what the preamble of the Constitution referred to as "the general welfare." A republic, wrote Thomas Paine, did not necessarily have any particular form of government but was rather that kind of system which was "established and conducted for the interest of the public, as well individually as collectively."[3] The prime question of late eighteenth-century political economy was thus how to accommodate both private interest and the public good.[4]

Answers to this question often began with the assumption that the American republic would present the mass of people with more opportunities for moral and material well-being than the Old World had provided. A better life for the common person would be possible, it appeared, if government policy created an economic structure in which citizens would have opportunities to prosper from their own initiative. "It is a well known truth that the riches and strength of a free Country does not consist in property being vested in a few Individuals," said a petition of Kentucky settlers to Congress in 1784, "but the more general it is distributed, the more it promotes industry, population and frugality, and even morality." The Kentucky petitioners, who were seeking statehood, complained that land was being monopolized by "several Gentleman . . . of fortune and influence" and that valuable salt springs had been "engrossed by Individuals" instead of being "held sacred and for the use of the community in general."[5] Such conflicts raised the perpetual problem of what was to belong to the person and what was to be shared with the community, but in the new context of a democratic republic it was for the people at large to decide.

I

Politicians did consider legislative solutions to social inequities. Thomas Jefferson, for instance, saw in the *ancien régime* the sort of conditions he had sought to avoid in Virginia by advocating public education, separation of church and state, and the end of primogeniture and entails. Walking in the countryside near Fontainebleau in the autumn of 1785, Jefferson, the minister to France after Franklin, had talked to a poor woman who had trouble finding work to support her children. He thought about "that unequal division of property which occasions the numberless instances of wretchedness" in Europe, and, describing his observations in a letter to Madison, asked why the poor should be left idle and hungry when the rich were keeping uncultivated lands for game. Although accepting "that an equal division of property is impracticable," Jefferson discussed a need to tax the wealthy at a higher rate, to divide inheritances equally, and to make lands available to the unemployed. "The small landholders are the most precious part of a state," he said.[6]

Not quite ready to accept the full thrust of Jefferson's egalitarian economics, Madison blandly replied, "I have no doubt that the misery of the lower classes will be found to abate whenever the Government assumes a freer aspect, and the laws favor a subdivision of property." Madison suggested, however, that a more equal distribution of land in a populous country would create troublesome surpluses and that the "greater simplicity of manners" that would result would mean less employment in manufacturing. The problem, he thought, was a "puzzling" one.[7]

Madison accepted the republican conception of virtuous, independent farmers moving across the continent and selling their crops on open world markets, but, in contrast to Jefferson and Franklin, he believed that the country's population would grow enough to force a turn to manufacturing within twenty-five years.[8] Americans, he thought, should plan their government accordingly with the checks and balances that could control the class conflicts that would develop in the future. The nation was already not "one homogeneous mass" and was beginning to show "symptoms of a leveling spirit," he told the delegates to the Constitutional Convention. "In framing a system which we wish to last for ages," he said, "we should not lose sight of the changes which ages will produce."[9]

In the 1780s, however, the design of the government was not always focused upon as the route to a just and stable republicanism. Disparities in wealth were not a particularly ominous concern to Americans who believed the nation's people would remain primarily agricultural for centuries. At the Constitutional Convention, Madison might warn of impending economic clashes and Hamilton might say that inequalities in property "would exist as long as liberty existed" and were "already great amongst us," but Charles Pinckney could calmly assert that there was "more equality of rank and fortune in America than in any country under the sun; and this is likely to continue as long as the unappropriated western lands remain unsettled."[10]

Americans thus inclined were able to contemplate with satisfaction the seemingly wondrous workings of the market described by free-trade theorists. In criticizing restrictive mercantilist policies and pointing toward unhindered exchange as natural and efficient, the French physiocrats and eventually Adam Smith, whose work Jefferson admired, had identified the consumable goods produced by labor as the actual wealth of nations, rather than unconsumable riches. Smith placed a less absolute emphasis on farming as the source of true national wealth than his French counterparts, but he nevertheless concluded that agriculture was the most genuinely productive of human enterprises.[11]

Franklin, who had congenial relations with the physiocrats while in Europe and may have had some influence on Adam Smith before the publication of *Wealth of Nations*,[12] reached similar conclusions about husbandry and trade. "Agriculture is truly *productive of new wealth;* Manufactures only change Forms," he wrote in 1768.[13] At the same time, in considering physiocratic principles, Franklin declared that "most of the Acts of Parliament, Arrets and Edicts of Princes and States, relating to Commerce, are political Errors, solicited and obtained by Particulars for private Interest under the Pretext of Public Good."[14] Countries that kept their ports open to all nations, he later observed, were likely to be "on the whole the most prosperous."[15]

With its aim of a more equal and self-adjusting economy understood to be based on labor, the American Enlightenment of Franklin and Jefferson presented a model of a largely agricultural nation able to sell its surpluses in foreign markets.[16] In eighteenth-century England, the breakdown of government control over selling practices had brought about considerable public unrest as buyers found themselves at times unable to obtain necessities at affordable prices,[17] but the United States could be seen as a nation of upright, self-sufficient farmers expanding across the West. One of the themes of Paine's *Common Sense* was that an independent America would profit from the unrestricted export of agricultural commodities, a trade he said would continue "while eating is the custom of Europe."[18] Jefferson began championing a policy of free exchange while secretary of state[19] and encouraged westward movement with the Louisiana Purchase in 1803. Franklin was interested in the experiments which were making agriculture more productive in his lifetime, but, having always been a city dweller, he admitted knowing little about the subject.[20]

In his writings, therefore, Franklin spoke of the importance of farming to the country's future, but he also gave attention to workers who, like himself, did not have experience tilling the soil. Having prospered as a tradesman and offered his wisdom to others, he set out to entify his principles in the one other life he could personally control—that of his grandson. As he demonstrated in preparing Benjamin Franklin Bache to be a printer, he hoped to see Enlightenment ideals realized in an urban context. While Jefferson might wish to see "our work-shops remain in Europe" so that city life would not corrupt government, Franklin could conceive of republicanism thriving wherever independent, capable, enterprising citizens knew their rights and responsibilities.[21] Outside of agriculture, however, the making of republicans would seem to require a more conscious effort.

II

Franklin was pleased by his role in his grandson Temple's life, having, as he saw it, "rescued a valuable young man from the danger of being a Tory, and fixed him in honest republican Whig principles."[22] Temple, however, never seemed quite ready to follow through on his grandfather's hopes that he would become a lawyer, gentleman farmer, or public official. He gained political experience as Franklin's private secretary and made himself a dashing figure among the young women of Paris, fathering an illegimate son, as his father and grandfather had.[23] Still, he only possessed, as Jefferson later observed, abilities "good enough for common uses but not great enough for uncommon ones."[24] Benny, on the other hand, appeared to have the steady character and aptitude necessary for achievement in the world. Franklin wrote to Richard Bache in 1779 that Benny was "a good, honest lad, and will make, I believe, a valuable man." The nine-year-old boy, he noted, had attained "as much proficiency in his learning, as the boarding school he was at could well afford him; and, after some consideration where to find a better for him, I at length fixed on sending him to Geneva."[25]

Benny was taken to Geneva by a Swiss diplomat, Philibert Cramer, who was a friend and publisher of Voltaire's. Cramer, who took a liking to the boy and was prepared to oversee his education, died not long after their arrival, but the child had been taken into the Rue Verdaine home of Gabriel Louis de Marignac, a one-time poet and military officer who was a regent at the college and academy of Geneva founded by Calvin in 1559.[26] In the first year, Franklin's letters sought to impress on Bache the "fine Opportunity" he had to learn what would be "reputable and useful" to him in later life. He assured his grandson that he thought of him every day and said that he wished he would return to the United States prepared with the knowledge and virtue he would need "to become an honourable Man." Franklin instructed the boy to do cheerfully what his mentors advised him to do and to understand that "by so doing you will recommend yourself to me, and all good People as well as we will love & esteem you for your dutiful Behaviour."[27] Bache told his grandfather that he would do all he could to be first in his class and that Monsieur de Marignac said he was "a good boy."[28] Franklin said, "I shall always love you very much if you continue to be a good Boy."[29]

At the college, Benny spent long hours translating Latin and Greek, the core of the curriculum for the school's five hundred students. Marignac reported to Franklin that he found a good heart and character as well as an observant eye in Benny, but also a tendency to take criticism harshly and to defend himself against anyone who treated him unjustly.[30] As a man who could admire the courageous kingbird and practice a Lockean psychology of esteem and disgrace,[31] Franklin had no reason to be disturbed by the suggestion that his grandson displayed valor in the face of injustice or mortification in response to a perceived failure. "Use your Skill to make his Will supple and pliant to Reason," Locke had advised for instructing a child, "Teach him to love Credit and Commendation; to abhor being thought ill or meanly of . . . and then the rest will come all easily."[32]

In letter after letter to Franklin, Benny said that he would always be grateful for his grandfather's generosity in providing for his education and would do everything possible to succeed in his classes.[33] After the first year, he was able to inform Franklin that he had won a school prize for translation from Latin to French and would receive a silver medal from the first magistrate in a ceremony at the Cathedral of St. Pierre.[34]

Franklin, like the Geneva college, followed Enlightenment educational theory by rewarding achievement. After the Latin prize, he authorized Benny to celebrate with a party for his friends.[35] On another occasion, he was pleased with some of the boy's drawings and sent Marignac money to buy books as a present. "But I expect you will improve," he cautioned, "and that you will send me some every half Year that I may see how you improve."[36] Willing to pay attention to details in a way he did not always do with his nation's diplomatic mission, Franklin supervised his grandson's education closely, treating it as a matter of considerable importance.

Franklin insisted on the respect due to parents and the public duties required of good citizens. When Sally Bache organized Philadelphia women to sew shirts for Washington's soldiers, Franklin wrote to Benny, "Be diligent in your Studies, that you also may be qualified to do Service to your Country, and be worthy [of] so good a Mother."[37] Another reason Franklin gave for closely supervising Benny's education was to influence the boy's fate. Franklin wrote to him in 1780 that there were two sorts of persons in the world, the virtuous, contented people, and the vicious, miserable ones. "The first had a good Education given them by their Friends and they took Pains when at School to improve their Time and increase their Knowledge," he warned, "the others either had no Friend to pay for their Schooling and so were never taught, or else when they were at School they neglected their Studies, were idle and wicked and disobedient to their Masters, and would not be instructed, and now they suffer."[38]

With his rewards and exhortations, however, also came mention of Benny's shortcomings and specific directions for self-improvement. In the same letter in which he expressed approval of the drawings, Franklin advised the boy to keep accounts of his spending throughout his life. He also said that he would be pleased to see his grandson's handwriting begin to have the "fair round" style. Noting for Benny that his younger brother William had made surprising progress in such penmanship for his age, Franklin announced, "I have sent to London for some Copy Books of that Hand for you, which you will try to imitate."[39] As if to make sure Benny did not miss the point, Temple wrote at the same time to suggest that he learn the "plain & distinct" handwriting of his father and grandfather. "Your Parents have great Expectations of your becoming a clever Man, & I am confident you will do your utmost, that they may not be disappointed," Temple reminded his cousin. "No Pains or Expence have or will be spared in your Education; what a Pity & what a Loss it would be were they not to have the desired Effect."[40]

The desired effect was clearly that Benny be an enlightened republican. Money would be spent on his education, but he was expected to be industrious and frugal. Americans, Franklin thought, were foolish to crave expensive goods. When Sally complained of wartime prices and asked him to send French linen, lace, and feathers, he replied that he was as disgusted "as if you had put salt into my strawberries." Having always preached hard work and economy, he said, he could not "in conscience or in decency encourage the contrary, by my example, in furnishing my children with foolish modes and luxuries." He insisted that Americans needed to be self-sufficient enough to make their own clothing, and added that if she wanted feathers, she could find them in every cock's tail, and if she wanted lace, she could wear her clothes until they had holes.[41]

When Benny requested a Swiss watch, saying that it would be practical, Franklin was only slightly more gentle in refusing. "When you are more of a Man, perhaps, if you have behaved well, I may give you one or something that is better," he wrote. "You should remember that I am at a great Expence for your Education, to pay for your Board and Cloathing and Instruction in Learning that may be useful to you when you are grown up, and you should not tease me for expensive things that can be of little or no Service to you."[42]

Taken away from his family at a young age and placed in the staid city of Geneva with instructions to live with monastic discipline, Benny Bache persevered, but he frequently wrote of his wish for English-speaking companions and more letters from his parents and grandfather.[43] His relationship with Marignac was cordial, but he wanted the easy familiarity of family and friends with similar backgrounds. Catherine Cramer, widow of the man who brought the boy to Switzerland, did take a parental interest in the young student and had him pay regular visits to her home. Her son Gabriel and Benny were friends at the pension Marignac, but the American boy was evidently not entirely at ease with Gabriel's mother, the daughter of a Russian ambassador to Vienna who had taken refuge in Geneva after falling into disgrace with Peter the Great. Madame Cramer informed Franklin early in Benny's stay that the boy, while "full of sense and reason," was indolent in his studies and timid to the point of being impolite. The answer, she thought, would be for the grandfather, for whom the grandson had "much respect and attachment," to write more often and correct his small faults.[44]

During Benny's second year, she worried again that he was not applying himself as he should in school, that he was a quiet boy and not affected by the rivalry among students that was, Madame Cramer thought, the great advantage of public education. Benny, she wrote to Franklin, "has an excellent heart; he is sensible, reasonable, he is serious, but he has neither gaiety nor vivacity; he is cold, he has few needs, no fantasies." He did not play cards and fight like other boys his age, she said, and, unless his character was late in developing, would lack both passion and great talent. Madame Cramer expressed astonishment that Benny showed little interest in having a larger allowance from Franklin to match what other boys had and that he said he regarded his Latin prize as just a matter of luck. "He does what is necessary so as not to be at fault," she maintained, "but no more."[45]

Such accounts may have prompted Franklin's missives about doing well in school, but they also could be interpreted by the grandfather as the picture of a self-contained, twelve-year-old republican. If Benny did not always seem to work hard, perhaps he was gifted enough to accomplish his tasks without extraordinary effort. If he seemed to be withdrawn, he may not have felt he could be particularly effusive as a guest in the Cramer house. When not within the college's regimen of learning ancient languages, he was still closely watched and judged by adults and was cautious enough to avoid mistakes.[46] He was expected to control himself and not disgrace his family. If he displayed emotion, as Marignac observed, it was when he was criticized or treated unjustly, but the grandson of the great Doctor Franklin did not wish to stray from good behavior. "I make all my efforts to please you and to have another prize next year," he wrote to his grandfather in the autumn of 1780. "I believe that my masters are satisfied with me or at least that I make all my efforts to satisfy them."[47]

III

The domineering demeanor that Benjamin Franklin typically brought to family matters may well have been intensified in his guardianship of Benny Bache by a nagging sense of personal pain and political failure in the final two decades of his life. Looking back, he could write in his memoirs that he would have "no Objection" to living the same life again, but would only ask "the Advantage Authors have in a second Edition to correct some Faults of the first." Yet, he recognized that the level of perfection he sought might be a ridiculous "Foppery in Morals" if always practiced.[48]

The admonitions he had so freely dispensed as a journalist and politician, moreover, had been of little use in preventing war with Britain. "I think it is Ariosto who says, that all things lost on Earth are to be found in the Moon; on which somebody remarked, that there must be a great deal of good Advice in the Moon," Franklin reflected in a discussion of the prospects for peace in 1778. "If so, there is a good deal of mine, formerly given and lost in this Business." The "mad War," as he then called it, continually brought to his mind an image of England's "present Ministers and their Abettors" with "Hands, red, wet, and dropping with the Blood of my Countrymen, Friends, and Relations." No peace treaty, he bitterly concluded, "can be sign'd by those hands."[49]

Feeling accountable for the "errata" of his own life[50] and troubled about the entrenched evils of Europe, Franklin took satisfaction in pondering the possibilities for a new kind of citizen and a new kind of nation in the United States. To a large extent, he himself represented that new person in France, where, he told his daughter, his portrait was appearing on snuff boxes, rings, and artwork of all sorts, making his face "as well known as that of the moon."[51] In Europe, the autocratic ways of the past were appearing ever more irredeemable. The England and France that Franklin knew were stirring with radical sentiments.[52] His own country was in a determined struggle to rid itself of policies it could no longer tolerate. At his dinner table in Passy, he told friends he wished he could be restored to life in fifty years to see how his country would be flourishing.[53]

To Franklin, America's emergence as a free and prosperous nation would begin with throwing off the past. The past, as he described it in rejecting Lord Howe's peace overtures of 1776, was Britain's "abounding Pride and deficient Wisdom" that drove it to blind conquest, domination, and monopoly instead of seeking its true interest, friendly relations with its colonies. Saying that "cool dispassionate Posterity will condemn to Infamy" those in Britain who promoted the war, he told Howe:

> To me it seems that neither the obtaining or retaining of any Trade, how valuable soever, is an Object for which Men may justly Spill each others Blood; that the true and sure means of extending and securing Commerce is the goodness and cheapness of Commodities; and that the profits of no Trade can ever be equal to the Expence of compelling it, and of holding it, by Fleets and Armies.[54]

Franklin was among those Americans who could readily perceive the Revolution as a blow to the mercantilist mentality. As far as could be foreseen, he thought, the United States should be a nation devoted to farms and free trade. As early as his pamphlet of 1729 on paper currency, he discounted the notion that agricultural surpluses were a danger. If too much wheat was produced, he wrote, then laborers could "proceed to the raising and manufacturing of *Hemp, Silk, Iron,* and many other Things the Country is very capable of, for which we only want People to work, and Money to pay them with."[55]

In his influential and often reprinted 1751 essay, *Observations Concerning the Increase of Mankind,* Franklin described an America which, in contrast to the fully settled nations of Europe, had open land that would make labor expensive by attracting workers to a thriving agricultural life and make the population grow by supporting large families, especially among the industrious and frugal.[56] Themes in his *Observations* were developed further in his pamphlet *Interest of Great Britain Considered,* published in England in 1760, which argued that American manufacturers did not have to be a threat to the mother country for centuries to come because of agriculture. Manufacturing may be proper in a country without available land, he maintained, but "no man who can have a piece of land of his own, sufficient by his labour to subsist his family in plenty, is poor enough to be a manufacturer and work for a master."[57]

In his writings before the Revolution, Franklin stated with increasing conviction that England, a seemingly wealthy and powerful nation, was, in fact, a "old rotten State" in contrast to a "rising" America of "glorious publick Virtue," that its only hope of retaining the colonies was the nearly complete removal of its economic restrictions.[58] In Britain, he insisted, government policies encouraged exports that were exploiting manufacturing workers and maintained low food prices that were hurting farmers.[59] In America, he believed, Parliament's laws and the sale of superfluous British goods were working against the development of colonial industry and frugality.[60] Government interference with natural economic forces, he argued, diminished rather than increased wealth and happiness.[61] The colonies had a brighter future than England, his writings suggested, because the North American continent had an abundance of fertile soil and productive waters, resources which were the ultimate source of prosperity.[62] Moreover, Franklin said, an agricultural life was more healthy than a manufacturing one[63] and, as he wrote in an essay published in England and republished by his physiocratic friends in France, was the most virtuous of three ways a nation could acquire wealth:

> The first is by *War* as the Romans did in plundering their conquered Neighbours. This is *Robbery.* The second by *Commerce* which is gener-

ally *Cheating.* The third by *Agriculture* the only *honest Way;* wherein Man receives a real Increase of the Seed thrown into the Ground, in a kind of continual Miracle wrought by the Hand of God in his Favour, as a Reward for his innocent Life, and virtuous Industry.[64]

The problem was not money itself, but how it was made and spent. While in England, Franklin defended the farmer's right to a profit. In a *London Chronicle* essay published in 1766, a poor crop year in which mob demonstrations forced the government to restrict British agricultural exports, Franklin complained that Parliament allowed manufactured goods to be shipped more freely than farm products. If the laboring poor needed bread, the essay suggested, the problem may have been that they had become too dependent on charity and on government economic policies that made farmers lose income. Contending that the poor were too idle and dissolute and needed "inducements to industry, frugality, and sobriety," Franklin wrote, "I think the best way of doing good to the poor, is not making them easy *in* poverty, but leading or driving them *out* of it."[65] People didn't have to be poor, he reasoned, if they only knew how to behave in their personal life and in their chosen occupation. Common people could strive for success and should not be hampered in seeking a fair gain for their work.

Franklin's writings for the public had long celebrated honest labor and careful judgment. His essay *Advice to a Young Tradesman,* for instance, explained that time spent in idle diversion was money lost and that "The Sound of your Hammer at Five in the Morning or Nine at Night, heard by a Creditor, makes him easy Six Months longer."[66] Much of what his twenty-six years of almanac journalism conveyed could be summarized by a saying in the *Poor Richard* of 1736: "God helps them that help themselves."[67] A compendium of the variations on that theme appeared in the preface to his final almanac in 1758. Reprinted in America and Europe at least 145 times by the end of the century under titles that included *The Way to Wealth* and *La Science du Bonhomme Richard,* the preface presented a speech of "Father Abraham," a "plain clean old Man," who advised a crowd at an auction to practice industry, frugality, and prudence, and to ask humbly for "the Blessing of Heaven." Among his specific suggestions was to start work early in the day. *"Early to Bed, and early to rise, makes a Man healthy, wealthy, and wise,"* Father Abraham said, quoting Poor Richard. He also emphasized avoiding debt for the sake of vanity because *"You give to another Power over your Liberty."* [68]

A republic, as Franklin understood it, suffered when its citizens lost their self-esteem and independence by being in unnecessary debt, working for others, or living in idleness and poverty. People unable to exercise control over themselves were unlikely to display the skill and public spirit needed to manage a self-governing nation. Fortunately, Franklin argued in a revolutionary-era essay circulated in Europe, Americans had the requisite qualities for happiness, the same qualities that made individuals good credit risks. In contrast to Britain, an "old, corrupt, extravagant and profligate nation," the United States had "general Industry, Frugality, Ability, Prudence and Virtue." While the English had acquired the habits of dissipation and misrule, he wrote, Americans were wise and peaceable cultivators of the land who were bred to honest, hard work. Not only did Americans really have public spirit, Franklin told Europeans, but they were also fighting for freedom of commerce and "the Cause of Liberty which is the Cause of all Mankind." [69]

Franklin's most ambitious effort to explain the United States to Europeans was his *Information to Those Who Would Remove to America.* Printed in English and French on his own press at Passy at the end of the Revolution and then reprinted by others, the essay brought together the observations and arguments of decades of thought on the nation's prospects. America, he told his readers, was not a place of rich and poor, as in Europe, but rather a country where "a general happy Mediocrity" of wealth prevailed. People were neither valued for their genealogies nor made corrupt and servile by their opportunity to hold profitable public office. They had the opportunity to profit from their own industry, the kind of industry and constant employment that "are great preservatives of the Morals and Virtue of a nation." Farming would expand with cheap land, and manufacturing would be kept small by competition from imports and by a lack of laborers willing to work for low wages. "The Husbandman is in honor there, and even the Mechanic, because their Employments are useful," Franklin wrote. "The People have a saying, that God Almighty is himself a Mechanic, the greatest in the Univers; and he is respected and admired more for the Variety, Ingenuity, and Utility of his Handyworks, than for the Antiquity of his Family." [70]

At the end of the war, Franklin's thoughts frequently turned to

ways of securing future peace and prosperity. He urged British nego-
tiators to agree to prohibit privateering in any subsequent conflict in
order to remove one of the inducements to war. Such plundering, he
said, was "impeding the mutual communications among men of the
gifts of God, and rendering miserable multitudes of merchants and
their families, artisans, and cultivators of the earth, the most peaceable and innocent parts of the human species." Franklin also asked that
in the event of another war, all unarmed fisherman, farmers, and others who labored for "the common subsistence and benefit of mankind"
be left unmolested by enemy forces.[71] Although realizing it might be
"in some respects chimerical," he published in 1782 at his press in
Passy *Project of Perpetual Peace* by Pierre-André Gargaz, a schoolmaster
who had spent twenty years as a galley-slave before approaching Franklin
with his manuscript. Gargaz proposed that a permanent representative
body be established to mediate disputes between nations, a plan the
author believed would "transform Europe into a veritable Earthly Paradise."[72]

Pondering the position of the United States at the end of his
peace negotiations, Franklin believed that with "the Fertility of our
Soil" and "with the Industry of our People, now that the Commerce
of all the World is open to us" the country would soon be thriving in
a way "which we hope Providence intends for us, since it has so remarkably favour'd our Revolution."[73] Finding that a "multitude of
People" were asking him for advice on moving to America, some of
whom mistakenly thought they would be offered substantial inducements to emigrate, Franklin seems to have developed a pat response.
"The only Encouragements we hold out to Strangers are, a good Climate, fertile Soil, wholesome Air and Water, plenty of Provisions and
Fuel, good Pay for Labour, kind Neighbors, good Laws, Liberty, and
a hearty Welcome," he observed in one of his standard answers, "the
rest depends on a Man's own Industry and Virtue."[74]

IV

Franklin, who spent twenty-five of his adult years in Europe, gamely
tried to realize his ideals for the new world with those he most loved.
He was unsuccessful in attempting to interest Temple in farming. After
the war, Franklin purchased land in New Jersey from his son William
in the hope that the young man would settle down and marry after

his escapades in France. Temple, however, saw in the property an opportunity to live the life of a European country gentleman. He sent to Paris for French deer to hunt and for wooden shoes for his workers. Remaining hopeful of some government appointment and devoted to his social activities, however, Temple neglected his farm, spending much of his time in Philadelphia. "I wish he would seriously make a business of it, and renounce all thoughts of public employment, for I think agriculture the most honourable, because the most independent, of all professions," Franklin sighed in a letter to Lafayette. "But I believe he hankers a little after Paris, or some other of the polished cities of Europe, thinking the society there preferable to what he meets with in the woods of Ancocas; as it certainly is." After his grandfather's death, Temple tarried away the rest of his days in England and France, where, except for publishing an edition of Franklin's writings, he lived in obscurity.[75]

Benny Bache took a more republican direction. Unlike his cousin, the illegitimate European child who valued the social graces and sought respectability, Bache began preparing himself for an industrious future. In Geneva, he did not repeat the honor of the Latin prize, but instead made it his goal to have the best notes, an accomplishment he told his grandfather he found "very glorious"—even though it was not rewarded with the presentation of a medal at the cathedral— because it showed that a student had worked hard all year. In a 1781 letter signed as usual "your very humble and obedient grandson," he sadly reported that he had the best notes, but that the recognition for good notes had not been given that year.[76]

Bache's last two years in Switzerland were not as dreary as the first two. Long-smoldering anger at Geneva's politically powerful aristocracy flared into an armed uprising over enfranchisement and other issues. For a time soldiers were garrisoned at the college and, as order was restored, Benny spent his nights at a country cottage obtained by Marignac. The boy reassured Franklin and told him he was having fun,[77] but another development also brought some excitement into his life. Benny, always anxious to have American companionship, welcomed the arrival of Samuel Cooper Johonnot, the grandson of Franklin's Boston friend, Rev. Samuel Cooper.

Brought to France in 1780 by John Adams, young Sammy, whose mother was dead and whose father was a footloose, failing merchant, had been left under Franklin's affectionate supervision. Before long, however, his new guardian noted for Cooper that he was giving his "best Advice," but that the twelve-year-old, although bright and genteel, was "too much of the Insurgent" in the minds of the schoolmasters in Passy.[78] After proving too demanding about his accommodations for Franklin's idea of economy, Sammy was sent off to Switzerland. By the end of 1781, the new student was being watched with some suspicion by Marignac who found him careless and obnoxious. Finally, when Sammy conspired to have the two boys moved to a French school he thought would be more to his liking, he received a stern rebuke from Franklin, who advised him "to think of establishing a Character for manly steadiness, which you will find of great use to you in life."[79]

Johonnot, who was facing high expectations from his own grandfather, did establish himself quickly as an outstanding student and soon let Franklin know he had won an academic award. Franklin, using the most elevated of tones, replied that with diligent study and the practice of "the Precepts of Religion and Virtue," the young Bostonian would have "the Promise respecting the Life that now is, as well as that which is to come" and would "possess true Wisdom, which is nearly allied to Happiness."[80] Sammy outpaced Benny in 1782, receiving the first prize for their class while Bache placed third.[81] Outside of school hours, Benny was evidently finding more to do because, perhaps at Johonnot's instigation, he asked Franklin to increase their allowance.[82] They wandered the narrow streets of the ancient walled city, taking little forays in which they might come across a magician performing his act or an underground passage to explore. Bache, perhaps inspired by Johonnot's keeping of a journal of his adventures while traveling to France, began keeping a diary to record his own adolescent observations and exploits.[83]

At the same time, however, concerns about Benny and Sammy were developing in distant America. Richard and Sarah Bache were alarmed that Benny was seemingly losing his command of English and inquired how much longer he would have to stay in Switzerland. Samuel Cooper wrote to caution Johonnot that his happiness depended on his grandson's doing well and that "the Temper and Behavior that tend to conciliate the Confidence and Affection of those around you" was "of more Importance to a Reputation and Figure in Life, than many are aware of." Cooper, who was dying, let Franklin know he was anxious to have the boy come home and receive a degree from

Harvard, which he had used his influence to arrange. (Hearing from Switzerland that Albert Gallatin, who had just completed his work at the boys' school in Geneva, was in Boston and in need of employment, Cooper had already arranged for the future Jeffersonian leader and secretary of the Treasury to teach French at Harvard.) On June 23, 1783, after learning that Bache was sick and was depressed at being away from his family so long, Franklin sent Benny a letter saying that the school's summer vacation would be a good time to have a visit.[84]

The boys may have been plotting their departure with the help of Robert Pigott, a wealthy and whimsically radical Englishman who regularly entertained them at his domaine de Penthes near Geneva. "They were both in perfect Health," Pigott wrote to Franklin after one visit late in 1782, "and I consider as two young plants which will produce good fruit when transplanted into their native Soil."[85] Seven months later, however, shortly before Franklin's already written summons to France arrived, Pigott suddenly sent Franklin a melodramatic account of the living conditions of his young friends. Bache, he wrote, had been suffering for "some weeks" from a fever "which may be reasonably attributed to his unhealthy dwelling improper diet & ignorance on the part of his Rulers." His room, Pigott continued, was no better than a prison cell and was crowded with other students in a way that would spread sickness. "Your Grandson demonstrates many *very* estimable qualitys which exclusive of other circumstances," the letter said, "entitles him to a very different management than he experiences."[86]

Once Bache and Johonnot arrived in Passy on July 19 after a ten-day journey, they were again under Franklin's management. He made the arrangements for Johonnot to leave quickly for Boston, but Sammy was slow in reaching Nantes and missed his ship. Franklin wrote to scold him for his "Wilfulness" and failure to follow directions. The letter concluded, "You are yet too young to reject safely the Advice of your Friends." Efforts meanwhile were being made in Boston to reach the boy with the news that Samuel Cooper wanted his dear grandson by his bedside, but with an unusually long voyage to Baltimore and his being in no hurry to reach Boston, he arrived two weeks after his grandfather's death. Writing to Franklin in his usual mannerly prose, Sammy admitted his mistake. "May the Lesson prove as useful as 'tis severe," he said, adding that Cooper had left him a third of his estate which would be used for his further education at Harvard and for getting started in the world as a lawyer.[87]

Bache was more pleasing to his elders. One letter he brought with him to Passy said that "his Sweetness of Temper & amiableness of Manners has rendered him here as universally beloved as Known & promises fair to be his portion under whatever Climate his lott is cast." In correspondence with the young man's parents, Franklin described his "great Satisfaction in finding him so well grown, and so much improv'd in his Learning and Behaviour." A visitor to Passy recorded Bache's reaction: "He found his G-Papa very different from other Old Persons, for they were fretful and complaining, and dissatisfy'd and my G. Papa is laughing & chearful like a young person." Bache told his parents that his grandfather and his cousin Temple were "very kind" to him and sent them accounts of his work on fencing, dancing, mathematics, Latin, and writing which "entirely fills up my time."[88]

Time was, nevertheless, also found for going down to the Seine to swim, a form of exercise that his grandfather had long ago mastered and still advocated, and for watching balloon ascensions, a novelty which was just then capturing the imagination of the Parisian public. Temple himself was experimenting with small balloons "filled with a certain lighter than the common air," as Benny informed his parents in the autumn. He watched in amazement as Temple "killed" a mouse with "fix'd air" and then brought it back to life with "some stuff in a bottle." "After it had run about for some time, he killed it again with an electric spark," Benny reported. "I am sure my cousin would pass for a conjurer in America."[89]

At the end of the summer, Franklin thought of sending Bache to school near London to restore his English, which his grandfather thought had "suffer'd for want of Use." Apparently forgetting his revolutionary disdain for the country he considered brutal and corrupt, he wrote to Polly Stevenson Hewson, his British "daughter" and a favorite correspondent, to ask if she might enroll Benny in school at Cheam. "He is docile and of gentle Manners, ready to receive and follow good Advice, and will set no bad Example to your *other* Children," Franklin cajoled. "He gains every day upon my Affections." His letter continued with counsel she had sought about her children's future and the suggestion that she and her family move to America:

All the means of good Education are plenty there, the general Manners are simple and pure, Temptations to Vice and Folly fewer, the Profits of Industry in Business as great and sure as in England; and there is one Advantage more, which your Command of Money will give you there, I mean the laying out a Part of your Fortune in new Land, now to be had extreamly cheap; but which must be increas'd immensely in Value, before your Children come of Age, by the rapid Population of the Country.[90]

Although Polly and her family did eventually move to Philadelphia in 1786 at Franklin's urging, the idea of having Bache come to England troubled her. "But how will my young Friend like to lay aside his powder and curls, and return to the simplicity of a rustic schoolboy?" she asked. "I fear he will think us all so unpolished he will scarcely be able to endure us, but if English cordiality will make amends for French refinement we may have some chance for making him happy."[91]

Bache did not go to England or even return to Geneva where he had left books and clothes. Instead, at Passy, he continued his studies and began to learn printing with the equipment his grandfather used to publish his bagatelles and diplomatic materials. Not only was printing considered a fine art in France, one which even royalty practiced, but it had been Franklin's original occupation and source of wealth. Franklin still set type, working a press himself on occasion, and consorted with printers. He particularly admired the work of the Didot family, which he thought had carried "the Art to a high Pitch of Perfection."[92]

By the end of 1783, Bache was doing his own printing, and the following year he began to receive instruction from master printers who came to the house. Franklin considered preparing his multilingual grandson for public service, as he had done with Temple, but he decided that Bache, who was good at notetaking and had an artistic bent, would be well suited to the printing business which he was learning quickly. To Richard Bache, who had served as postmaster general through the Revolution only to be replaced abruptly in 1782, Franklin wrote that "being now convinc'd that *Service is no Inheritance*, as the Proverb says, I have determin'd to give him a Trade that he may have something to depend on, and not be oblig'd to ask Favours or Offices of anybody." Benny, the grandfather said, was very well behaved and very much loved and would "make his way good in the World with God's Blessing." [93]

When Polly Stevenson Hewson visited Franklin at Passy in 1785, she found Temple "just fit to be employed in a court and to be the galant of the French ladies," but the tall, dark-haired Benny "one of the most amiable youths I ever knew." Despite the foppery and licentiousness of Paris, she observed in a long, descriptive letter to her sister-in-law, Benny "with the simplicity of his dress retains a lovely simplicity of character." Manly, sensible, and a good companion for her children, he worked at printing "with uncommon diligence," getting up before dawn and continuing until evening. Unlike Temple, who was so vain and so devoted to pleasure that he was "not an amiable nor a respectable character," Benny made pleasant conversation and did not assume any self-importance. The older grandson looked like Franklin, Polly concluded, but Bache resembled him "in mind." [94]

Benjamin Franklin Bache and the Rise of Jeffersonian Journalism

5

Newspapers for the New Nation

SEEING THE POTENTIAL OF THE PRESS TO DELIVER IDEAS AND INFOR-mation to the general public, Benjamin Franklin believed develop-ments in publishing would open up a brighter future. Poor Richard, noting how words had come to conquer time and space, remarked, "What an admirable Invention is Writing, by which a Man may com-municate his Mind without opening his Mouth, and at 1000 Leagues Distance, and even to future Ages, only by the Help of 22 letters, which may be joined 5852616738497664000 Ways, and will express all Things in a very narrow Compass." In one of his almanac's poems, a free press was described as an enemy of arbitrary power and super-stition which could, "Like Water carriage, cheap convey" the nation's art, wit, and "philosophic Goods."[1]

Franklin's sense of the importance of the press was particularly acute at the end of the Revolution. In 1782, while commenting on the way patriot newspapers had helped establish political "truths," he portrayed the press as a greater force than the oratory of the Greeks and Romans, which could only reach a limited audience. "Their writ-ings had little effect, because the bulk of the people could not read," Franklin continued. "Now by the press we can speak to nations; and good books and well written pamphlets have great and general influ-ence." The art of printing, he told one correspondent in 1783, pro-duced a light "so general" and "so penetrating" that "despotism and priestcraft" could not block it out. A few days later, in a letter prais-ing his British acquaintance Thomas Hollis, an editor and promoter of republican literature, Franklin said that it was possible for even one publisher of libertarian opinion to do a great amount of good: "Good, not only to his own nation, and to his cotemporaries, but to distant Countries, and to late Posterity; for such must be the effect of his multiplying and distributing Copies of the Works of our best English Writers, on subjects the most important to the Welfare of Society."[2]

Franklin, in deciding to prepare Benjamin Franklin Bache for a career as a printer-publisher, was training his grandson in a trade he regarded not only as a public service, in that it educated citizens of the republic, but also as an influence on foreign relations. He worried about the press's role in creating the image of America, saying in a 1782 letter to Francis Hopkinson that he thought an editor should "consider himself as in some degree the Guardian of his Country's Reputation, and refuse to insert such Writings as may hurt it." He said that before giving Europeans his newspapers from the United States, he set aside the issues that disgraced the country with the personal defamation "so scandalously common" in political essays.[3] On the other hand, Franklin was distressed by the negative depictions of the United States in the English press. In a stern letter to British negotiator David Hartley in 1783, he wrote:

> You have deceived yourselves too long with vain expectations of reaping advantage from our little discontents. We are more thoroughly an enlightned people, with respect to our political interests, than perhaps any other under heaven. Every man among us reads, and is so easy in his circumstances as to have leisure for conversations of improvement, and for acquiring Information. Our domestic misunderstandings, when we have them, are of small extent, tho' monstrously magnified by your microscopic newspapers. He who judges from them, that we are falling into anarchy, or returning to the obedience of Britain, is like one who being shewn some spots in the Sun, shou'd fancy, that the whole Disk would soon be overspread by them, and that there wou'd be an end of Daylight. The great body of Intelligence among our people surrounds and overpowers our petty dissensions, as the Sun's great mass of fire diminishes and destroys his Spots.[4]

Franklin's successor in representing the United States at the court of France, Thomas Jefferson, likewise condemned the "lying newspapers of London," saying in 1786 that they made it appear that Americans were "a lawless banditti, in a state of absolute anarchy, cutting one another's throats, and plundering without distinction."[5] Hearing of Shays' Rebellion, he wrote to Edward Carrington in 1787:

> The way to prevent these irregular interpositions of the people is to give them full information of their affairs thro' the channel of the public papers, and to contrive that those papers should penetrate the whole mass of the people. The basis of our governments being the opinion of the people, the very first object should be to keep that right; and were it left to me to decide whether we should have a government without newspapers, or newspapers without a government, I should not hesitate a moment to prefer the latter.

Maintaining that the population of Europe was divided into "wolves and sheep," he continued:

> Cherish therefore the spirit of our people, and keep alive their attention. Do not be too severe upon their errors, but reclaim them by enlightening them. If once they become inattentive to the public affairs, you and I, and Congress, and Assemblies, judges and governors shall all become wolves. It seems to be the law of our general nature, in spite of individual exceptions; and experience declares that man is the only animal which devours his own kind, for I can apply no milder term to the governments of Europe, and to the general prey of the rich on the poor.[6]

To two of the foremost theoreticians of the American Enlightenment, then, the success of their causes as well as their new nation's credibility abroad depended greatly on the press and public opinion. Benjamin Franklin Bache, the American journalist most prominently associated with libertarian change in the 1790s, learned his profession from Franklin and practiced it fiercely, advancing the political onslaught of Jefferson and his supporters. Bache's editorial demeanor evolved from serene and philosophical to outraged and partisan, but his principles and his hopes for human progress remained intact. He and other opponents of oligarchy gradually began to see the extent to which their new age would not simply create itself through general historical forces, improved understanding, or the rightness of the movement's objectives, but would rather require considerable organization, agitation, and accommodation. The country's founding ideals were being transformed into parties, propaganda, and programs.

I

Franklin's instruction during Bache's four years in Geneva was confined to letters discussing the general principles of good work and the
specific skills expected of a capable citizen. Once he had chosen the
trade of printing for his grandson, however, the fundamentals of politics came into play. The first printing Bache was given to do was
"An Ode in Imitation of Alcæus," a poem by linguistic scholar William Jones decrying England's corruption and misuse of monarchical
power. Jones, a British friend of Franklin's who was upset by his country's policies toward America, asked, "WHAT constitutes a State?"
The poem said it was not fortifications, cities, navies, or a court:

> No:—MEN, high-minded MEN,
> With pow'rs as far above dull brutes endued
>   In forest, brake, or den,
> As beasts excel cold rocks and brambles rude;
>   Men, who their *duties* know,
> But know their *rights*, and knowing, dare maintain,
>   Prevent the long-aimed blow,
> And crush the tyrant while they rend the chain:
>   *These* constitute a State.[7]

The idea that high-minded citizens who knew their duties and
rights were the real strength of a state was one which Franklin could
endorse. Yet, having had a long career in sometimes bitter controversy, he was evidently not anxious to push his young printer toward
political journalism. He instead arranged for Bache to learn typefounding, first from a typefounder who came to the house in Passy,
then briefly in 1785 as an apprentice to François-Ambroise Didot in
Paris. "I am now learning to Print at Mr. Didot's the best Printer that
now exists & maybe that has ever existed," Bache told his parents,
"his son is also an excellent engraver of Types and gives me lessons."
Impressed with his grandfather's willingness and ability to do such
things for him, Bache had great admiration for Franklin, a respect
and wonder which could extend to the smallest matters. Apologizing
to his mother for writing with a dull quill, he said his grandfather was
"the only Man who can write with a bad pen."[8]
    Approaching the age of eighty, Franklin was delighted at the way

Ben was becoming a "good Man," but dejected by his absence while in Paris, especially when Temple fell ill and Franklin found himself "very *triste* breakfasting alone, and sitting alone, and without any Tea in the Evening." The apprenticeship was cut short, however, when Franklin received permission to return to the United States. Bache was put in charge of packing and making other arrangements, and in July 1785 Franklin and his grandsons sailed for America. They went by way of England, where they met the exiled William Franklin. William was pleased to see his nephew, regarding him as likely "to make a good solid man," but the reunion was a brisk one mainly concerned with settling his debts to Franklin. The party was also greeted by a number of well-wishers, including Jonathan Shipley, bishop of St. Asaph. "Your promising Grandson, who has the Courage to tread in your early Steps I hope will preserve the same generous emulation thro his life," the bishop wrote to Franklin later that year. "Few Professions are in my Eyes more respectable than the Character of a Printer who excells in his Art."[9]

Franklin's arrival at the Market Street wharf in Philadelphia on September 14 was celebrated with cannon fire, the sound of bells, and cheers from the citizens who escorted him to his home. For the next several days he received formal congratulatory messages extolling his devotion to the common good through his philanthropy, philosophy, and patriotism. In response to the address presented to him by the provost, vice-provost, and professors of the University of Pennsylvania, he expressed his "extreme Pleasure" at the thriving condition of higher education in America. "The Instruction of Youth is one of those Employments, which to the Public are most useful; it ought, therefore, to be esteem'd among the most honourable," Franklin said. "Its successful Exercise does not, however, always meet with the Reward it merits, except in the satisfaction of having contributed to the forming of virtuous and able Men for the Service of their Country."[10]

Recording his joy at seeing his family again after nine years and at the acclaim his grandfather received, Bache ended his diary saying he would be prevented from continuing it by "more serious occupations." Still certain he would become a printer, he spent two years studying for his bachelor's degree at the University of Pennsylvania, then located in two buildings at Fourth and Arch Streets in Philadelphia. His first tuition payment, recorded a month after his return from France, was made in wood for heating classrooms. Bache was able to go back to the familiar disciplines of Greek and Latin and to take courses in natural philosophy, history, and English. Students heard notable guest lecturers, including lexicographer Noah Webster, and read works of Xenophon, Epictetus, Cicero, and Livy. Like other American colleges at the time, the institution offered instruction in moral philosophy which stressed the importance of republican government promoting the common good and of the sovereign and self-restraining people retaining their virtue. Franklin, with his affection for his grandson and his desire that he serve his country as a printer, was gratified to see that Bache was "very diligent in his Studies."[11]

The commencement of Bache's class of eight Bachelors of Arts was delayed four months by the Constitutional Convention three blocks away, in which alumni, faculty, and trustees were involved. Having been elected president of the Supreme Executive Council of Pennsylvania in 1785, Franklin himself was the *ex officio* president of the Board of Trustees. Finally, on November 22, 1787, the graduation took place, with the members of the state-ratifying convention forming a procession to the university for the ceremony. At the age of eighteen, Bache was slightly older than the average graduate of the time. Among Bache's classmates was Samuel Harrison Smith, later the editor of the *National Intelligencer,* the newspaper Jefferson favored during his presidency. After Bache completed the degree, Franklin was able to write to European correspondents that the young man had entered "the original Occupation of his Grand-father." To one, he wrote, "I am too old to follow printing again myself, but, loving the business, I have brought up my grandson Benjamin to it, and have built and furnished a printing-house for him, which he now manages under my eye." Working in a shop at the family's Franklin Court property on Market Street, Bache was compliantly becoming the man he had been raised to be.[12]

The nation itself also appeared to be sufficiently secure and republican in the philosopher's eyes. While in France, Franklin had written to George Washington that he expected the country to flourish "amazingly and rapidly" after the war, like a field of parched Indian corn that after a storm "recovers fresh Verdure, shoots up with double Vigour, and delights the Eye."[13] When he returned to the United States and found a painful postwar depression with business failures and financial disruption, he was still optimistic, choosing to tell one correspondent about farmers, "the bulk of the nation," having plentiful crops and high prices and about working people having full employment and high wages. Saying that England's papers "to please honest *John Bull,* paint our situation here in frightful colors," he pointed to America's respect for the law, secure property, westward expansion, and ability to buy cheap goods from Europe "since Britain has no longer the monopoly of supplying us." The letter concluded, "In short, all among us may be happy, who have happy dispositions; such being necessary to happiness even in Paradise."[14]

Franklin was also able to tell the public that the United States had developed a sound political economy. In a *Pennsylvania Gazette* essay published in 1786, a year after Jefferson's *Notes on the State of Virginia* was privately printed in Paris, Franklin described Americans as "Sons of the Earth and Seas" who need only be "quiet and thankful" for the wealth of farming and fishing that flowed from divine providence. No country had a greater share of human happiness, he thought, and in no part of the Old World were "the labouring Poor so well fed, well cloth'd, well lodg'd, and well paid." If merchants were suffering, he wrote in the *Gazette,* they should turn to the productive life of the farmer or mechanic and leave the few stores necessary in a predominantly self-sufficient America to be run by widows and other women. A seemingly ruinous amount of imports need not be considered a major problem in a nation consisting primarily of "industrious frugal farmers" who would grow wealthy gradually with the sale of surpluses and the rise of land values. "The great Business of the Continent is Agriculture," Franklin declared.[15]

II

As much as he might be satisfied with his grandson and his country, however, in the last years of his life Franklin became uneasy about his former trade and about politics. Toward the end of the 1780s, as he became more involved in his country's domestic realities, his picture of America's future was tarnished by the journalism he read and by a classical republican anxiety about the misuse of power for self-interest. Although he and his son William had once held profitable positions in colonial administration, Franklin had gained firsthand knowledge of corruption in England, seeing, as he put it, large "Emoluments of Office" destroy good government by creating a "stormy Sea" of factions controlled by powerful individuals. In France he had observed the operation of courtly life and arbitrary rule in the extreme. Accordingly, at the Constitutional Convention, he warned that there was "a natural Inclination in Mankind to kingly Government" and, realizing that his preference for a plural executive was not shared by the majority of delegates, he worked to deny the president an absolute veto and even a salary.[16]

In his *Pennsylvania Gazette* essay of 1786, written after he was chosen president of Pennsylvania's Supreme Executive Council, Franklin had been able to take a forbearing approach to political dissension in America. Having been nominated for the Council not only by the Mechanical Society, but also by both factions in the extended controversy over altering Pennsylvania's extremely democratic revolutionary-era constitution,[17] he could tell the newspaper's readers that parties were "the common Lot of Humanity" and naturally went along with political liberty. "By the Collision of different Sentiments, Sparks of Truth are struck out, and political Light is obtained," he wrote. "The different Factions, which at present divide us, aim all at the Publick Good; the Differences are only about the various Modes of Promoting it." Eleven months later, however, in the wake of Shays' Rebellion, Franklin was less composed. He wrote to Jefferson that the "Insurgents" in Massachusetts had been quelled, that the Articles of Confederation were considered defective, and that he hoped the federal convention being called would do some good. "Indeed if it does not do Good it must do Harm," he said, "as it will show that we have not Wisdom enough among us to govern ourselves; and will strengthen the Opinion of some Political Writers, that popular Governments cannot long support themselves."[18]

Shortly before the convention, some Americans were certain that independence and confederation had not carried the country far enough toward its realization as an epoch-making republic. Early in 1787, leading citizens of Philadelphia—including William Bradford, Francis Hopkinson, Tench Coxe, Jared Ingersoll, Thomas Mifflin, Robert Morris, David Rittenhouse, Benjamin Rush, and James Wilson—formed the Society for Political Enquiries, which met at the house of its president, Benjamin Franklin, to discuss political economy and government. The organization's express purpose was to rescue political science from politicians and individual theorists, but many of the actual discussions were on matters as specific as prison reform, taxation policies, and freedom of the press. Its statement of rules and purposes, a document drafted by Thomas Paine, asserted that the United States still retained too much reverence for the political ideas and manners of corrupt monarchies. "In having effected a separate government, we have as yet effected partial independance," the statement said. "The Revolution can only be said to be complete, when we shall have freed ourselves, no less from the influence of foreign prejudices than from the fetters of foreign power."[19]

The foreign power that haunted Franklin was England. He believed that America's friendship with France was "of the utmost importance to our security" and that it "should be carefully cultivated." Franklin thought that Britain still had hopes of recovering its former colonies. "A breach between us and France would infallibly bring the English again upon our backs," he wrote in 1784, "and yet we have some wild heads among our countrymen, who are endeavouring to weaken that connexion!" In the portion of his memoirs written after his return from France, Franklin complained of the "pernicious Consequences" of newspaper attacks on "our best national Allies."[20]

In the year before his death in 1790, however, circumstances changed dramatically—although not necessarily for the worse in Franklin's mind—with the outbreak of the French Revolution. After writing to one French friend that he found the news from Paris "very afflicting" and saying he hoped "it may all end well and happy," he commented that the United States Constitution "has an appearance that promises permanency; but in this world nothing can be said to be certain, except death and taxes." In another letter, he observed:

> The Convulsions in France are attended with some disagreeable Circumstances; but if by the Struggle she obtains and secures for the Nation its future Liberty, and a good Constitution, a few Years' Enjoyment of those Blessings will amply repair all the Damages their Acquisition may have occasioned. God grant, that not only the Love of Liberty, but a thorough Knowledge of the Rights of Man, may pervade all the Nations of the Earth, so that a Philosopher may set his Foot anywhere on its Surface, and say, "This is my Country."[21]

The United States also appeared to be at a momentous juncture. By 1789, Franklin feared that reciprocal reactionary and turbulent forces were arising in the new American republic. He prepared a point-by-point essay in defense of Pennsylvania's constitution, saying that its

opponents' desire to have a single executive with a long term and a
divided legislature with an upper house restricted to the wealthy was
monarchical and betrayed "a Disposition among some of our People
to commence an Aristocracy." On the other hand, having witnessed
the acrimonious anti-Federalist campaign against ratification of the
federal Constitution, he told Senator Charles Carroll:

> I am glad to see by the papers, that our grand machine has at length
> begun to work. I pray God to bless and guide its operations. If any form
> of government is capable of making a nation happy, ours I think bids
> fair now for producing that effect. But, after all, much depends upon
> the people who are to be governed. We have been guarding against an
> evil that old States are most liable to, *excess of power* in the rulers; but
> our present danger seems to be *defect of obedience* in the subjects. There
> is hope, however, from the enlightened state of this age and country,
> we may guard effectually against that evil as well as the rest.[22]

In addition to his fears about the development of monarchical
tendencies and unruly or self-serving conduct, Franklin worried that
a reckless press could disrupt the broad-minded equanimity of the new
nation, undermining the kind of consensus and action that would be
necessary to achieve the public good. Since his days as a printer's
apprentice he had regarded unfettered journalism as a force against
political injustice, but, after being a target of the press, particularly as
a diplomat and as a delegate to the Constitutional Convention,[23] he
began to think that unrestrained publications could be a threat to
enlightened republicanism as well. Republicans, seeing themselves as
moral leaders, had, after all, a strong interest in preserving their reputations. As Jefferson would eventually do during his presidency,
Franklin railed against printed defamation in the last years of his life.
In the part of his autobiography written after the ratification debates,
he complained about the "Libelling and Personal Abuse, which is of
late Years become so disgraceful to our Country" and said that printers
were making "no scruple of gratifying the Malice of Individuals by
false Accusations of the fairest Characters among ourselves."[24]

Franklin's feelings about the press were apparent in a 1788 case
involving Eleazer Oswald, a spirited Philadelphia editor whose anti-
Federalist newspaper had portrayed him as a doddering old fool for
backing the Constitution. When Oswald printed comments on a libel

case brought against him by another editor and was then jailed for contempt of court, his wife Elizabeth appealed to Franklin for help and advice. Franklin flatly refused to become involved, saying that it would not be proper for him to do so in his official capacity as president of Pennsylvania and that she should try to make her husband avoid the kind of journalistic behavior that "made and provok'd so many Enemies." A year later, Franklin wrote his "Court of the Press" essay for the *Federal Gazette* which denounced what he felt was the press's ability to ruin at will the reputations of good, honest citizens and to find support in "the depravity of such minds, as have not been mended by religion, nor improved by good education." The court of the press, he said, could condemn its victims as easily and unfairly as the Inquisition and so should be subject to the restraints of personal libel law. He supported the right to discuss public issues, he explained, but not a liberty of "affronting, calumniating, and defaming one another." [25]

In deteriorating health and with decades of public service behind him, Franklin had little patience left for the disagreements troubling the nation he had helped to create. Always an advocate of cooperation for the sake of progress, his sense of the American achievement was such that he did not want to see it undermined by bias and bickering. Early in 1787, he told Jefferson that "Boutdefeus are not wanting among us, who by inflammatory Writings in the Papers are perpetually endeavouring to set us together by the Ears about Taxes, and Certificates, etc." [26] He thus could accept a federal Constitution he found flawed and encourage others to support it as he did in his closing speech at the convention of 1787 saying, "The opinions I have of its *errors* I sacrifice to the public good." When citizens of the state of Franklin, named for him, but later called Tennessee, asked for his advice on their difficulties in separating from North Carolina, he simply deferred to Congress, saying it was "a wise and impartial Tribunal" and that the more it was respected "the more able it will be to answer effectually the Ends of its Institution, the quieting of our contentions, and thereby promoting and securing our common Peace and Happiness." [27]

One issue Franklin knew Congress could not resolve, however, was slavery. As early as 1729 Franklin printed an antislavery tract, and he advocated education for blacks. The Franklin family did have black servants from time to time, but his revulsion toward slavery grew, and he argued that the practice was not only immoral but also impractical for the owners.[28] In 1787 he was elected president of the Pennsylvania Society for Promoting the Abolition of Slavery, and the Relief of Free Negroes Unlawfully Held in Bondage. Several of his last public writings were about the status and condition of blacks and the need to provide education and employment. He signed the society's 1789 plea for funds, which pointed hopefully to "the daily progress of that luminous and benign spirit of liberty, which is diffusing itself throughout the world," but also signed its 1790 memorial on the subject to Congress which a committee rejected, deeming it interference with the authority of the states. The final newspaper essay of his career, written for the *Federal Gazette* a month before his death, was a parody of a speech made in Congress by James Jackson of Georgia that presented the customary justifications for slavery. Franklin facetiously used the same arguments to justify the enslaving of whites in Algiers. He concluded with a somber prediction that petitions against slavery would continue to meet the same fate as his own.[29]

III

Benjamin Franklin Bache would display a similar antipathy to aristocratic authority and slavery in his journalistic career, just as he also was to share the nearly euphoric sense of national identity and individual purpose that infused Franklin's political thought. He was part of a political culture that was celebrating itself in public displays of enthusiasm for the changes that were occurring. At Philadelphia's Federal Procession in honor of the ratification of the Constitution, Franklin and his council were among the dignitaries in a massive parade along the city's streets. As in other cities, tradesmen participated in great numbers, believing that the new national government would protect them from the competition of British manufactured goods.[30] The Philadelphia parade included forty-four units of tradesmen, ranging from coach painters and nailsmiths to printers and stocking makers. The Constitution also offered to weary Americans the possibility of harmony after years of upheaval. Richard Bache, riding behind flags depicting events in the revolutionary period, appeared in the procession as a herald "attended by a trumpet, proclaiming a New Æra" with a banner saying:

Peace o'er our land her olive wand extends,
And white rob'd Innocence from Heaven descends;
The crimes and frauds of Anarchy shall fail,
Returning Justice lifts again her scale.[31]

But if Benjamin Franklin Bache reached adulthood at a time when
the country's political prospects were lauded, he also lived in a nation
where, with the advance of commercial capitalism, the economic and
social breach between rich and poor was expanding and widespread
demands were being made for debtor relief, equitable taxation, and
land for small farms.[32] In his city of Philadelphia, while fortunes were
being made in maritime ventures and real estate and being spent imitating the fashions and pastimes of Britain's upper classes, the lives
of laborers in the lower ranks were close to subsistence level and easily
disrupted by imports, immigration, and downturns in business activity. During the revolutionary crisis, the artisans of Philadelphia organized to enlarge their political presence through the 1776 state constitution, but split—sometimes violently—over the issue of wartime
price controls, which were intended to protect impoverished citizens
from soaring inflation. The more affluent workers upheld the principles of free trade in the face of restrictions on profits, but the more
needy demanded economic regulations that they argued were for the
common good. Even before the Pennsylvania constitution, communitarian sentiment was evident among lower-class members of the militia.[33] A broadside from the Committee of Privates told other militiamen:

> A Government made for the common Good should be framed by Men
> who can have no Interest besides the common Interest of Mankind. It
> is the Happiness of America that there is no Rank above that of Free-
> men existing in it; and much of our future Welfare and Tranquillity will
> depend on its remaining so for-ever; for this Reason, great and over-
> grown rich Men will be improper to be trusted, they will be too apt to
> be framing Distinctions in Society, because they will reap the Benefits
> of all such Distinctions.[34]

In creating a unicameral legislature, plural executive, and broad
franchise, the Pennsylvania constitution of 1776, a victory for the
state's egalitarians, reversed the classical republican notion that only
those with substantial assets would be independent enough to judge

the needs of society properly. While recognizing general protections
for property, the state's new declaration of rights said, "That government is, or ought to be, instituted for the common benefit, protection
and security of the people, nation or community; and not for the
particular emolument or advantage of any single man, family, or set
of men, who are a part only of that community." The declaration,
which Franklin as a participant in the state's convention had a hand
in writing, also stated that liberty depended on "a firm adherence to
justice, moderation, temperance, industry, and frugality."[35] Responding to criticism that too much faith was being placed in majority rule,
defenders of the document argued that it aimed at the common good
in the efficient way of enlightened republicanism. In a newspaper series on the constitution published in 1778, Thomas Paine wrote that
real riches came from the increased population and cultivation that a
just government would bring and said:

> I have heard it advanced, by those who have objected against the pre-
> sent constitution, that it was a good one for a poor man. I reply, that for
> that very reason is it the best government for a rich one, by producing
> purchasers, tenants, and laborers, to the landed interest, and consumers
> to the merchants. . . . I am not pleading the cause of the one against
> the other . . . for I am clearly convinced that the true interest of one
> is the real interest of both.[36]

Paine, who had a cordial relationship with Franklin and relied
on Bache to circulate a number of his works in America in the 1790s,
often articulated in his writings a simple, harmonious view of American politics operating without the kind of class tensions that Madison
thought were inevitable. He saw, like Adam Smith, a mass of small
competing producers who would prosper through initiative but not
tend to acquire the kind of great wealth that would lead to inequality
and conflict. A self-regulating market in this sense was natural, egalitarian, and liberating. Yet, like Franklin, he saw a need for government to impose economic regulation on occasion for the sake of the
common good. Although both Franklin and Paine thought unicameral legislatures and plural executives were the most likely to defeat
selfish interests, they supported—as did Bache—ratification of the federal Constitution with its stronger national government.[37]

The advocates of enlightened republicanism considered proper taxation and good wages to be crucial in securing what Franklin's *Information to Those Who Would Remove to America* essay proudly called the "almost general Mediocrity of Fortune" among citizens of the United States, a description that was more apparent for European audiences than American ones. While observing the gap between rich and poor in Europe, Jefferson discussed with Madison a need to tax in "geometrical progression" with increased wealth, a policy which would take more from the rich than the poor. Franklin similarly believed that taxation should be in proportion to wealth. He did not think that money could be acquired without incurring obligations, and he articulated a theoretical foundation for raising government revenue for the common good, a rationale that sought to define what belonged to the individual and what belonged to the society. Informed in 1783 that some Americans were unwilling to pay their taxes, he wrote:

> All the Property that is necessary to a Man, for the Conservation of the Individual and the Propagation of the Species, is his natural Right, which none can justly deprive him of: But all Property superfluous to such purposes is the Property of the Publick, who, by their Laws, have created it, and who may therefore by other Laws dispose of it, whenever the Welfare of the Publick shall demand such Disposition. He that does not like civil Society on these Terms, let him retire and live among Savages.[38]

The conflict over wages, as identified by Adam Smith, was simply that workers wanted them to be high and employers, complaining that they must compete, wanted them to be low. Smith pointed out that high profits were as much or even more to blame for high prices as high wages. "No society can surely be flourishing and happy, of which the far greater part of the members are poor and miserable," he said in *The Wealth of Nations*. "It is but equity, besides, that they who feed, cloath and lodge the whole body of the people, should have such a share of the produce of their own labour as to be themselves tolerably well fed, cloathed and lodged." Franklin from time to time expressed dismay over poor wages in Europe, but tended to believe that America would not have to face such difficulties until its range of opportunities narrowed. As he related in his memoirs, his reaction to a clash over his pay as a young journeyman printer was to start his own business.[39]

IV

By the mid-1780s, the practitioners of the printing trade were finding their options more limited and defending their sometimes varying interests. After Bache and his grandfather returned from France, Franklin's honors included a birthday observance by a large gathering of Philadelphia printers at the Bunch of Grapes tavern on Third Street. They not only toasted him as the "venerable Printer, Philosopher, and Statesman," but also lifted their cups to "Thomas Paine, Esq. Author of COMMON SENSE," to liberty of the press, "preserved forever inviolate," and to printers throughout the world.[40] When the city's journeymen printers—the compositors and pressmen—voted to strike over wage cuts later in 1786, Franklin might have taken their side, since they conducted the drinking festivities at his next birthday. In 1788 he participated in the founding of the Franklin Society, a combination of credit union and insurance company for printing workers which met at his house with Bache in attendance. One of the members, Isaiah Thomas, later recalled, "He evidently had much at heart the success of his grandson, who was then printing, at the recommendation of his grandfather, an edition of the minor classics."[41]

Bache's first ventures in commercial publishing, carried out with Franklin's advice and encouragement, were school texts. In addition to the collection that Thomas saw of writings by Aesop and Erasmus for classics courses, Bache reprinted a series of four *Lessons for Children* books by Anna Letitia Barbauld, an English woman who used Lockean behavioral techniques of esteem and disgrace to instill wisdom and virtue. Franklin thought they were "very pretty little Books for Children" and "really valuable for the purpose of teaching Children to read."[42] The children in Barbauld's works learned that they were not to cry, mistreat animals, or be idle. In one story, a child is told not to fear a storm because the family's house has been furnished with a lightning rod. In another, three boys at a boarding school each receive cakes from home. Harry greedily eats his and becomes sick. Peter hoards his cake until it becomes stale. Billy shares his with the other students and eventually with an old blind man, an act of generosity which makes the boy "more glad than if he had eaten ten cakes." Barbauld's young readers are then asked to decide which of the three boys they like the best.[43]

Franklin, who believed American typography was in need of improvement, also handled the business affairs of Bache's typefounding enterprise. Both the children's books and the typefounding, however, were more personal Enlightenment crusades for the old printer-philosopher than profitable ventures. When Franklin sent one hundred and fifty copies of each volume of the Barbauld books to a relative to sell for the benefit of his sister Jane Mecom in Boston, the booksellers admired the quality of the paper and printing, but found sales slow. Bache, in turn, performed secretarial tasks for his grandfather, including making handwritten copies of the autobiography.[44]

Franklin's prodigious energy was at last waning toward the end of the 1780s and he was becoming more reliant on others. He wrote to Polly Hewson that seeing "our well-furnished, plentiful market as the best of gardens, I am turning mine, in the midst of which my house stands, into grass plots and gravel walks, with trees and flowering shrubs." He told her that he sometimes worried about passing too much time in idle diversions, but thought that with an immortal soul he had all of eternity before him. "So, being easily convinced, and, like other reasonable creatures, satisfied with a small reason, when it is in favour of doing what I have a mind to," he said, "I shuffle the cards again, and begin another game." In January 1788 Franklin sprained his wrist in a fall on the steps to his garden and for several months could barely hold a pen. In the autumn of 1789, weary from years of pain from his "stone" and taking opium, he wrote to congratulate Washington on "the growing Strength of our New Government under your Administration." He added, however, "For my own personal Ease, I should have died two Years ago; but tho' those Years have been spent in excruciating Pain, I am pleas'd that I have lived them, since they have brought me to see our present Situation."[45]

Bache meanwhile had fallen in love with Margaret Markoe, the woman he would marry in 1791 despite expressions of doubt in both families. In a letter to Margaret, he confided that his grandfather "struggled with Death . . . longer than his Friends could wish." Franklin's last public business was a letter dictated to Bache to answer an inquiry from Jefferson about the northeast border of the United States that the British had agreed to after the war. For the following nine days the grandson saw him "in the greatest Agonies" and having trouble breathing. On the morning of April 17, 1790, Franklin, no longer able to talk, shook his head when offered food. "Whenever I approached his Bed, he held out his Hand & having given him mine he would take & hold it for some time," Bache remembered. That night, at the age of eighty-four, Franklin died with his grandsons Benjamin and William at his side. "I think there is something remarkable in his End," Bache told Margaret. "His mental Faculties unimpaired or but little impaired, at his Age. His Resolution unshaken. His Principles fixed even in Death, shew a Man of a superior Cast." Franklin's death would be "universally lamented," the grandson wrote, but for him the loss would be "irreparable."[46]

V

Although an advocate for the rights and economic advancement of the common citizen, Franklin was one of the wealthiest Americans of his time. Despite his prolonged absences from the country, he accumulated an estate that Benjamin Franklin Bache estimated to be worth fifty thousand pounds. After making provisions for a number of favorite people and causes, Franklin left most of his fortune to Bache's parents and to Temple. Bache received several specific bequests, but the main thing of value, he noted for Margaret, was all of Franklin's printing supplies and equipment "that his Industry are to put in Motion assisted by his Father's Aid." Bache's friends expected him to receive more, but he insisted the inheritance did "square perfectly" with his expectations. He thought the will, which included such provisions as a fund for silver medals to honor students of the free schools in Franklin's native Boston, was "a great Man's *Will* it is of a piece with his Life."[47]

Bache was not yet twenty-one at Franklin's death, but, unlike most novice printers, he was free of debt and able to make use of considerable family resources. He also had the name and example of the most celebrated tradesman of the age, the man who began his will, "I, BENJAMIN FRANKLIN, of Philadelphia, printer. . . ." Three months after his grandfather died, as Congress was planning to make Philadelphia the nation's capital for ten years, Bache took the opportunity to establish himself in the public eye. He issued a prospectus for the publication of a newspaper. "This Paper will always be open, for the discussion of political, or any other interesting subjects, to such as deliver their sentiments with temper & decency, and whose motive appears to be, *the public good*," Bache told potential subscrib-

Franklin regarded drawing as "a kind of Universal Language" and encouraged his grandson to practice sketching people and places. Bache sometimes drew Franklin, as in this sketch (center), which was probably done near the time of his grandfather's death in 1790. (Reproduced with the permission of the American Philosophical Society, Philadelphia) ers. "The strictest impartiality will be observed in the publication of pieces offered with this view."[48]

Pledging public-spirited impartiality, a principle of classical republicanism, was a routine practice of editors, especially those Franklin had set up as partners before the Revolution. What was new in Bache's plan was the extent to which the paper was intended to cover the work of scientists and artists, a mission that with Franklin's encouragement had been undertaken earlier in France by the periodical *Nouvelles de la république des lettres et des arts.* Such a venture might not be lucrative, but starting a newspaper could lead to more shop business and job printing even if the publication's advertising and subscription income did not offset the costs. President Washington and members of Congress were committed to keeping postal rates low for newspapers in order to help keep citizens informed.[49]

When his paper appeared on October 1, 1790, with the name *General Advertiser, and Political, Commercial, Agricultural and Literary Journal,* Bache explained in a statement of editorial policy that friends had encouraged him to give more attention than other newspapers to the sciences, literature, and the useful arts. "These wishes, coinciding with the advice which the Publisher had received from his late Grand Father," he said, "suggested the idea of the present work." Bache maintained that while newspapers were the best kind of publication to inform the sovereign people on political matters and to allow "zealous patriots" to express sentiments "for the good of the Community," their "general circulation and cheapness render them also very proper vehicles for every species of information in the *Arts, Sciences, &c.*" He promised news of agriculture, "being, with justice considered as the main support of a young country," and commerce, because of "the assistance which it affords to Agriculture, by furnishing an outlet for the productions of the earth, and from the tendency which it has to extend human knowledge, and to promote liberality of sentiment and universal philanthropy, by the intercourse which it occasions between the most remote nations."[50]

The notion that newspapers improved the lives and raised the political awareness of the public had been a basic tenet of libertarian thought for most of the eighteenth century and had been propounded with enthusiasm by Franklin and Jefferson in particular. For decades, American printers had spoken of providing such wide-ranging intellectual fare in their newspapers, but they had tended to seriously attempt to do so in the more open format of magazines. Admitting that he was imitating the successful English periodicals, which included *Gentleman's Magazine,* Franklin had raced to bring out America's first magazine in 1741, but his Philadelphia rival Andrew Bradford beat him by a matter of days. After both publications failed in their first year, other printers tried to produce magazines, but most were also not profitable. One of the more successful efforts was *The New-York Magazine* founded by Thomas and James Swords in the same year as Bache's paper. Saying that their purpose was the diffusion of all kinds of knowledge to all classes of society, the brothers in their eight years of publication were able to attract subscribers ranging from President Washington to barbers and bakers, despite the fact that a year of the magazine cost almost five days' wages for the common laborer.[51]

At five dollars a year, Bache's *General Advertiser* was twice as expensive as *The New-York Magazine,* but it was published six days a week rather than monthly and, like other newspapers, was able to attract local advertising. The use of *"Advertiser"* in the nameplate, which was not very descriptive of the venture Bache described, may have been chosen out of a desire to encourage an important source of income, or perhaps because the usual names were already in use in a city where a dozen other papers were competing for attention in 1790. Despite such a glut of publications, Bache was able to claim a healthy initial circulation of four hundred, a number which grew to seventeen hundred over the next eight years. Of course, getting either subscribers or advertisers to pay what they owed was not easy. When Jane Mecom learned of Bache's project, she remarked to Sarah Bache that "it may soon create for him an Estate in the clouds as his Venerable Grandfather usd to say of His Newspaper Debpts."[52]

With his ideals apparently as important as his income, Bache sought to position his newspaper as the publication that would, like the various discussion clubs and learned societies Franklin had attended, serve to bring together ideas and discoveries in different fields for the benefit of all. "If the PEOPLE are enlightened the Nation stands and flourishes," Bache said in the first issue, "thro' ignorance it falls or degenerates." At the same time, however, he recognized that the variety in content would mean that what was interesting to "one person may be useless or unintelligible to another." He asked his readers to be patient with material that did not interest them and to know that he did not want to print personal defamation or the merely interesting, "the circumstantial account of a horrid murder, shocking suicide, or hard fought boxing battle, which only serves to turn our thoughts to the dark side of human nature, and put us out of humour with mankind."[53] Bache's plan, which he said was formulated with his grandfather's advice, was to create a pristine, positive newspaper that would see and work for what enlightened republicans believed to be the bright future of a free country.

The matter of money did nevertheless cross Bache's mind as he was preparing to publish his first issue. In August 1790, knowing that the secretary of state made agreements with selected newspapers to print the federal laws, he wrote to offer his services. Jefferson was not only an admirer of Franklin, but had already taken an interest in the career of his grandson. While in France, Jefferson had wondered if "young Mr. Beach has begun to exercise his destined calling of a printer" and, through Franklin, arranged for him to sell editions of "the most remarkable of the English authors" being prepared by Pissot, a French printer who published a newspaper of English and American affairs named the *Général Advertiser*. In contrast to Temple, who would soon inform Jefferson he wanted to represent the country in France and remind him that he was "the Friend of my deceas'd Grandfather," Bache sent a brief, polite note saying that if he decided to employ him, he "would endeavour to merit your approbation." Jefferson, who thought little of Temple and even came to suspect him of intrigues with the British, merely told the older grandson he would make the wish known to the president.[54] A newspaper editor, on the other hand, could be a valuable political asset and worthy of serious attention.

VI

Worried, as Franklin had been, about the presence of "monarchical" or "aristocratic" ideas in public debate and about the bias of British news sources, Jefferson had used his patronage powers in the spring of 1790 to make John Fenno's *Gazette of the United States* a publisher of the federal laws. Fenno, in return, had agreed to publish foreign news from the *Gazette de Leide*, a Dutch publication with republican leanings which Jefferson regarded as more accurate than the other French-language international newspapers and which he supplied with information while he was in Europe. Interested in preventing an important, but reactionary New York newspaper from slipping entirely into the enemy camp, Jefferson hoped to keep more than one side represented even as Fenno that summer offered his readers *Discourses on Davila,* John Adams' defense of social ranks and property rights. By August, when Washington signed the controversial bill for the federal assumption of state debts, and partisan schisms were becoming obvious along lines of wealth and geography, Fenno gave up printing the Leyden articles and embarked on a course of attacking the spirit of democracy and praising "energetic" government in general and Hamilton's funding system in particular. As Fenno moved his paper to the new capital, Jefferson was ready to change printers.[55]

Instead of paying Bache, an editor whose loyalties were not likely to be in question, for publishing the laws, Jefferson then gave his patronage to Andrew Brown of Philadelphia's *Federal Gazette,* an adroit move which ushered an able editor into the ranks of administration critics. Bache, who knew French, began receiving Jefferson's copies of the *Gazette de Leide,* which the secretary of state had previously had to translate or have translated for publication. After Bache had been in business for half a year, Jefferson asked him if he could make the *General Advertiser* "a paper of general distribution, thro' the states" so that the country would have "a purely republican vehicle of news established between the seat of government and all it's parts."[56] Jefferson, as he explained to a relative in Virginia, had been unsuccessful in offering the project to Philip Freneau, an experienced writer and satirist recommended by Madison:

> I inclose you Bache's as well as Fenno's papers. You will have percieved that the latter is a paper of pure Toryism, disseminating the doctrines of monarchy, aristocracy, and the exclusion of the influence of the people. We have been trying to get another *weekly* or *halfweekly* paper set up excluding advertisements, so that it might go through the states, and furnish a whig-vehicle of intelligence. We hoped at one time to have persuaded Freneau to set up here, but failed. In the mean time Bache's paper, the principles of which were always republican, improves in it's matter. If we can persuade him to throw off all his advertisements on one leaf, by tearing that off, the leaf containing intelligence may be sent without over-charging the post, and be generally taken instead of Fenno's.[57]

Bache had already given up a weekly version of his paper for distant subscribers, finding it difficult to please both sets of readers.

Following through on Jefferson's suggestion proved disappointing. In 1792 Jefferson described his dealings with Bache in a letter to Washington and told about his efforts to bring the Leyden paper's "juster view" of European affairs to the president and the public. "Mr. Bache essayed it for me in Philadelphia, but his being a daily paper, did not circulate sufficiently in the other states," Jefferson said. "He even tried, at my request, the plan of a weekly paper of recapitulation from his daily paper, in hopes that that might go into the other states, but in this too we failed."[58]

Jefferson continued to court Freneau with inducements that included an undemanding translator's position in his department. By the autumn of 1791 Freneau had accepted and he began to publish a newspaper that met his sponsor's specifications, the *National Gazette.* Jefferson did not write for the paper himself but helped gather subscriptions. For two years the *Gazette* was in the vanguard of advancing Jeffersonian principles. Madison contributed theoretical essays extolling the nation's experiment with political equality, and he spoke specifically in an essay on "PUBLIC OPINION" of the need for "a *circulation of newspapers through the entire body of the people.*"[59]

At the time the country had more than one hundred newspapers, with the clearly Federalist journals, which were strong in the commercial areas that gave support to Hamilton's economic programs, outnumbering recognizably Republican papers by about two to one. Madison and Jefferson evidently perceived a need for a publication that would reach potential supporters in the sparsely populated agrarian regions where they could count on opposition to the administration. In the *National Gazette,* writers articulated the emerging Republican view that Hamilton's financial policies added up to a conspiracy for speculators in the public debt and would be the foundation of a new aristocratic order. One of the more gifted contributors was George Logan, a Pennsylvania friend of Franklin's and Jefferson's who espoused physiocratic principles on agriculture and trade and argued that the masses would be oppressed where wealth was concentrated in the hands of a powerful few.[60]

Freneau's *National Gazette* lost money and gradually became an embarrassment to the cause as the editor's penchant for caustic wit began to prevail over reasoned discussion, and his hatred of Britain blinded him to the implications of Edmond Genêt's disastrous diplomacy. Jefferson, with his position in the government undermined by what he said to Washington were Hamilton's "machinations against the liberty of the country," resigned in 1793. Annoyed by Hamilton's charges against him in the press, including that of misuse of office for partisan purposes in appointing Freneau, the secretary of state told the president that his rival in the cabinet had wanted to have a king and house of lords in 1787 and had created a massive and corrupt patronage machine in the Treasury. Freneau's paper expired as Jefferson prepared to leave office and the editor-translator resigned his government post. With the *Gazette* gone at the end of 1793, Bache's *General Advertiser* became the nation's leading Republican newspaper, a position it would retain for the rest of the decade.[61]

The *National Gazette* disappeared at a time when Bache too was struggling. As early as 1791, the editor of the *Advertiser* told his readers about the "fatigue and anxiety" he experienced in publishing a daily newspaper. His difficulties increased as his parents toured Europe in 1792–1793 and he was given the responsibility of managing Richard Bache's extensive financial affairs. "I work hard, that's clear yet perhaps am not as economical as I ought to be, and want regularity in my business," the son wrote to his father early in 1793. "Not having been brought up as a man of business has proved a considerable disadvantage to me." A yellow fever epidemic at the end of the year made him suspend the *Advertiser* for two months. When he resumed publication, he stated in the paper that he could have continued printing and remained safe himself, but that it would have been criminal to endanger the lives of his four apprentices and seven workmen and assistants for his own private interest.[62]

Bache did not have the benefit of the kind of patronage dispensed to Brown or Freneau. Indeed, providing government funds to Franklin's grandson undoubtedly would have angered the political enemies Franklin had acquired over his decades of public service. Following Franklin's death, Bache was in the position of reporting on the mixed reactions to the event in the realms of national and international politics. The House of Representatives passed a motion by Madison that members wear badges of mourning for a month, but a similar motion fell under attack in the Senate and was withdrawn. The matter did not end there, however, as the two houses of Congress, the president, and members of the cabinet became enmeshed in the issue of how to respond to elaborate condolences sent by France's National Assembly to honor an "immortal" father of "the great human family." Reflecting the growing split in the country's attitudes toward France in the midst of its revolution, Hamilton wrote a reply for Washington which spoke of the French monarch as a "friend of the people" and of the need for "public order," while Jefferson's letter on behalf of Congress spoke warmly of Franklin, regretted the "arbitrary Lines of Separation" between countries, and referred to "the Friendship and the Interests of our two Nations."[63]

The divisiveness of the issues that would dominate the partisan debate of the 1790s—Hamilton's financial system and relations with the European powers—was becoming apparent before the end of Washington's first term. In Jefferson's mind, France was a countervailing force to Britain and to what he came to see as a British conspiracy against freedom and independence in America.[64] With the weapon of the press and increasing political mobilization, Jefferson, Madison, and their allies were seeking to impel the United States away from what they regarded as the inequitable realities of British government and economics toward a revolutionary future they thought possible for all enlightened nations.

Benjamin Franklin, the most venerable American associated with such sentiments, had left a particular journalistic legacy to a young printer and had given intellectual inspiration to a rising politician, a democratically minded leader who would be elected to the presidency in 1800. In a letter to Franklin's eulogist in Philadelphia that was incorporated into the tribute arranged by the American Philosophical Society, Thomas Jefferson remembered that whenever he was asked at the French court if he was replacing Dr. Franklin, he would reply that he was only his successor, that no one could replace him. Jefferson wrote that the country could be thankful that his life was so long "as to avail us of his wisdom in the establishment of our freedom, and to bless him with a view of it's dawn in the east, where they seemed till now to have learned every thing, but how to be free."[65]

CHAPTER

6

World Revolution and American Reform

IN THE FIRST FEW MONTHS OF PUBLICATION, BENJAMIN FRANKLIN BACHE attempted to follow his announced plans for making the *General Advertiser* an educational newspaper. The second issue, for instance, had articles on calculating erosion and checking the quality of gunpowder. Having promised in the first issue "to gratify the Public" with anecdotes about his grandfather, he also inserted an account from an English newspaper of some of Franklin's accomplishments. Stories about Franklin and instructive items continued to find a place, but Bache was not satisfied with the merely informative. With fundamental conflicts arising over national goals, he wanted to publish a paper that would report the thrust and parry of contending conceptions of the future. In his fourth week as an editor, he complained to readers about a temporary shortage of exciting news. Heads were not then being cut off in France, he said sarcastically, and in domestic politics he found no party disputes, legislative debates, or "even so much as a piece of private abuse to grace a paper." Saying that contentious times were happy ones for editors, he exclaimed, "Zounds, people now have no spirit in them."[1]

For a political journalist of the 1790s, there was seemingly no greater shortcoming than failing to paint subjects in the most arresting hues. Bache, like Franklin and Jefferson, was affable and self-assured, but angered by injustice and provoked by affronts to his moral principles. Anxious to contribute to a revolution of hearts, he lost much of his interest in stocking readers' minds. On January 1, 1791, after

three months of publishing, he dropped the word "Agricultural" from
the paper's full title and removed a motto—"Truth, Decency, Utility"—from beneath the nameplate as he expanded the size of the pages.
Bache told his readers that he needed space to cover Congressional
news and that he was unable to offer the variety of material he had
originally proposed as long as "more important matter" was at hand.
He was raising the price of an annual subscription to six dollars, he
said, but the paper would be a third larger. Later in the year, Bache
dropped the words "Political, Commercial and Literary Journal" from
the nameplate.[2] The paper was becoming increasingly polemical and
was promoting reforms in line with enlightened republicanism.

Although Benjamin Franklin Bache was not alone among American editors in advocating libertarian solutions to societal problems,
his *General Advertiser* was in a position to be an important channel of
information and opinion. Its potential impact was not limited to those
who subscribed or otherwise managed to see a copy; the news and
essays Bache published were read by political leaders and reprinted
elsewhere. Making use of the free postal exchange of newspapers among
editors, eighteenth-century journalists simply gathered much of what
they printed by selecting press material from other states.[3] The *General Advertiser* offered pointed analysis, and, on occasion, a scandal or
some striking development in government policy. As a daily located
in the nation's capital, the paper was well situated to dramatize issues
and assign blame. In conveying the hopes and animosities of those
seeking a more egalitarian world, Bache demonstrated how well he
had learned the kind of political and economic lessons taught by
Franklin and Jefferson.

I

Educated in Europe, where dancing and fencing were considered valuable branches of learning, and in the home of one of the century's
most agile writers, Bache was not about to produce plodding journalism. The view he and his correspondents offered in the first years of
the decade was that it was a time of extraordinary promise for citizens
of all nations, particularly America. An editorial in the newspaper's
second month declared that "nature has done everything on her part
to render the United States more fully competent to supporting an
independent empire, than any other country whatever." Other com-

ments at the same time rejected doubts about the viability of democratic government and stated that in no part of the globe did "new truths have a better prospect of being attended to and received than America." The nation was, the paper contended over the next several years, a refuge where the oppressed were welcomed and differing religions tolerated. "May this prospect never be clouded," one editorial said, "but may it extend more and more until the lights of Philosophy, Liberty and Philanthropy shall eradicate the benighted corners of the whole world."[4]

With as much fervor as any newspaper of the period, the *General Advertiser* gave credit to the former British colonies on the shores of a largely unexplored continent for beginning an era of worldwide revolution. The founding of the United States was a "triumph of reason and liberty—the harbinger of universal freedom and happiness to the race of mankind." The paper said that America's Revolution had already inspired the French upheavals and would continue to provide an example of a free people's ability to achieve peace, stability, and general prosperity. In one issue the United States, an "Eden in the West," was described as enjoying "the SMILING RADIANCE of Heaven" while "the expansive energy of principles" was sweeping across the Earth with the force of an earthquake that "must overthrow the Colossus of despotism."[5] In another editorial, France was pointed to as the country which had "hitherto set the pattern to all Europe in matters of taste and fashion" and was now prepared to afford the more "noble example" of liberty:

> France was the brightest gem in the crown of tyranny—the monarchy in which the arts and sciences most flourished, and which presented the most favourable prospect of arbitrary power in the world. An Empire so respectable, from whom tyranny derived her chief ornament and support, embracing the side of freedom, will serve to bring her cause into great credit and reputation.[6]

Believing that the progress of history could nevertheless take various paths in different countries, Bache was, like his grandfather, not always too particular about the exact form a free government took because its ultimate success would depend on the people's attitudes and behavior. In 1792 the *Advertiser* stated that the three "enlightened nations" of the world—England, France, and the United

States—were in a sense competing to show which kind of system would best achieve public liberty and happiness. "Perhaps we shall see that each plan has its merit," the paper said, "who has a right to decide dogmatically that there is but one right way in politics?" Readers were then cautioned against "a persecuting spirit" that would try to impose political orthodoxy by force. Later in the year they were told that the American Revolution had succeeded because of the "general light and information of the people of the United States" and their "singular magnanimity, which nothing but superior wisdom could have inspired." Bache insisted, "On knowledge and virtue then are raised the pillars of this rising republic."[7]

Enlightened people naturally wanted freedom, the paper argued, and freedom produced greatness. "It is an established principle, that wherever reason and philosophy prevail, liberty will insensibly flourish," said one brief essay, "nor is it a practicable measure, or in the power of man to establish a system of oppression by military force, unless a nation is previously reduced to its original meanness by ignorance and superstition." In the time of the Grecian commonwealth, when "liberty was in its zenith," Greece was consequently an "emporium of arts and sciences" and "raised mankind to the highest summit of grandeur and independence." As relaxed and confident as Bache could be about the development of democracy, however, he was extremely intolerant of those who would degrade others. Assessing the "present posture of affairs in Europe" in 1792, he presented a vivid scene of old wrongs being eliminated:

> An universal effervescence is apparent—kingdoms, states, and empires are convulsed—the struggles of reason, right and liberty have produced the fermentation—the fæces of despotism, superstition and prejudice will be pursued away, and the pure waters of life, transparent and invigorating, will remain: these will be imbibed in copious draughts by an enlightened race of men, who have for ages been drinking the enervating and intoxicating potions prescribed for them by the emissaries of darkness—the traitors to the dignity of human nature.[8]

Bache and his writers spoke of the American and French Revolutions as if their fates were intertwined. Failure in France, they reasoned, would give new life to monarchical power. "Few people have a proper sense of the importance of the success of the French revolution to the welfare and happiness of America," said one of Bache's editorial paragraphs in 1792. "Should a counter-revolution be ultimately effected in France, the advocates of hereditary government and titular dignities here may again be emboldened to come forward with their pernicious doctrines." On the other hand, a successful outcome in such a populous and powerful nation would "crush those plants of ambition which have been long hatching for us on the hot-bed of European depravity." A month later, after noting the celebrations on the Fourth of July, Bache was able to say with satisfaction that the fourteenth of July had been given "almost equal attention by the patriots of America, and will no doubt in future be considered as our second day of eminence in the calendar of Liberty."[9]

Bache accordingly made his paper a champion of the revolutionary change in France and a leader of Republican opinion on the issue. The United States should be grateful for the French help it received during its own revolution, the paper maintained repeatedly. "An Old French Soldier," for example, wrote to remind Americans that "the blood of Frenchmen drenched the foundation of the temple of your liberty." In addition, readers were urged to see France's potential as a principal market for the nation's merchants and farmers. Bache reported on demonstrations of support for France in America, printed the words to "The Marseillaise," and, like many of his correspondents, identified the French struggle as "the cause of humanity." Responding to doubts expressed in less radical publications in the summer of 1792, he stated that no one could "seriously suppose that the present struggle of that nation is not the beginning of that universal reformation which is about to take place in the world for the general benefit of the human race."[10]

Soon, however, came news of the September 1792 massacres in Paris, the execution of Louis, the beginning of the French Revolutionary Wars, and the Reign of Terror. One of the victims of the Terror was Condorcet, the Enlightenment philosopher and revolutionary politician who spent the last months of his life in hiding, writing his moving *Esquisse d'un tableau historique des progrès de l'esprit humain.* Anticipating that he and his wife Sophie would be arrested, he wrote a testament recording his last wishes for his daughter Eliza, that she practice republican virtue and love liberty and equality. Having admired Franklin's philosophies and been one of his eulogists in France, Condorcet suggested that Eliza learn English and recommended her to Thomas Jefferson and to Franklin's grandson, Benjamin Franklin Bache. Shortly after being captured and confined, Condorcet was found on the floor of his cell, dead from a stroke or perhaps from suicide by poison.[11] Bache did not have to help Condorcet's daughter, but he was one of the American publishers of his *Esquisse*, a polemical history of human thought which upheld reason and justice, as infrequent as they may be in human conduct, against ignorance and superstition.

As early as 1790, Bache had worried about the "unbridled licentiousness" of a vengeful populace unaccustomed to the "novelty of freedom." In 1793, with the administration attempting to distance itself from the Treaty of Amity and Commerce that Franklin had negotiated with France, Bache wrote to his father that Hamilton was striving to have the document interpreted narrowly, "that is, the British interest has by far outweighted the French with the government, the commercial, the monied interest carries all before it." By the summer of 1794, one of Bache's correspondents began a letter to the editor saying simply that the "friends of liberty and mankind" ought to pray for the French Revolution. "The citizens of the United States are peculiarly interested in their cause and its triumph," the writer continued. "Our peace and prosperity depend greatly upon it; and nothing else will prevent the unjust aggressions of Britain, in the present temper of her vindictive rulers."[12]

As the turmoil in Europe intensified, Americans became increasingly divided in their attitudes toward England and France. Shortly after France declared war on England and a coalition of European countries early in 1793, Edmond Genêt arrived in the United States with hopes of gaining American support. Despite Washington's proclamation of neutrality and warnings from Jefferson, the French minister dispatched privateers to attack British vessels and made plans to invade British and Spanish territory. Bache's newspaper attempted to shore up Genêt's position with pro-French essays and war reporting, but the administration took steps to stop the diplomat's actions and enforce neutrality. When "A Jacobin" wrote in the *Advertiser* that France's treaty of alliance with the United States allowed the minister's activities, Alexander Hamilton responded with a "No Jacobin" series in *Dunlap's American Daily Advertiser*. Identifying Genêt himself as "A Jacobin," the secretary of the treasury charged that the French minister had privately *"threatened to appeal from The President of The United States to the People."* [13]

Americans—many of whom were initially sympathetic to the French cause—were distressed by Genêt's apparent recklessness. Accounts in Bache's newspaper maintained that the minister never intended to meddle in domestic politics or to insult the president and, moreover, was being persecuted by a conspiracy of government officials who seemed to find him "too *democratic*" for their liking. Washington was criticized for accepting a policy that would anger a good ally and force Americans into "the protection of the English, who having already acquired considerable influence in the large towns, will find it an easy task to subject this country anew." Most of the blame, however, was placed squarely on "the crooked politics of a treasury officer to add one more to the disgraceful list of perfidious nations" opposing France. Hamilton and others in high positions had descended to spreading gossip against the representative of an important nation "instead of attending to the important concerns of a great and rising commonwealth." [14]

Bache had, in fact, turned down the opportunity to publish Hamilton's "No Jacobin" jab at Genêt, writing in the *Advertiser* that he had not wanted to print a personal attack "which we, indeed, positively knew to be ill founded." When Hamilton sent Bache a warning that its rejection would be considered evidence that the paper was " 'devoted to the support of a foreign interest, in opposition to the government of our country, and to its real welfare,' " Bache published the threat and said of the secretary in a reply:

> Whether our correspondent is, in any degree, actuated by *foreign* influence, we are not so ungenerous as to hazard even a surmise, but we can honestly disclaim all such undue or improper influence, as much as he, or any of our fellow-citizens; nor will we yield to him, or any man, in warmth of regard for the 'real welfare' of our country. [15]

The *Advertiser* writers presented the Republican view that a cabal of Hamiltonians was guiding the country back to British domination, or at least shaping society in the English mold, and that the people needed to be roused and their enemies confronted. Bache and other prophets of world revolution did acknowledge from time to time that their victory was not always assured, especially in Europe where "the attainment of universal freedom" was being hampered by "corruption in every form, gigantic prejudices, and the darkness of ignorance among the great mass of the people" who had only recently glimpsed the "rays of reason." In a letter which spoke of "the depressed and servile condition of the wretched peasantry" of Ireland, for instance, a correspondent stated that "as free Americans, we ought to look with a fraternal eye on the efforts of every people, who are nobly endeavouring to shake off the yoke of tyranny, and to assert those rights of which they have too long been despoiled, by the ruffian band of despotic power." The writer wondered, however, if the Irish people were too weak to fight "a monstrous aristocracy, in *church* and *state.*"[16]

Pro-administration papers, meanwhile, were expressing horror at the brutality in France and mocking Bache for his unwearying support of the revolution. Bache and his fellow Republican editors responded by trying to give the best appearance to the purges and executions. Finding that America's "aristocratic prints" exulted in the fall of Robespierre, Bache's *General Advertiser* contended that republicans were attached to principles rather than individuals and would not miss a man who stifled public opinion and concentrated authority in his hands. American "papers under British influence" had been pleased at the suppression of popular political societies in France, the paper pointed out, and had argued for abolishing the pro-French Democratic-Republican societies that were forming in America. Restrictions on free inquiry might occur in France, the editor said, but "no man in our enlightened republic would be swayed by the force of so pernicious an example and be tempted tamely to give up that right because it had been tyrannically wrested from his brethren the French."[17]

Bache professed shock at what he regarded as the "calumnies on the French revolution" published in the "British prints" of the United States. The London newspapers they relied upon for war news gave "truly laughable" accounts of French victories in which "a severe beating is called a check" and flight "a change in position." In Britain "ministerial" papers received government subsidies which, Bache observed, would explain their survival and their "doctrine of passive obedience and non-resistance," but support for "principles so subversive of popular government" in America was surprising. "There is undue influence some where," he said. In fact, Federalist printers were routinely given postmasterships as rewards for their political sentiments. John

Fenno, the premier Federalist editor, had received a substantial amount of printing business from the Treasury and the Senate, and Hamilton raised a considerable sum to keep him from bankruptcy in 1793. The *Advertiser*'s reaction was to dub Fenno's paper the *"pensioned Gazette"* and its editor the tool of "the American Chancellor of the Exchequer." The *Gazette* returned the compliment by periodically asserting that Bache was supported by French gold, a charge that Bache ridiculed and denied.[18]

The *General Advertiser* was also able to deride its chief rival's portrayal of the emerging American opposition as incendiary factions and *"blood-thirsty Jacobins,"* but defending France was a greater challenge. The frenzied killing was said to be necessary for liberty and to be expected as the result of the atrocities that had been inflicted on the French people. One correspondent, quoting a speech in the National Assembly, pointed to the "feudal rights" which had allowed lords to seize the property of their vassals, hunt poor peasants for pleasure, and usurp the role of the husband on the wedding night. Bache explained that the French populace had more cunning, determined enemies at hand than Americans had fought. America did not have so much misery, he wrote, and a "royal puppet, on this spot, did not dance on the wire of a band of courtiers, the most despicable and abandoned wretches that ever disgraced mankind." In a statement that could have been used to explain his own later journalistic ethics, he excused a Paris mob's "insult" to Lafayette by saying: "When parties run high, the good cause must be supported with enthusiasm and absolute violence, to outweigh the activity and extravagance of opposite partizans."[19]

II

Since Federalist policies and practices seemed to ignore the fundamental moral framework of enlightenment egalitarianism, Republicans, like Bache, gave up the classical ideal of impartiality and recognized the enduring partisan conflicts that would exist under the Constitution. In Hamilton's stated outlook on political economy, self-interest was the driving force, democracy was a disease, and the pursuit of property naturally gave rise to a division into the few and the many. In his *Report on Manufactures* submitted to the House late in 1791, Hamilton had emphatically rejected the idea of America as an

agricultural nation and denounced the specific physiocratic arguments
that supported it, saying that foreign demand for farm surpluses would
be too uncertain, that the population had reached a level allowing for
diversification into manufacturing, and that government would have
to be involved, because other nations did not practice free trade and
Americans would need incentives to enter new enterprises.[20]

Faced with heavily indebted federal and state governments and
an enfeebled economy, many Americans shared the secretary's desire
to secure the public credit, but critics interpreted Hamilton's ambitious funding system as a windfall for speculators in depreciated notes
and the creation of the Bank of the United States as a boon for wealthy
investors. Madison, who led an unsuccessful effort in Congress to offer
payments to the original holders of the debt as a matter of fairness,
used the pages of the *National Gazette* to launch a strident attack on
the Hamiltonian program and its implications in 1792. He contrasted
the healthy, uncorrupted life of farming with the miseries and uncer-
tainties of relying on manufacturing. A society of idle rich and struggling poor was not a proper basis for a democratic republic, Madison's
writings suggested, as he scorned measures that were "pampering the
spirit of speculation" and that "might smooth the way to hereditary
government." Already, he said, the country was split into two groups—
the republicans and those favoring the "opulent" who thought "that
government can be carried on only by the pagentry of rank, the influence of money and emoluments, and the terror of military force."[21]

Bache and his correspondents analyzed Hamilton's policies with
a mixture of praise and contempt. A restoration of public credit was
considered beneficial, and the development of some manufacturing
was seen as a means of making the United States more independent.
On the other hand, *Advertiser* essays generally reflected egalitarian
inclinations by displaying more faith than Hamilton had in free trade
and less tolerance for economic privileges and a continuing public
debt. The idea of government giving special incentives and protection
to some commercial ventures of the wealthy violated republican principles and seemed "a production of the dark ages" rather than "the
present enlightened æra." The nation would come to realize that the
debt should be eliminated, the paper said, and that the investors should
put their money to more productive uses. "It is bad policy for them
to retire on their 6 per cents," commented an editorial. Speculation
on the national bank, another opinion essay said, "drained all the

natural channels of business" and produced a "prostitution of morals."[22]

When bank shares went on the market and quickly rose in price, some of the *Advertiser*'s contributors lamented that honest republican industry and frugality would succumb to the lure of easy wealth. One wit wrote to ask Bache why he did not sell his shop to buy bank stock. "I know that this advice is contrary to certain maxims deeply impressed on your mind by the venerable Doctor Franklin!" the letter said. "But, with all respect for the memory of that great Philosopher, I think, with a majority of Americans, that his maxims of prudence, economy, honesty, &c. are too abstract for actual practice, and too narrow for the policy of this Rising Empire." Bache was a fool, the writer said sarcastically, for slaving day and night when gentlemen were letting their money work for them. Bache did not take the situation so lightly. "The spirit of speculation, and the desire of amassing fortunes rapidly, without awaiting the slow but sure progress of industry and frugality, is ever attended, in any state or country, with a multiplicity of evil consequences," he observed. "Among these, a thirst for rank and distinction is not the least, and may justly be termed the child of speculation."[23]

Hamilton's most egregious error, in Bache's mind, was failing to recognize the place farming should have in the nation's priorities. In his second week of publication, after listing Franklin's reasons for thinking agriculture "the basis of all real power in a state," Bache remarked, "The Americans have felt the blessings of their attention to that great man's advice, which, if they continue to follow, it will lead them to every national advantage, to a continuance of peace, to an increase of wealth, to a redoubled population, and to a degree of consequence in the world, to which no other pursuit can possibly raise them." Bache's investment advice for anyone with available cash was "a snug farm near a good market."[24]

When Hamilton's *Report on Manufactures* appeared, Bache made a point of contrasting its conclusions with Jefferson's wish that American "workshops remain in Europe," as well as with Franklin's opinion that the United States "attend principally to agriculture." Franklin, the *Advertiser* noted, had been upset by the "pale and sickly" condition of English factory workers and only approved of America having "domestic manufactures" that would not injure health or take necessary time away from the household and farming. For his own part,

Bache provided a classic portrayal of nations abandoning hard work and equality as they grew rich and dissolute. "Too great attention to commerce will soon introduce idleness and luxury," Bache wrote, "and though it may enrich a few particular persons, it will impoverish the country." A national reliance on agriculture, he said, would preserve industry, liberty, and the virtues of strength, patience, and courage.[25]

Bache's primary sociopolitical objective was a moral cleansing of the world, one which would engender not only liberty and equality, but also the feeling of brotherhood and benevolence that Franklin in particular had thought necessary for the maintenance of a democratic republic. The virtue of treating fellow citizens with decency and compassion was seen as the responsibility that went with Americans' new freedom. Writings published and republished in the *General Advertiser* said that the more individuals controlled themselves and acted properly, the less government would have to do. "Conscious virtue is the only solid foundation of all happiness," stated the paper in a list of aphorisms. "If thou regardest thine own welfare, health of body, and peace of mind, observe this short precept,—be always doing good." The rewards of virtue and costs of vice were clear to Franklin's grandson, as was a need to do more than just talk about the subject. In the early years of his paper, as he was setting out his philosophy, Bache wrote:

> The supreme sense and relish of virtue, or whatever is lovely and heroic in affections and conduct, is not to be obtained by perusing dull, formal lectures on the several virtues and vices, and declaiming loosely on the effect; but by exhibiting to the moral eye living examples, or what is nearest to those pictures genuine copies of manners, that it may learn easily to separate between the fair and harmonious, the deformed and dissonant.[26]

Bache wanted Americans to remember that "without frequent pruning of vicious shoots, the most virtuous governments will degenerate, and bear bad fruit." One essay described the need for societal efforts to restrain vice as medicine checked disease, especially as the country becomes "more extensive and populous; more civilized & refined, more opulent and commercial, and is farther removed from the simplicity of nature." There was, the *General Advertiser* said, a "moral use to be made of history," a chance to learn from examples in order to "shun the paths of vice and immorality, cruelty and barbarism: or implant in our minds the more refined sentiments of benevolence and philanthropy." Advancing nations, republicans such as Bache suggested, always faced a contest between the enlightenment and the corruption of the public. "The prognostics of national prosperity or decline, do not vary more than those which indicate a wholesome or destructive change in the constitution of different individuals," he wrote. "Justice, wisdom, love of liberty, and an honest national zeal will ensure prosperity and power to every people whom they influence."[27]

Bache feared—as his grandfather had—that America had not fully escaped the attractions of the English form of government and its social hierarchy. In the classical republican paradigm, a complex, commercial nation like Britain might naturally produce inequality and therefore political friction, but a balancing of monarchical, aristocratic, and democratic elements resulted in stability. Hereditary authority had disappeared in America, but the Constitution seemed to recognize the traditional concept of mixed government with the strength of the one in the president, the wisdom of the few in the Senate, and the liberty of the many in the House. In Bache's brand of enlightened republicanism, however, the mass of people—with enough education and economic security—could be trusted with the ultimate, predominant power in society. "The English government is like the American, as a Cheshire cheese is like the moon; they have the same form, but are very different in substance," an *Advertiser* editorial said. The British had "the will of the legislature for a constitution," while the American government was framed by the people, and officials were servants who "are chosen from among the people by the people, return to the people and are responsible to the people."[28]

The editor and his correspondents did find aspects of the nation's new political structure to praise. Abuses of authority could be checked, they agreed, with three branches of government, two houses of Congress, and state and federal levels. Yet, they were at their most exuberant in extolling the principle of *vox populi, vox dei*. Government needed to have "the GOOD of the PEOPLE in view as the *end*, and the WILL of the PEOPLE as the *guide*," wrote "A Republican." "It is the glory of a Democracy that every question arising; is determined by the only just mode of decision the *voice* of the MAJORITY." The writer allowed that the will of the majority could be "fairly given by

Representation," but said, "The moment the government contradicts
this voice from that moment it is no longer republican." Bache produced similar statements about the paramount importance of majority
rule. Americans fought for such liberty in the Revolution and were
"rapidly rising to greatness" under their present system, he said, "but
should a majority of the people at any time think that they could
enjoy greater political happiness by a change of government, the principles of the Constitution would not be looked on as fixed principles."[29]

By the middle of the decade, Bache was concluding that the
American political system had not given enough power to the people.
Noting that the "American Constitution is said to resemble the fabled
constitution of Great Britain" with "*monarchy, aristocracy* and *democracy* blended," he stated that the "seeds of destruction lurk in a constitution that has engrafted on it incompatible principles." One of the
elements must eventually predominate, he thought, as indeed Britain
had found with monarchical rule "daily swallowing up the privileges
of the commons." In the United States, where the Federalists were
asking for more "energy" in the exercise of authority, Bache said, "It
might be asked whether a form of government containing opposite,
or in other language, *balancing* principles is adapted to a people, where
there are no *grades* in society, where all are equal, and no royal or
noble privileges are to be created or secured?" The framing of the
Constitution itself had to be viewed with suspicion. "Was it *wisdom*
that planned a government containing within its own bosom the elements of eternal discord?" Bache asked. "Or was it designed, that the
people might become weary of their condition and at length call out
for a king?"[30]

After the ratification of the Jay Treaty of 1795, with terms Republicans angrily regarded as too favorable to Britain and as disregard-
ing the public will, Bache reached the point of backing arguments for
democratization of the Senate and presidency, two institutions which
had, his paper said, acted against majority will in approving the agreement. Bache published an impassioned, anonymous pamphlet, *Remarks Occasioned by the Late Conduct of Mr. Washington*, which maintained that America did not want a new King George, but that the
nation's thinking had remained too monarchical at the time the Constitution was written and was still indolent enough to be deceived by
Washington's stature as a hero. A chief executive had enormous re-

sponsibilities, readers were reminded, and yet could be brought down by ill health, the corruptions of power, the machinations of evil advisers, and the difficulties of mastering complex issues. The vice-president was "an inert personage" while some appointees were "*too active*" in governing. The pamphlet's solution was one Bache's grandfather had endorsed at the Constitutional Convention, the plural executive. A model, the *Remarks* said, was the new French Directory, which had shown the requisite "vigor, secrecy, and celerity" in battling the forces of monarchs and had united its country while Washington had divided his.[31]

Although Bache's newspaper noted that Franklin had supported unicameralism, and even seemed to agree with his standard story that two houses would act like a two-headed snake and die of thirst trying to decide which direction to take, the pamphlet did not propose eliminating the Senate. Single houses might be considered more democratic, but they had produced questionable results under the Articles of Confederation and under Pennsylvania's state constitution in effect from 1776 to 1790, both of which had plural executives and annual elections for representatives. Still, in the *Remarks,* senators were labeled as a "class of men more advanced in *political* corruption" than any other and the Senate itself was traced to British practice. The pamphlet therefore recommended Virginia's "wise resolutions" for constitutional amendments in response to the treaty controversy, changes which would reduce the term of senators to three years, give some authority for accepting treaties to the House of Representatives, and establish a tribunal other than the Senate for impeachment trials.[32]

The idea of altering the Constitution to undercut the administration and its adherents had little appeal. As the 1796 election approached, the Democratic-Republican societies were rapidly disappearing not only because they had failed to defeat the Jay Treaty and Washington had denounced such "self-created" organizations after the Whiskey Rebellion, but also because they had to fight charges of being anti-federalist. Bache and his scribblers, said a correspondent in the *Gazette of the United States,* were part of "that inveterate antifederal junto who exerted every nerve to prevent the people of the United States from adopting the present Constitution of Government." Another *Gazette* writer, "PLAIN DEALING," added that if the young editor thought of the president as a traitor and of the Senate as corrupt for accepting the treaty, then it was time for "this *magnus apollo*

Citizen Bache to *unfold* his great plan of *political redemption.*" If the
Constitution had undone the country, "PLAIN DEALING" continued, then Bache should offer a new one, one which would resemble
the legislative work of Robespierre and make "us poor oppressed
Americans *leap* for joy." The contributor accused Bache of wanting
the people to act for themselves, without representatives, and of seeking a system where no aristocrat would have a head after three months.[33]

Opposition journalists and politicians were anxious to deny Federalist allegations of their having radical, French-inspired ideas for
subverting the Constitution. The correspondence of the two presidential candidates took up the matter as Jefferson and Adams agreed that
a plural executive like the French Directory would only foment new
divisions and that corruption was the real danger to elective governments. Expressing a wish that there could be an "ocean of fire" between the United States and the venal oligarchy of Britain, Jefferson
told Adams that he had come to hate politics. The "morals of a people," he hoped, could be the foundation of government in the United
States:

> Never was a finer canvas presented to work on than our countrymen.
> All of them engaged in agriculture or the pursuits of honest industry,
> independant in their circumstances, enlightened as to their rights, and
> firm in their habits of order and obedience to the laws. This I hope will
> be the age of experiments in government, and that their basis will be
> founded on principles of honesty, not of mere force. We have seen no
> instance of this since the days of the Roman republic, nor do we read
> of any before that.[34]

Bache and his writers were also content to concentrate less on
the abstractions of political structure than on the reality of political
behavior. The discussion of constitutional alternatives he published
was only a few pages in the midst of an eighty-four-page pamphlet
castigating Washington for lacking ability as a general and for abandoning republican practices as president. The underlying problem was
not so much the form of government as the sentiments and conduct
within it. Washington's failures, the *Remarks* said, stemmed from a
pompous attitude that the people should remain in their place and
the aristocrats in theirs. "He loves good faith in pecuniary transac-
tions being himself a man of property," the pamphlet commented.

"He has no hatred of the lower orders of society, but neither has he any active philanthropy for them; since few really *love* what they do not also *respect.*" Bache's most basic objection to the Senate was that it also showed contempt for the public by meeting behind closed doors, particularly as it met in secrecy to consider the Jay Treaty. Both Bache and Freneau had campaigned to open its meetings to the public, saying that republican government required that the people know what their representatives were doing.[35]

The persistent theme of Republican journalism of the 1790s—the leitmotiv of papers like the *Advertiser,* Boston's *Independent Chronicle,* and the New York *Argus*—was that the federal government had fallen into the hands of an aristocratic party aligned with Britain and hostile to the interests of the general public. When a harshly worded letter from Thomas Jefferson to Philip Mazzei made similar accusations and in 1797 found its way into a Federalist paper, Noah Webster's New York *Minerva,* Bache said he could only agree with the vice-president's conclusion, that there was "a Monarchical and Aristocratical party" in America. "We also think, and many good citizens throughout the United States think with us," the editor added, "that the Federal Constitution is not perfection, that it is too much on the model of the British." When Webster, one of Bache's usual sparring partners, decided to declare Jefferson's correspondence *"treasonable,"* Bache retorted that if that were the case, then "every page" of his newspaper had been treasonable for years.[36]

In fact, the *Advertiser* had wasted few opportunities to disparage what Bache and his contributors identified as regressive tendencies in the country they had touted as the harbinger of enlightened change. The paper's outlook thus could shift quickly from revolutionary optimism to a more traditional republican solemnity. "I begin to tremble for my countrymen," said a 1792 editorial concluding that Congress was taking an expansive view of its powers under the Constitution, "I fear there is an irresistable propensity in all governors to slide into despotism." In another issue, readers were told that the "idea of the necessity of a nobility for preserving decorum in, and giving eclat to a nation, has been so assiduously propagated through the world, and the minds of men have been so dazzled by the tinsel splendor of courts," that many people were reconciled to the existence of social distinctions. "It takes some time for a root to be eradicated from a soil where it long uninterrupted grew," said a correspondent, "and it will yet be some space, before the most baneful and poisonous of all roots, viz. the root of royalty is entirely grubbed up in America."[37]

III

Some of the antiadministration rhetoric coming from Bache's press put a classical republican stress on plain, honest manners and on the press's role in maintaining vigilance against corruption. The "most virtuous should be the real nobility of every nation," stated one essay, and the "only effectual check upon the monied interest" was the public awareness made possible by the wide circulation of information. "Remember that had not Rome slumbered," said an editorial in the classical mode, "Cæsar would never have enslaved his country." Writings spoke of the need for the pure republican habits of industry and frugality and of the importance of sacrificing personal comfort to battle liberticide in all its forms. Replying to the frequent Federalist assertion that Bache and his fellow Republicans were pursuing liberty and libels to dangerous extremes and inviting repression, the editor of the *Advertiser* said:

> Anarchy never sprung from a state of rational liberty, it is the child of ignorance and despotism. The history of all nations exhibits the same picture nearly: Government first established for the good of the greater number, too often degenerates into an instrument of ambition and oppression in the hands of the few over the many. It is only by constant watchfulness that its original intention can be preserved, and not by *lullabies* to republicanism.[38]

Along with such traditional libertarian sentiments about popular involvement in governing, however, went the enlightened republican emphasis on social and economic equality. "It has been a favorite, and undoubtedly a just principle, that, in Republics, equality in the property of individuals should be preserved as much as possible," said an editorial by Bache. The way to prevent disparities was to diffuse knowledge to "every class" in society. "Industry and economy, it is true, may lead to wealth," he explained, "but when they come to the assistance of *talents* and *ingenuity* the rise is certain." In an essay blaming monarchy for ignorance and the unequal distribution of nature's "abundant feast," the paper said that the unenlightened mind was "of the nature of a machine, which, to be of any service, must be ac- tuated by some co-ercive power." Equality, *Advertiser* correspondents contended, was enlivening. "What a happiness for America, that the sparks of her liberty kindled the flame in France; for her example has reverberated, and the glow of our late revolution is again upon us," observed "A Republican" in 1793. "Frenchmen, who have just bro- ken the fetters of despotism, have given an example to Americans; they have taught them that distinctions among citizens are incompat- ible with the spirit of a Republic."[39]

Of particular, continuing concern for the paper's writers was what they saw as the imperious nature of the administration's style and of Federalist complaints about citizens meddling in government affairs. In 1792, "Mirabeau" listed ten "FORERUNNERS of Monarchy and Aristocracy in the United States," which included Washington's for- mal levees, observances of the president's birthday, and ostentatious displays that supposed the people "to be children, and that they are governed by their senses and imaginations, and not by their reason." Mirabeau complained that the officers of government wanted public matters to be their exclusive business. "It is well enough in England to run down the rights of man, because the author of those inimitable pamphlets was a stay-maker," he wrote, referring to Paine, "but in the United States all such prescriptions of certain classes of citizens, or occupations, should be avoided; for liberty will never be safe or durable in a republic till every citizen thinks it as much his duty to take care of the state, as to take care of his family, and until an indifference to any public question shall be considered as a public offence."[40]

Bache took the position that understanding the "principles of fair, equal government" was within anyone's ability, that good and evil were easily discriminated and that only self-interest distorted the picture. "The mass of mankind, even those classes which have been degradingly denominated the *herd*," he wrote, "are more to be trusted in the operations of government, than those classes which assume a superiority, and whose prejudices and passions are continually at war with plain reason." Over and over again, the *Advertiser* stated that government policies were allowing "paper noblemen" to feed on "the toil of the useful classes" as they selfishly speculated in land and fi- nance. The "dishonest traffick of land-jobbing" encroached upon "the permanent source of individual competence and independence," said "A Back-woods Man," and the funding system turned a successful speculator into an aristocrat who "wishes arbitrarily to rule over those whom he has cheated."[41]

As a solution, Bache did not necessarily rule out taking from the rich, which Franklin and Jefferson had proposed in a limited sense and which was promoted in an unbounded fashion by some English radicals and, in France, by François-Émile "Gracchus" Babeuf, the leader of the communistic Conspiracy of the Equals in 1796. In 1797, Bache published an American edition of Thomas Paine's *Agrarian Justice*, a pamphlet which began innocuously enough with the Franklinesque statement, "Practical religion consists in doing good; and the only way of serving God is, that of endeavouring to make his creation happy." Paine made a point of rejecting Babeuf's notion of eliminating all property distinctions between rich and poor, but he did say that wealth beyond what a person's hands produced came from society and was, at least in part, owed to society. Affluence resulted from paying low wages and from owning land, which was the natural inheritance of all, Paine reasoned. His proposal for advancing human happiness was that landowners be taxed in order to create a fund which would help the young get a start in the world by providing fifteen pounds to each person at the age of twenty-one and would assist the elderly by giving annual pensions of ten pounds to everyone who had reached the age of fifty.[42]

Ideas for reform published in Bache's paper sometimes followed similar, specific lines. In one case, an editorial noted the scarcity and expense of wood fuel for cities and suggested that farmers pay a special tax if they did not plant "useful trees" along the borders of their fields. Proposals put forth to alleviate other problems of urban dwellers ranged from establishing places where lost children could be housed temporarily to hiring a constable to see that building excavations were covered at night so that pedestrians would not fall in. Officials were urged to clean up the filthy alleys where the poor lived and to provide free and universal public education. In an essay titled "BENEVOLENCE," readers were told that being willing to help those in poverty was an honorable, "god-like affection" and a duty everyone owed to society. "How often do we see men of opulence," the paper asked, "one moment bestowing costly presents on their equals in wealth, and the next spurning from them an unfortunate fellow mortal, whose modest necessity, perhaps, requests but a shilling."[43]

General advice was given in moralistic essays about drinking, gambling, and dueling, but Bache's publication gave attention to the particular needs of the poor. While agreeing that outright charity was appropriate for those who could not help themselves, the paper's writers agreed, invoking Franklin's opinions, that the impoverished who could work should not become dependent on donations. One contributor, citing the views of Jefferson and others, argued that workhouses, with their miserable conditions, were not the answer, but rather assisting the poor in their own homes or boarding them with farmers. Honest work and the resulting individual dignity were the basis of good health and good behavior, essays said, and labor, after all, was "the only fountain of wealth." The Franklin gospel of helping one's self and one's neighbors and believing in the importance of the productive majority was thus being preached in the Philadelphia of the 1790s.[44] Bache's most sustained editorial crusades, however, were against the systematic brutalities of slavery and harsh criminal justice.

With a ringing condemnation of human oppression, Pennsylvania became the first state to pass legislation for the gradual abolition of slavery in 1780. Only a small number of slaves were left in Philadelphia by the 1790s, and citizens organized to assist and educate the city's freed and fugitive blacks. Looking elsewhere, however, Bache's newspaper found much to condemn. The slave trade, which the Constitution had protected until 1808, was assailed in explicit stories of blacks being seized in Africa and subjected to hideous conditions aboard vessels crossing the Atlantic. One of the accounts described a woman who, after delivering a baby, "gave her son the first and last kiss, and precipitated herself with him in the waves." Slavery, writers said, also degraded the masters and was inconsistent with the nation's ideals. As Franklin had begun to do decades earlier, Bache not only supported abolition, but also defended the intelligence of blacks and urged Americans not to buy slave-produced commodities.[45]

The frequency and nature of such articles may well have limited the appeal of the *General Advertiser* in the South and other areas where Jefferson and Madison wanted a national newspaper with a Republican message to circulate. Saying that defenders of the slave trade had paid little attention to right and wrong, Bache complained, "When we speak of doing justly and mercifully towards poor Africans, they talk of their property being injured thereby, and when we profess a regard to these sacred principles, they call us fanatics." Bache invited additional disgust by showing respect, as Franklin and Jefferson had, for the rights and abilities of the Indians who conducted intermittent warfare with white settlers. Among the stories of the mistreatment of native Americans was one which ended by asking, "How is peace to be expected on our frontiers when our own citizens thus provoke hostilities?" The paper outpaced most Americans on women's rights by considering female participation in politics and praising Mary Wollstonecraft, the author of *A Vindication of the Rights of Women.*[46]

Editorials about criminal justice were nearly as vehement as those about slavery. Crimes, the *General Advertiser* said, were committed by the desperately poor and hungry. "Let the division of property be made as nearly equal as possible, or advantages given that will form an equivalent, and mankind will become virtuous instantaneously," one essay asserted. Bache supported the efforts of Pennsylvania's prison reform movement to release honest debtors and to teach criminals the value of morality and industriousness. The newspaper praised the state for limiting the death penalty to four crimes and expressed the hope that "enlightened and humane" citizens would eliminate capital punishment entirely. The fear of solitary confinement and hard labor would do more to prevent crime than "human sacrifices," the *Advertiser* maintained. The death penalty was a proof of ignorant government, especially when imposed for an "artificial crime" against property which was "in a manner created by society."[47]

Taken together, then, what Bache and other writers were condemning as immoral and inconsistent with the revolutionary promise of the American republic was greed, domination, and intolerance. Wealthy white men, it appeared, were shaping the nation for their own power and benefit. A "POLITICAL CREED" Bache published in 1797 stated that a country where "one description of men is privileged, and another debased" was in a state of slavery. "Those, who set themselves up as a gazing stock to the rabble, and excite a species of admiration by affecting some frivolous distinction from other people," said an *Advertiser* editorial, "are under the influence of the meanest kind of ambition."[48] Bache followed Franklin in offering a philosophical prescription for more egalitarian conditions that was less interested in creating a constitutional structure to control or eliminate class struggle than in reforming old habits and promoting particular national policies. To achieve new outlooks and opportunities that favored the common person, Bache, like his grandfather, saw a need for the cultivation of minds through education and the press and for greater and more principled participation in the political system.

Defending the Democrats

AMID THE AFTERSHOCKS OF THE AMERICAN AND FRENCH REVOLU-
tions, little about the idea of democracy seemed entirely secure. The
public good would be served in an antagonistic fashion, classical republicans had reasoned, if the people periodically arose to make probity prevail among public officials. The idea of enlightenment republicanism, however, was that the people would be more than an occasional
check on a governing class, that, in fact, a large measure of equality
and popular participation was possible and beneficial as long as citizens were responsible, discerning students of public affairs. Involvement, of course, could be interpreted as interference.

The *General Advertiser* was one of the newspapers of the early
republic that had to defend critical journalism and democratic thinking against charges of being subversive to the hierarchy necessary to
all government. Papers that supported the administration, Benjamin
Franklin Bache asserted in 1792, operated "upon the principle that
whatever is, is right,—that a government established by the people,
must ever act for the best good of the people." This, the editor said,
was like "the old doctrine of passive obedience and non-resistance,
now almost universally exploded even in Europe."[1]

Bache, like other proponents of enlightened republicanism, believed that readily available education would help prepare for true
democracy, and he frequently wrote in favor of establishing public
schools as a means of reducing inequalities and instilling republican
virtues. Where public opinion was the basis of government, he ar-

gued, "the great mass of people" had to be informed through formal instruction. "That the streams of power may flow pure," he said, "the source must be clear." The other major means of enlightening citizens, he contended, was the wide circulation of newspapers so that readers, thinking for themselves on political subjects, could find truths about "the important science of government, and that part of national policy which respects the general interests and individual happiness of mankind." In 1791, "A Friend to Merit," told the paper's readers that liberty was preserved by diffusing knowledge and that the two ways of diffusing knowledge were "namely, by the industry of teachers in their schools, and by that of authors from the press."[2]

In an era of developing party machinery, when personal political ambition was considered so inappropriate that presidential candidates did not make their own direct appeals to voters, the press's role in conveying programs and perspectives was paramount. The making of America's second democratic revolution, the Jeffersonian one, thus largely depended upon the partisan battles over public opinion waged in newspapers and pamphlets. Journalism, long practiced for moral as well as self-serving purposes, had become a mature art of advocacy and attack by the 1790s. While continuing to say for some time that he was impartial and independent, Benjamin Franklin Bache also stated that newspapers had a republican responsibility to expose the failures of those in office. Acknowledging that his criticism of Washington and others had made him enemies, Bache depicted a free press as the "palladium" of the people's rights and declared that "neither the frowns of men, or allurements of private interest" would make him "swerve from the line of his public duty."[3]

Consistent with much of what Franklin taught, Bache's idea of public duty was an egalitarian urge to protect the general public from the prosperous and powerful. He evidently relished the role of the people's champion, publishing at one point a letter from "Pluto" who told him that his "stiff democratic principles" were costing him the emoluments of offices and government printing available to Federalist editors. The correspondent facetiously chastised Bache for upholding the "inflexible republicanism" of his grandfather, saying, "Never mind the applauses of the people; abandon this cause for the *golden* one of aristocracy, and let the swinish herd take care of themselves." Bache later remarked that as a printer in a commercial city like Philadelphia he could have made more money publishing in "compliance with the

General   AURORA   Advertiser.

SURGO UT PROSIM.

PUBLISHED (DAILY) BY BENJ. FRANKLIN BACHE, AT No. 112, MARKET-STREET, BETWEEN THIRD AND FOURTH STREETS, PHILADELPHIA.

(Six Dolls. per ann.)   FRIDAY, NOVEMBER 28, 1794.   (Num. 1241.)

For the Information of the MERCHANTS.

In behalf of the Committee,
THOMAS FITZSIMONS.

To the Merchants of the United States.

For JEREMIE,

THE SCHOONER
BETSEY,

apply to,
DANIEL & VINCENT THUUN.

VINCENT DUCOMB,

No. 53, WALNUT-STREET,

PERFUMERY.

MONEY LENT,

At No. 46, Spruce-street,

On all Deposits of Dry Goods, Plate, Watches
Wearing Apparel, &c.
LOFTHOUSE, & Co.

ARGENT PRETE,

Au No. 46, Spruce-street,

Sur Depots en Merchandises, Vaiselle d'or et
d'Argent, Montres, Vetements, &c.
LOFTHOUSE, & Co.
Nov. 12.

MADEIRA WINE.

FOR Sale, by JOHN SWANWICK, 10 pipes London Particular Madeira Wine, now at imported.
Nov. 15.

NOTICE.

ALL Persons indebted to The Estate of JAMES REYNOLDS, Carver and Gilder, deceased, are requested to make immediate payment—And all persons who have demands thereon, are requested to render their accounts properly authenticated.
THOMAS REYNOLDS,
JAMES REYNOLDS,
JAMES REES.
Nov. 26.

CARVING and GILDING.

JAMES and HENRY REYNOLDS inform their friends and the public, that they have commenced the business of CARVING and GILDING in all their various branches, at their father's late dwelling, No. 147, north Third-street.

ASSHETON HUMPHREYS,

ATTORNEY at Law, Notary Public and Conveyancer, at his Office, No. 65, on the north side of Walnut-street.

CONSULSHIP OFFICE of the FRENCH REPUBLIC

THOSE who have any claims against the following Estates, are requested to deliver their claims at the said office, within four months from this date, agreeable to the Consular Convention, viz.

For the Merchants of the United States.

ENGLISH AND DUTCH CROSS-CUT AND MILL
SAWS,
VERY CHEAP, by the Box or less number, also, LARGE
SCALE-BEAMS.
THOMAS RYERSON,
No. 177, Market-street.
Nov. 27.

TO BE SOLD,

A Large and Commodious House, IN FRONT-STREET.

A THREE STORY BRICK MESSUAGE and Lot of Ground on which the front stands, situated on the back side of Front-street, near sixth Chestnut-street.

A Corner Lot of Ground,

ON MARKET-STREET.

A LOT of GROUND on the South side of Market-street and at the corner of Eighth-street 240 feet, or half the square from Market to Chestnut-streets.

A Lot of Meadow Ground.

A PIECE of MEADOW GROUND, Situated in Moyamensing Township, on Stamper's Lane, containing about FOUR ACRES.
JOHN WILCOCKS,
No. 90, north Third-street, or at his Counting-house, in Lodge-Alley, near the Pennsylvania Bank.

MUSCAVADO and Loaf Sugar, Coffee, and to have of Chocolate, Brandy, Molasses and Shrub, Muscatle, Teas, Corks, and a few boxes fresh Muscadel RAISINS.
Nov. 17.

Twenty Dollars Reward.

RAN AWAY, on Saturday night the 15th instant, a kind of Madeira Rolt-India boy, named CRISPIN, about 16 years old, five feet four inches high, slender built.

The cargoes of the ship Good Friend and snow Voiture, from BOURDEAUX, for sale by
STEPHEN GIRARD,
No. 83, North Water-street.

BRANDY, in pipes, of an excellent quality.

He has also for sale,

FLAX SEED,

FOR Sale by, for subscriber, 400 hogsheads of FLAX SEED, in good order.
LEVINUS CLARKSON.
Nov. 27.

SUCH PERSONS

ARE desirous of disposing of their SHARES in any of the Canals in Pennsylvania, are informed, that the average being paid up, they may find a purchaser by applying at the Canal Office, near the Bank of the United States, by
WILLIAM COMPTY.

PORT WINE.

A CHOICE parcel of fresh OLD RED PORT WINE, may be procured, by the TWENTY Cask or QUARTER, from Onsets, apply to PETER BLIGHT.

St. Ubes' SALT.

NEW THEATRE.

THE Managers of the New Theatre respectfully inform the Public, that the Entertainments for the Season will commence, on MONDAY, the FIRST of DECEMBER.

Red Morocco Pocket Book.

LOST, on the 11th instant, out of his pocket, by a gentleman at Mr. French's Hotel, Fourth-street, a large Red Morocco Pocket Book, containing several Bonds and Papers and about FORTY DOLLARS in specie.

BOARDING and LODGING.

GENTEEL BOARDING and LODGING, for four or five Gentlemen, may be had at No. 125, south Water-street.
Nov. 26.

WANTS EMPLOY.

A YOUNG MAN, accustomed to the MERCANTILE Business, with necessary recommendations; would wish to be addressed to a Store, and apply on true terms. Enquire at this office. In this direction to A. B. and left at the Office of the General Advertiser, will be duly attended to.
Nov. 1.

Notary and Lawyer.

A FRENCHMAN from Paris, who has been employed five years in the Notary's business, and is acquainted with Law and Commerce, wishes always. Address to A. B. and left at No. 10, Brent's Alley, will be attended to.
Nov. 14.

WANTED, A MAN SERVANT,

A WAITER, in a small family. He must be well recommended. Apply at the Office of the General Advertiser.
August 14.

WANTS A PLACE,

A YOUNG MAN who has been regularly brought up as a COACHMAN in England. For particulars, enquire for I. S. at No. 56, south Water-street.
Nov. 13.

WANTS A PLACE.

A WET NURSE, a young woman with a fresh breast of milk, in a good household, and can be well recommended. Enquire at the Office of the General Advertiser.
Nov. 21.

Wants Employment,

A YOUNG MAN, regularly bred to the PRINTING Business, understands the French and English languages perfectly; possesses the necessary qualifications of a Translator, would either engage in that capacity, or at a Compositor in a Printing Office. For further particulars, apply to apply at No. 53, south Third-street.
Nov. 17.

LECTURES on CHEMISTRY.

Mr. THOMAS HENRY, Jun. Surgeon.

FORMERLY Secretary to the Literary and Philosophical Society of Manchester, and Assistant to his Father, the Professor of Chemistry, in the College of Arts and Sciences instituted there, Proposes, early in November, to commence a COURSE of LECTURES on CHEMISTRY, in which he particularly intends to.

NORRIS COURT,

back of New-Library, between Chestnut & Walnut Streets,
GEORGE RUTTER

RESPECTFULLY informs his friends and the Public in general, that he continues carrying on his business of SIGN & ORNAMENTAL PAINTING.

JUST LANDED,

FROM on board the ship Washington, captain Collins, from BOURDEAUX, lying at Mullett's wharf, near the Conduit Bridge, a range of WHITE WINES, in bottles and Claret in bhds and cases, for sale by
F. COPPINGER,
No. 56, Spruce, near Front-street.
August 14.

COLE & GOODLUCK's

CORRECT Numerical Book of this drawn of the Ticket of the Washington Hotel Lottery, Second state, on the.

views of the wealthy," but that he had other principles about what the press should be doing. In November of 1794, as he announced he was renaming his paper the *Aurora and General Advertiser,* Bache said the *Aurora* would "diffuse light within the sphere of its influence,— dispel the shades of ignorance, and gloom of error and thus tend to strengthen the fair fabric of freedom on its surest foundation, publicity and information."[4]

I

Although the northern lights appear at night, Bache did not think the new name was "unapplicable to a diurnal morning print." The aurora borealis, which Franklin had studied while his grandson was with him in France, was depicted on the newspaper's nameplate as Franklin had represented the phenomenon, with luminous electrical rays emanating through the Earth's atmosphere. In the spirit of Franklin's famous remark that the sun on the back of Washington's chair at the Constitutional Convention was dawning with the republic rather than setting, Bache assured his readers that the light his newspaper was offering was in ascent. Below the word *Aurora* was the motto "SURGO UT PROSIM," which Bache translated as "I rise to be useful." Bache's usefulness was in publishing what James Monroe, in a letter written in 1794, called the "best political paper" for national issues. Monroe approvingly described the editor as "the gr.son of Dr. Franklin & a republican."[5]

Bache was linked to Franklin in the public's perception and worked to preserve his grandfather's ideas and fame, noting the profuse international praise he had received after his death, quoting him on issues such as the threat Britain posed to America, and defending his memory from attack by Federalist writers. On one occasion, printing a letter in which Franklin had discussed his own efforts and hopes for a better nation, Bache used the headline "FROM FRANKLIN—ERGO—

←————————

Like many editors, Bache obliged advertisers by placing their notices on the front page of his newspaper. Most news stories and opinion essays appeared on the second and third pages. (Reproduced with permission of the State Historical Society of Wisconsin)

GOOD." In another issue, an editorial ventured the opinion that perhaps no other American had "effected so much general good" in his writings as Franklin and that "his maxims most strikingly shew, that he toil'd for the good of the whole human race." Bache himself tried his hand at aphorisms but rarely matched Poor Richard's simple, easily remembered adages. "In a free country," Bache wrote in a typical example of his more complex and philosophical axioms, "there is little to be done by force: Gentle means would gain you those ends, which violence would forever put out of your power."[6]

In his response to one of the volatile issues of the Washington administration, the Whiskey Rebellion, Bache publicly practiced the kind of nonviolence and trust in an informed people that his grandfather advocated. He admitted that the tax placed on liquor by Congress in 1791 might not bear equally on everyone, but noted, as Franklin often had, that alcohol "maddens the brain and weakens the body." Laws had to be obeyed even if unfair and obnoxious, he argued, so that critics of free governments could not say democracy naturally ran into licentiousness. "A free people, therefore, by refusing obedience to the laws," he wrote, "do an injury not only to themselves, but to mankind." In 1794, his paper joined the farmers, tradesmen, and manufacturers opposing the extension of federal excise taxes, but consistently condemned the insurrection in western Pennsylvania, warning that it might have been encouraged by the British or might be exploited by aristocrats as a means of attacking democracy. Bache himself was presiding at a stormy meeting of the Democratic Society of Pennsylvania on September 11 when a resolution was passed saying that the strength of the state should be exerted where the power of reason failed. The *General Advertiser* congratulated the government for ending the rebellion peacefully but endorsed an opponent of the taxes at the next Congressional election.[7]

The battle over excise taxes continued to occupy Congress for years, but Bache's faith in the administration was not entirely lost until the signing of the Jay Treaty. After the Senate had approved it, but before Washington made the contents public, Bache published an abstract of the treaty and then issued a pamphlet with the entire text, provided by Senator Stevens T. Mason, a Republican from Virginia. Hoping to see public opinion kill the treaty before Washington signed the document, the editor set off on a trip through New York and Hartford to Boston with a large supply of the pamphlets to sell. Reporting to Alexander Hamilton that Bache had passed through Hartford a week before, Rep. Jeremiah Wadsworth noted that "the greatest industry and pains" were being used "to disturb the public Tranquillity." In fact, effigies of Jay were burned and protest meetings were held in cities across the country. Hamilton himself was pelted with stones when he tried to defend the treaty in New York.[8]

Bache delighted in the spectacle of public pressure being put on Washington. Anticipating one of the Philadelphia meetings held to object to the treaty, he said it would be "conducted, no doubt, with the order and decency which ought always to attend the deliberations of the enlightened citizens of the Metropolis of America." As he reported the mass protests that were being held elsewhere, the editor gave the treaty little chance, at least in the columns of his paper. Bache thus professed to be stunned when the news of Washington's decision arrived. "We are assured that the President has signed the Treaty," the paper announced in a one-sentence story in large type, "but cannot yet believe it." The paper claimed that nine-tenths of the people opposed the Jay Treaty and that Washington had given weight to a "priviledged class" of merchants and traders in opposition to the good of the whole. The paper warned that the people should "be lulled no longer into a dangerous security by the arts of those whose interest it is to deceive them."[9] The time for cool reasoning was over. For the next two years Bache attempted to assassinate Washington's character.

In setting out to destroy the president's name, Bache deviated from the pattern his grandfather hoped republicans would follow. At the end of his life, Franklin, as usual an advocate of unity and cooperation, had warned against the divisiveness of personal attacks on national leaders. Having been subjected to vehement recriminations himself, he had publicly complained about the way "the court of the press" could damage reputations as abruptly and unjustly as the Inquisition. Bache, on the other hand, was zealous enough to be more interested in social justice than in mercy for people in public life. He and his contributors began to portray political figures in the starkest terms, as forces for good or evil. "Public men are all amenable to the tribunal of the press in a free state," he declared in 1794, "the greater, indeed, their trust, the more responsible are they." The *Remarks* pamphlet Bache published in 1797, an effort to disparage virtually every aspect of Washington's character and abilities, said that those with

the power to affect many lives had to submit to press scrutiny, that to
be too "tender of the individual is to be unpitying towards the public." [10]

Bache's tribunal was one in which politicians were judged on
whether the editor thought they were helping or hindering human
progress. Bache maintained that a free press and a free government
were inseparable, that lapses in republican morality had to come to
light. "No man loves to be under the power of a master," he observed. "Therefore, to become free men have only to let their passions
loose; to secure freedom, they must contrive to put them under prudent restraints." Commentary he published suggested that a newspaper should offer "moral instruction" and political information. How
far such writings could go was another question. Bache sometimes
expressed a dislike of defamatory journalism early in his career, but
essays in the paper noted that libel law offered no clear distinctions
between protected and unprotected writings on public persons. As the
Aurora's treatment of Washington's administration became more vituperative, Bache told his readers that his "strictures upon men high
in office" were being regarded as licentious by some, "but surely the
evils of that reputed licentiousness are not to compare to the danger
of nursing that foe to Republicanism—excessive idolatry; which might
insensibly lead to the establishment of the maxim—'That a public
officer can do no wrong.' " [11]

Republicans like Bache were concluding that much of the Federalists' success was due to Washington's prestige and that a way to
improve the odds was to dismantle the president's reputation as a hero
and leader. Those in favor of democracy had sufficient numbers to
prevent Americans from restoring monarchy and aristocracy "as the
dog turns to his vomit," the *Remarks* said. Everything, the pamphlet
insisted, "demands the extinction of the Washington credit, the passport of so many weak or bad measures." Much of the *Remarks* itself
was devoted to making Washington appear to have been a mediocre
general and misguided president, especially for backing the Jay Treaty.
Similar charges were made in a pamphlet written by Thomas Paine
and published by Bache. Bache also reprinted a collection of forged
letters, purportedly written by Washington in 1776, that expressed
despair over American prospects in the war and hope that a reconciliation would occur between the two countries. [12]

The reappearance of the spurious correspondence, which was first published in England in 1777 and in America in 1778, infuriated Washington. He issued denials through friends and in a formal letter that he filed with the secretary of state on his last day in office and had published in newspapers. "This man has celebrity in a certain way," he said of Bache in one of his letters at the time, "for His calumnies are to be exceeded only by his Impudence, and both stand unrivalled." Washington was also enraged by the "malignant industry, and persevering falsehoods" with which he was assailed in Bache's paper. Among the *Aurora* statements on the president's departure was one which said Americans could rejoice "that the name of WASHING- TON from this day ceases to give a currency to political iniquity, and to legalize corruption." The correspondent said it was astonishing to see that "a single individual should have cankered the principles of republicanism in an enlightened people." Another writer, recounting the Genêt affair and the Jay Treaty, urged readers to think that Ham- ilton was not alone as "chief juggler" of foreign relations, that Wash- ington too had "the most hostile and unworthy designs against the French Republic." [13]

II

Bache's attitude toward the first president was not originally so bitter. Washington was a frequent visitor to Franklin Court during the Con- stitutional Convention, and Franklin himself was on excellent terms with the former general. Although Washington had disappointed Richard Bache in 1789 by not nominating him for the office of post- master general which he had held during the Revolution, Benjamin Franklin Bache's initial treatment of the chief executive was usually laudatory. In the autumn of 1791, he wrote that "confidence in the administration of this government pervades all classes and denomina- tions of men" and that Americans could anticipate public happiness and honor "maturing to a perfection, hitherto unknown." Four months later, despite the view of some of his correspondents that the balls, suppers, and parades in honor of Washington's birthday were too mo- narchical, Bache printed an editorial approving of the celebrations, saying that the day would be remembered as long as Americans felt the blessings of liberty. Bache commended Washington for making his southern tour of 1791 rather than indulging in fox hunting or other genteel pursuits favored by European heads of state. Yet, he did not approve of the president's being "perfumed with the incense of *addresses*" from citizens along the route of the tour, a practice which had "too much of Monarchy to be used by Republicans."[14]

Soon after Washington was reelected without opposition in 1792, contributors to the paper began an editorial campaign to deny that the president, who was taking advice from Hamilton, was a man of the people. He was, critics said, encouraging aristocracy with his aloof manner and acceptance of public adulation. "A Farmer" wrote an account of how he was surprised to see "the *plain and republican George Washington*" in a cream-colored coach with six bay horses and servants in livery. So transformed was the president, he said, that his neighbor had mistaken him for King George's son, Prince Edward. A satirist addressed an advertisement to the "NOBLESSE AND COURTIERS OF THE UNITED STATES" soliciting a poet laureate to compose birthday odes and to extol "certain *monarchical prettinesses*" such as "LEVIES, DRAWING ROOMS, STATELY NODS INSTEAD OF SHAKING HANDS, TITLES OF OFFICE, SECLUSION FROM THE PEOPLE, &c. &c." The notice said the poet should know the causes of the decline of republics in order to praise them as favorable to prosperity. "It is a wretched and mad opinion that some high-flying republicans maintain," the advertisement remarked, "that officers of government ought to deport themselves as the *equals* of the people."[15]

Some of Bache's contributors invoked the spectre of the democratic hero Franklin to demean the president. "Mirabeau" wrote that Washington was receiving the glory for the Revolution's success instead of the many people who fought it and instead of "that venerable sage" Franklin, "whose labours have enlightened mankind, and added to their portion of felicity." "A Subscriber" wondered why Franklin's laurels were "torn from his brow, and entwined around the brow of another." The same writer told Bache that the "republican simplicity of your illustrious sire is well deserving, not only of your imitation, but of the imitation of every man who wishes to preserve the principles of liberty uncorrupt." When "Q." protested that personal matters such as the president's equipage and Tuesday afternoon levees were not proper subjects for newspaper commentary, Bache replied that "manners have been considered so far of a public nature, as to be made objects of sumptuary laws in republics" and that he could not shrink from his duty even if "interest might point out a safer line of conduct."[16] "Equality" agreed with Bache:

As this is said to be the age of reason, as well as of equality, every custom however trifling in itself, ought to be tried by these two touch-stones, to ascertain whether they assimilate with the principles which we profess: If men who profess to be governed by reason, and who ac-knowledge no other superior than the laws of their country, are counte-nancing follies which put reason and equality to shame, we may be allowed to suppose that, either they do not fully understand the conse-quences which may result from such indulgencies, or that they have some sinister views.[17]

During the fusillade of postelection invective, Washington read in the *Gazette of the United States* that a Federalist writer was planning to assail Franklin's character, apparently as a reprisal against the Re-publicans in general and Bache in particular. Troubled at the prospect of a clash of political personalities, the president discussed his appre-hensions with his cabinet. Hamilton and Edmund Randolph volun-teered to speak to Fenno about suppressing the piece. "Both observed that they had heard this declaration mentioned in many companies," Jefferson said of the anticipated smear, "and that it had excited uni-versal horror and detestation." Washington objected to the essay, Jef-ferson noted, because "the party seemed to do it as a means of de-fending him (the President) against the late attacks on him." When the president told Jefferson that he was upset by the criticism he had received and was wondering how to conform to the public's wishes in matters of social style, Jefferson told him he was sorry to see the hurt being inflicted, but the secretary of state, as suspicious as anyone about monarchical tendencies, evidently made no effort to stop the journal-istic aspersions.[18]

Washington retained warm feelings for Franklin which dated back to the war, when Franklin had corresponded with the often frustrated commander to let him know that the old generals of France were studying his maneuvers and highly approved of his conduct. Writing to Sarah Bache in January 1781 to thank her for sending 2,005 shirts made by Philadelphia women for his poorly equipped soldiers, Wash-ington recalled Franklin's compliments, remarking that nothing gave "more rational and exquisite satisfaction, than the approbation of a Wise, a great and virtuous Man." Franklin's securing of French aid and his conciliatory influence at the Constitutional Convention would have been difficult for the first president to forget. In his will, Frank-lin had left "to my friend, and the friend of mankind, *General Wash-*

ington," a walking stick topped with a gold cap of liberty. "If it were a Sceptre, he has merited it, and would become it," Franklin wrote.[19]

When the tensions arose over the Genêt affair and relations with the European powers in the summer of 1793, Washington wrote privately to Governor Henry Lee that Bache's publications were "outrages on common decency" and had a disruptive tendency that should alarm the country. A year later, as the villification of Washington continued, Bache printed a letter from "An Unfeigned Democrat" stating a similar worry that the berating of the president had passed the bounds of decency and that the country seemed to be on the verge of anarchy. Reminding the editor of Franklin's bequest of the walking stick to Washington, the correspondent said, "The shade of Franklin, must with grief and sorrow see his grand-son so far differ in opinion from him." Bache responded that he knew his grandfather's opinion of Washington, but that it was his duty as an "impartial printer" to print censure of the public conduct of public servants and to let the public decide if it was unmerited. The next day "A Republican" wanted it recalled that Franklin opposed "every aristocratic excrescence in our State and general constitutions" and that the sceptre he had in mind was a trophy of victory over tyranny, not a symbol of despotic authority.[20]

During his last years in office, Washington continued to be maligned as a monarch-in-the-making. Shortly after the Jay Treaty was signed in 1795, "Pittachus" complained that the president's aloof stateliness and his coach and six—"to take him from his house to the Senate Chamber, a distance of about two hundred yards"—were "the trappings of royalty" and that the intent of such deportment appeared to be to dazzle the people and to deify money. "Did he sanction the plans of speculation which have grown out of his funding and bank systems to countenance and support the pageantry which he established?" the writer asked. At the same time "Casca" called for Washington's impeachment, citing his sanctioning of Hamiltonian finance and the Jay Treaty, his proscribing of Democratic-Republican societies, and his using a show of military force in the Whiskey Rebellion which should have been used instead against the enemies who had "plundered our merchants in every part of the globe." The Senate would not convict, Casca said, but that was an argument for a unicameral legislature and a plural executive—"the favorite propositions of Rousseau and Franklin."[21]

A week after Casca's call for impeachment, "A Calm Observer" disclosed that Washington had, several times during his presidency, accepted salary payments before they were earned. The next day an editorial noted that administration critics had been accused of finding fault with trifles, but that A Calm Observer had found serious misconduct. "Coaches and six are not there the theme," the *Aurora* said, "but breaches of the laws, of the constitution and of a solemn oath are talked of." The paper printed defenses of the Treasury Department disbursements written by Alexander Hamilton and his successor, Oliver Wolcott, Jr., but neither could refute the evidence that advances had been made on the application of the president's secretary to cover household expenses. The public, a correspondent noted, had been led to believe that Washington did not accept a salary. Writers continued to say the president should be impeached for failing to respect the Constitution or that he should retire to preserve the country and what was left of his reputation. "You now, like Cæsar, stand on the banks of the Rubicon," wrote "Scipio."[22]

The *Aurora* punctuated the year before the election of 1796 with regular reminders that Washington was a slaveholder and with specific charges that he was servile to Britain and hostile to France. The president, who was deciding not to run for a third term, found the paper's denunciations of his motives in foreign policy as "indecent as they are void of truth and fairness." With considerable anger, Washington told Jefferson in the summer of 1796 that he was being portrayed in terms "as could scarcely be applied to a Nero; a notorious defaulter; or even to a common pickpocket." Noting that newspapers were trying to turn the public against him and that Jefferson and his friends had denounced him for being under a "dangerous influence," he told his former secretary of state that he had only sought to make the right decisions and was "no party man." To another correspondent, he acknowledged a fear that Bache's attacks would affect the public as "drops of Water will Impress (in time) the hardest Marble" and that there could be "no doubt" that "his attacks on the Government" would continue.[23]

In the first draft of his farewell address, written as the *Aurora* was leading the republican onslaught against him, Washington included a self-pitying statement on how he had chosen to treat with silent contempt "all the Invective that disappointment, ignorance of facts, and malicious falsehoods could invent" in the press "to misrepresent my politics and affections; to wound my reputation and feelings; and to weaken, if not entirely destroy the confidence" of the people in him. As he worked with Hamilton on the final draft, however, Washington decided that eliminating the "egotism" of his reaction to harsh journalism would be a "more dignified" approach that would be "less exposed to criticism" and "better calculated" for foreign readers and "the Yeomanry of this Country." Perhaps out of embarrassment at the kind of barbs he had received in Bache's newspaper, Washington also decided to omit a portion of the address which spoke of his concern that America, as a young, agricultural nation, had progressed too far in luxury and opulence. Among the sentences he crossed out, saying they were "not sufficiently important," was one which warned, "Cultivate industry and frugality, as auxiliaries to good morals and sources of private and public prosperity."[24]

With its themes of peace and national unity, the address, which circulated through most of the nation's newspapers, met its requirements. Hamilton was seeking "sentiments as will wear well" and "redound to future reputation," while Washington wanted a placating, high-minded defense of his policies that would be the appropriate length "for a News Paper publication." Not intending to deliver the address as a speech, Washington worked out the details of the initial publication with the editor of *Claypoole's American Daily Advertiser*, where it appeared on September 19, 1796. Without any commentary, Bache reprinted the address over the next two days. He could hardly have faulted a moving statement that referred to the benefit of education in enlightening public opinion, the mischief of trade restrictions and foreign influence, and even the personal failings of the president himself. The *Aurora* did, however, question the president's sincerity as he left office, saying he delivered "the profession of republicanism, but the practice of monarchy and aristocracy." Arguing that the nation had been "debauched" by Washington, another editorial remarked that "the masque of patriotism may be worn to conceal the foulest designs against the liberties of a people."[25]

Although he could employ the enlightened republican rhetoric of the opposition party, Washington was vexed by those who used it against him. A primary purpose of the farewell address may have been to disarm his detractors with what he said to Hamilton was an appeal to the yeomanry "in a language tha[t] was plain & intelligable to their understand[ing]," but Washington was not entirely forgiving toward his political and journalistic enemies. In retirement, he took the time to write angry, defensive annotations in his copy of James Monroe's *View of the Conduct of the Executive of the United States*, a blistering 1797 book on what the author, minister to France for two years before he was recalled in 1796, called the "great derangement" of America's foreign relations. Monroe had advanced Bache the money to print the nearly five-hundred-page work and received advice on the project from Jefferson, who also oversaw the book's distribution in Virginia. Washington had abundant cause to despise the Republicans who were seeking his disgrace, particularly the young printer in Philadelphia. Until the end of his life, he sputtered in his letters about Bache and "Bachite Republicans."[26]

Bache's own reputation suffered in the fray. Mathew Carey, another Philadelphia printer who had once worked for Franklin at Passy, wrote in his memoirs that before his campaign against Washington, Bache had been "popular on account of his amiable manners and his descent from Dr. Franklin." The "violent measures" against the president, Carey observed, did more to injure the democratic cause than all its enemies could have done. "The Aurora was ably conducted, and had had a very extensive circulation," he continued. "But the attacks on Gen. Washington blasted Bache's popularity, and almost ruined the paper. Subscribers withdrew in crowds—and the advertising custom sank to insignificance." Elizabeth Hewson, the young English woman Franklin had hoped Bache would marry, kept her brother Thomas informed of the developments, noting how Ben, who had been "the flower of the family" and still had a "very cool and rational manner" of discussing politics, had been losing business by printing "detestable abuse." She told her brother that at least Bache had his wife Margaret's support:

> I have staid with Mrs B. Bache since I have been in town. She has frequently asked me. Poor woman, her old acquaintance have almost all deserted her. She is luckily of opinion that her husband is quite in the right she does not therefore suffer the pain of entertaining a mean opinion of him which I am sorry to say most people do. What a pity a few years should make so great an alteration. At the time of Dr. F's death Ben was universally beloved and esteemed and now he is as much despised even by some who are warm Democrats.[27]

Bache nevertheless remained adamantly attached to the principles his grandfather had taught him. Responding in late 1795 to Federalist charges that he was an anarchist in the pay of the French, he
outlined a "political profession of faith" in which he said government
officers were fallible, the Constitution good but not obviously "stampt
with the seal of perfection," and that a free press was "one of the first
safeguards of Liberty." He was, he said, therefore resolved to preserve
the character of the *Aurora*. Reacting at the same time to intimations
that he would be prosecuted for libel, he challenged his enemies to
try. "Unawed by those threats," Bache said of himself, "the EDITOR is
determined, THAT THE FREEDOM OF THE PRESS SHALL NOT
SUFFER THRO' HIS PUSILLANIMITY." In another issue in the
autumn of 1795, he denied an assertion by Fenno that the *Aurora* was
losing readers. Bache maintained that he had gained ten subscribers
for each one lost since the Jay Treaty was promulgated, and he challenged Fenno to a public comparison of gains and losses in circulation
since the controversy began.[28] Fenno merely continued to berate Bache.

III

One reader not driven away was Thomas Jefferson. While out of national office, Jefferson corresponded with Bache to subscribe, to order
bound sets of the newspaper, and to ask when Franklin's collected
works would be published. Jefferson had reason to remain loyal to
Bache. The paper had printed discreet praise of his political views and
expressed regret at his resignation from the Washington cabinet. His
withdrawl from an administration tainted with antirepublican principles, the paper's writers contended, was an honorable decision for
"the enlightened friend of liberty and France." "Mirabeau" praised the
departing secretary of state for his "republican simplicity" and "respect
for the people," saying that "the armour of virtue" would defend him
against detractors.[29]

One of the facts his opponents tried to exploit in the press was
that the professed champion of equality owned slaves. In his *Notes on
the State of Virginia* and proposals for legislation, Jefferson took antislavery positions, but he was vulnerable to press accusations on both
sides of the issue. Federalists were able to tell abolitionists that he had
a black "harem" and supporters of slavery that he had dangerous plans
for emancipation. Although Bache's paper castigated Washington for

using forced labor at Mount Vernon, it was almost entirely silent about the presence of slaves at Monticello. In 1792, the *General Advertiser* did, however, publish a letter to Jefferson from a free black almanac writer and mathematician, Benjamin Banneker, who asked why the author of the Declaration of Independence should keep slaves "under groaning captivity and cruel oppression." [30]

Jefferson nevertheless remained the best hope of the Republicans. During his career as a legislator in Virginia and as a member of the Continental Congress, he had become known as a strong advocate of establishing public education, reforming property and penal laws, and barring slavery in new territories. "We are happy to be informed, that Mr. JEFFERSON that good patriot, statesman & philosopher, is perfectly recovered from his late indisposition," the *Aurora* reported early in the presidential election year of 1796. "May he long live, and in the moment of necessity re-appear and save his country from the unhappy effects to which it is exposed." [31]

When Washington declined to run for a third term, the paper accurately surmised that Jefferson and John Adams would be the leading contenders for the presidency. This meant, Bache's *Aurora* said, that the people would have to choose between "a steadfast friend to the Rights of the People, or an advocate for hereditary power and distinctions." Repeating arguments it had used in 1792 that Adams was an improper choice for office because his writings advocated "artificial balances and unjust distinctions, destructive of the foundations of that Constitution which he has sworn to support," the paper dramatized the race as a struggle between republicanism and monarchism. One editorial argued that Jefferson's party should be known as the Democrats in the future since republican, aristocrat, and monocrat were "synonimous terms in the vocabulary of Adams." While "Franklin" maintained that Adams would try to establish a British constitution, other contributors were suggesting that Jefferson would keep the country independent of Britain and out of war while concentrating on peaceful pursuits of education, the mechanical arts, and agriculture. [32]

Although not yet thirty years old, Bache himself was among those nominated at a meeting of mechanics and tradesmen to run in a large field of candidates for common council in Philadelphia in 1796. "A Citizen" wrote to admire the "truly republican" spirit of such gatherings and to say it was proper to draw public servants from the majority rather than accept the European idea that "a certain description of men ought always to manage the public concerns." Censuring the council for making aristocratic decisions, "A Mechanic" presented a long list of citizens' grievances, including improper handling of financial affairs, "worse than useless" constables who profited from heavy and sometimes illegal fines for "very trivial faults," restrictions on building inexpensive housing in some places, and an attempt to fix wages for labor. The *Aurora* exhorted every voter "who has the cause of republicanism at heart" to turn out at the polls and to "use every endeavour to carry the JEFFERSON ticket." Although the Republicans did not achieve a victory, they were encouraged by their show of strength. Jefferson lost to Adams by only three electoral votes and became vice-president. During the same election and again a year later, Bache and most of the other candidates on the Republican ticket for the common council fell about three hundred votes short of being elected.[33]

The *Aurora*'s initial commentary on Adam's victory gave the best appearance to the outcome by suggesting that the new administration was at least a step in the right direction. Although Adams was a "professed aristocrat," an editorial said, he was to be preferred to Washington who had declined to run again "to save himself from the mortification and disgrace of being superceded." Washington was a slaveholder who had "the ostentation of an eastern bashaw," while Adams lived in republican simplicity. It was well known, the paper said, that "ADAMS is an Aristocrat only in *theory*, but that WASHINGTON is one in *practice*." The *Aurora* complimented the new president for the "republican plainness" of his inauguration and noted that he remained friendly with Jefferson and had disappointed the Federalists who wanted a tool of Hamilton in the office. James Thomson Callender, a journalist who assisted Bache in editing the paper, later remembered that Adams was regarded by some of his enemies as an honest man who was above party. " 'Let us give him a fair trial,' " Callender recalled Bache observing, " 'and then, if he actually does wrong, our censures will fall with the greater weight.' "[34]

Bache did not have to wait long for Adams to do wrong as far as Republicans were concerned, and, indeed, the president himself told his wife he expected to "soon be acquitted" of the accolades the *Aurora* had given him. Adams took office at a time of crisis. France's anger over the Jay Treaty had prompted raids on American ships and a break in diplomatic relations with the United States. At a special session of Congress which Adams called to meet in May 1797, he urged the country to undertake defense measures while further negotiations were attempted. *Aurora* writers immediately expressed horror at "the President by *three votes*," saying that his views were not those of the people. Suggesting that he resented a country as democratic as France and was seeking to establish British influence, correspondents insisted that he was trying to plunge the country into war on trivial pretexts. The paper subsequently denounced the measures Congress took to protect commerce as costly and foolish. Making fortifications and preparing eighty thousand militiamen, said one contributor, made little sense in a naval conflict. Adams was depicted as a senile warmonger and, after he informed Congress early in 1798 that peace negotiations had failed, he was told to resign for the good of the country.[35]

Attempts to resolve the conflict between the United States and France, however, soon played into the Federalists' hands when it became known that the countries' diplomatic dealings had degenerated into an attempt by unnamed agents of Talleyrand's to obtain a loan and a bribe from the American envoys. As revelations of the "XYZ Affair" caused war hysteria and anti-French sentiment to erupt in the spring of 1798, John Fenno informed his readers that Jefferson was "in daily and secret conference" with the "Gallic Editor of the Aurora." The "fruits of this republican connection," Fenno said, would be a bastard "brat" that "may gasp but it will surely die in the infamy of its parents." Jefferson continued to meet through the summer with Bache and with Dr. Michael Leib, an *Aurora* contributor and Republican political organizer in Philadelphia. "I received them always with pleasure, because they are men of abilities, and of principles the most friendly to liberty & our present form of government," Jefferson wrote to a Maryland congressman after further reports of the meetings. "Mr. Bache has another claim on my respect, as being the grandson of Dr. Franklin, the greatest man & ornament of the age and country in which he lived."[36]

With the public outcry over the XYZ revelations came difficult, dispiriting times for Republicans. Jefferson, who had begun seeking subscribers for the *Aurora* shortly after taking office as vice-president, wrote to Madison that Bache's newspaper and James Carey's *Recorder* "totter for want of subscriptions" and that the two Virginians would

have to "really exert" themselves to procure them, "for if these papers
fall, republicanism will be entirely brow beaten." The *Gazette of the
United States* learned of the effort and reported that the vice-president
was *"earnestly soliciting his partizans and all their influential men in his
part of the country to exert themselves to procure subscriptions to the AU-
RORA, or the paper must fall, many Subscribers having lately withdrawn."*
It was strange, Fenno remarked, that the *Aurora* "that rose to profit
all, should fail to profit herself!" Bache admitted that the paper had
"never been a very lucrative establishment," but told his readers that—
unlike Fenno—he had not relied on outside financing. Still, his newspaper had never had a greater circulation or made more money, Bache
said, adding that he had at least as many subscribers as the *Gazette*.
As for Jefferson, he observed, it should come as no surprise that a
person "friendly to the cause of liberty and equal rights, & to the
genuine principles of the constitution" should want to promote the
Aurora.[37]

Bache and Jefferson certainly shared a veneration for Franklin
and his ideals, but the vice-president, clearly in need of journalistic
backing, had immediate political reasons for turning to the young editor. The French crisis was a serious blow to the opposition party, and
Jefferson found himself "a constant butt for every shaft of calumny
which malice & falsehood could form, & the presses, public speakers,
or private letters disseminate." He and other Republicans, however,
sensed an opportunity as the Federalists split over how aggressive to
be with France. With an eye toward future elections, Jefferson made
quiet efforts to rally his supporters and to distribute Republican pamphlets and newspaper essays. "The engine is the press," he told Madison. The time had come for "systematic energies & sacrifices." With
efforts to orchestrate partisan activity still often regarded with suspicion, Jefferson deliberately maintained a low profile. Fearing that Federalist postmasters would intercept his correspondence and make it
available to unfriendly editors, the vice-president was careful to avoid
mailing letters with unguarded statements that could be used by his
enemies.[38]

Jefferson demonstrated less caution in supporting journalists who
would do battle for him and his causes. Although a careful politician
who rarely produced anything for publication himself, he appreciated
writers with visions as democratic as Franklin's and his own. One had
been Philip Freneau, a nationalistic poet whose brutal treatment aboard

a British prison ship in 1780 did nothing to abate his hatred of Old World behavior. As editor of the *National Gazette*, however, he proved to be so obsessed with his republicanism that he exasperated readers and eventually despaired of his own ability to conduct a newspaper. Answering Hamilton's accusation in the *Gazette of the United States* that he had set up Freneau to attack the administration, Jefferson told Washington in September 1792 that he had given his translating clerk help in procuring news and subscriptions. His expectation, he said, was that Freneau would chastise "aristocratical & monarchical" writers, not that the *National Gazette* would criticize the government. Yet, Jefferson ventured to add,

> No government ought to be without censors: & where the press is free, no one ever will. If virtuous, it need not fear the fair operation of attack & defence. Nature has given to man no other means of sifting out the truth either in religion, law, or politics. I think it as honorable to the government neither to know, nor notice, it's sycophants or censors, as it would be undignified & criminal to pamper the former & persecute the latter.[39]

Another favorite was Thomas Paine, whose *Rights of Man*, an answer to Edmund Burke's attack on the French Revolution, appeared in its first American edition in 1791 with a strong endorsement from Jefferson. Probably printed in Bache's shop, the edition was published by Samuel Harrison Smith who later went to Washington at Jefferson's request in 1800 and received his patronage and advice as editor of the *National Intelligencer*. In 1791, however, Smith caused Jefferson considerable political discomfort by including the secretary of state's appraisal of the *Rights of Man* in the pamphlet without his permission. The endorsement, taken from a letter, spoke of Paine's work as a proper answer to the emerging "political heresies" of national leaders, a statement which angered Hamilton and Adams and helped identify Jefferson in the public's mind with the developing opposition to the administration. The pamphlet, which continued to carry the endorsement in subsequent editions, also linked Jefferson with an adamantly egalitarian and harmonious worldview that proved popular with the laboring classes of England and America. Even after Paine had acquired a reputation as a drinker and infidel near the end of his life, he stayed at the White House as Jefferson's guest.[40]

Bache not only praised Paine's work, but also recommended that it be read by the poor and, in 1791 and 1792, reprinted many extracts from the two parts of Paine's *Rights of Man*. When his former school-mate in France, John Quincy Adams, wrote his "Publicola" essays to depict both Paine and Jefferson as rigid-minded visionaries after the publication of the American edition of the *Rights of Man* in 1791, Bache reprinted the letters, as did many other editors, from Boston's *Columbian Centinel*. The *General Advertiser*, however, accompanied the first of the "Publicola" series with an answer to the first question Adams raised—what Jefferson meant by *"political heresies."* Assuming, as many did, that John Adams was the author of "Publicola," Bache made references not only to what the vice-president had written in support of social distinctions, but also to his title campaign of 1789 in which he had tried to convince Congress and the country that the president and vice-president should be addressed as "His Highness" or "Majesty." An example of political heresy, Bache declared, was sup-porting aristocracy and titles because they were "diametrically oppo-site to the spirit of a great majority of the people, and to the princi-ples which form the basis of the state and federal constitutions."[41]

By the election of 1796, the treatment of Washington's vice-president had descended into sarcasm. A proper title for the corpulent Adams, suggested an *Aurora* story ridiculing the candidate, would be *"his rotundity."* When Adams, as president, proclaimed a national fast day in response to the troubles with France, a tactic Hamilton pro-moted to take political advantage of the public's religious sentiments, one of the paper's correspondents commented that the only fault that the country had to repent was electing Adams. When the *Aurora* refused to observe the fast's restrictions on regular activities and sent the president his paper as usual, Adams returned it, the only person to do so, the paper noted. Angry at such treatment of her husband, Abigail Adams could hardly write a personal letter without unleashing some imprecations against the editor of the *Aurora*. "In short we are now wonderfully popular except with Bache & Co who in his paper calls the President old, querilous, Bald, blind, cripled, Toothless Adams," she wrote to her sister after the XYZ Affair came to light. "Thus in Scripture was the Prophet mocked, and tho no Bears may devour the wretch, the wrath of an insulted people will by & by break upon him."[42]

IV

Jefferson's consulting openly with Bache at an early point in the Adams administration was another example of his willingness to stand behind journalists with republican fervor. Bache's relationship with Jefferson and his taunting of Adams, however, were indications of how much his initial intention to be an impartial printer had been eroded by events and his own predispositions. In a 1791 *General Advertiser* editorial on party spirit, truth was said to be "a stranger to passion and haughtiness." Rather than "search calmly after truth" as an individual would "according to his own fancy," parties produced quarrels and ridicule in the "fanatic tone" of foolish minds. Nevertheless, by 1795, an *Aurora* correspondent could answer the contention of one of Fenno's writers that parties were dangerous by quoting from "the immortal" Franklin's 1786 *Pennsylvania Gazette* essay which suggested that parties produced truth by the collision of sentiments. "Candidus" concluded that "there never did and never will exist a real and pure republican government, without, and independent of parties."[43]

During the first decade of government under the new Constitution, the proponents of democratic republicanism were increasingly aware of the need to organize politically, especially among the artisans and mechanics, if they were to overcome their opponents. To Jefferson and his followers, the press appeared to be the primary means of influencing the voters who could effect change. "So long as elections are free, and made by a full vote of an enlightened community," said a 1791 election-day editorial in the *General Advertiser*, "so long will their liberties, constitution and laws, which are all inseparably connected, be safe." On the same day, Bache printed a list of worthy candidates for the state legislature and wrote of the importance of a representative having the ability to pursue "whatever will tend to the good of his country." As his frustration over administration policies grew, Bache gave more specific advice. In 1792, he warned against electing "jobbers in paper" and "office hunters" who would not have "common interest and feeling with the people." After printing the tickets formed at various public meetings, he urged on election day "a full attendance of the enlightened citizens of this Commonwealth." Five years later, the paper was offering sophisticated prognostications of party strength in local, state, and national elections and urging "union and perseverance" in supporting Republican tickets.[44]

Thinking in opposition party terms began in earnest after Washington was elected to a second term. Late in 1792, the *General Advertiser* stated unequivocally, "The question in America is no longer between federalism and anti-federalism, but between republicanism and anti-republicanism." As the Democratic-Republican societies began to appear, dozens of *Advertiser* articles defended their legitimacy in the face of attacks from the Federalist press and eventually from the president himself. One of Bache's correspondents asked sardonically who the Democrats were to "dare to intrude their sentiments upon the public" instead of leaving political affairs to "officers of government, speculators, stock-holders, stock-jobbers, bank-directors, or British agents." It was, the writer said facetiously, "exceedingly unpleasant to have a parcel of ragamuffins looking about, like the devil, seeking whom they can devour." People should understand, the piece insisted, that having a public office indicated "the unerring wisdom and virtue of the man of your choice."[45]

Such essays goaded readers to abandon deference politics and to believe that a favored few were secretly conspiring to defeat the interests of the many. The *General Advertiser* contended that Republicans were only using their First Amendment rights to assemble, speak, and publish. The purpose of the Democratic-Republican societies, said "A Democrat," was to awaken Americans from a political lethargy that began after the Constitution was ratified. "It afforded an opportunity for designing men to take advantage of our negligence," the writer maintained, "and, had not the French revolution commenced, we know not to what lengths this spirit might have been carried." Before the presidential election of 1796, an editorial expressed satisfaction that American aristocrats' "underhand, dark proceedings" had been detected and disapproved of by "the class of citizens out of the vortex of governmental influence." If the term "faction" meant "adherence to interests inconsistent with the general interest," the paper concluded, then the Federalists were the dangerous influence to be detested and eliminated rather than the Republicans.[46]

In its election stories of the 1790s, the paper condemned suffrage restrictions, bribery, intimidation, and ticket-forming tactics that the editor and his contributors interpreted as attempts to undercut the voting power of the laboring classes. After Jefferson's near victory in 1796, which writers thought would have been a Republican triumph with a more democratic voting process, the *Aurora* was emphatic about the difference that a better turnout by the less affluent could make. Social and economic tensions were particularly felt in the 1797 election for state senator from the Philadelphia area. The Federalist incumbent, Benjamin R. Morgan, a lawyer, faced Israel Israel, a tavernkeeper active in Democratic-Republican politics and in relief efforts for the sick and poor. Noting objections to Israel's candidacy from "the *well born* of our city, on account of his occupation," the paper said that suffrage was fortunately not confined to gentlemen in learned professions. "The great body of our citizens," said an editorial, "the useful classes among us, the artisans and mechanics have too much respect for themselves to object to ISRAEL ISRAEL because he is not a merchant or a lawyer."[47]

As the election approached, yellow fever struck the city and many of what the paper called "the fugitive gentry" departed for safer surroundings, leaving laborers to gather in a tent community on the banks of the Schuylkill. Dr. Michael Leib, a county member of the assembly, proposed an appropriation of twenty thousand dollars to assist the distressed, the *Aurora* pointed out, but some of the city's legislators objected and demonstrated their lack of "feeling for their more indigent fellow citizens" by reducing the amount by half. Bache said that the public was still waiting to see them join the lists he was publishing of those who were making donations for the suffering poor. Israel, one of the contributors, took a prominent role in the relief efforts and, with the help of support from working class districts, was elected by a narrow margin. The state senate, however, was not prepared to have the tavernkeeper join their ranks. After hearing charges of voting irregularities and complaints that Israel would represent a threat to the rights of property, the Senate decided to hold a new election for the seat.[48]

During the second campaign, Morgan's supporters warned that Israel was not only not as fit for office as their candidate, but that he also represented the kind of dangerous democratic ideas that had led to anarchy and bloodshed in France. Israel's backers said that they were cheated of a victory and that the interests and liberties of the common citizen were at stake. More than twice as many ballots were cast in the second election, ending in a 357-vote majority for Morgan. *Aurora* correspondents accused the Morgan partisans of hiring carriages to bring voters to the polls, paying taxes in some cases, and threatening tenants with being turned out, creditors with ruin, and employees with losing their jobs if they supported Israel. The paper ridiculed Fenno for printing an apparently inaccurate report that a horseman with a drawn sword had paraded in front of one polling place wearing *"Israel or Death"* on his cap with a skull and crossbones. Bache attributed Israel's loss to "the influence of wealth" and said that he felt "the republican spirit of this city is rising." "Cassius" told *Aurora* readers that the democrats had the "revolutionary virtues" of *"nerve and fortitude"* on their side. "You now know your strength," the writer added, "and let the British faction beware how they rouse the Lion by endeavouring to ensnare him."[49]

V

Bache's revolutionary fervor, his attacks on Washington and Adams, and his electioneering were all scorned in the Federalist press. He was regularly accused of being a threat to the nation's well-being, but the nature of the attacks degenerated with the appearance of William Cobbett's *Porcupine's Gazette* on the day of the Adams inauguration. Born in Britain and inimical to all that the Enlightenment represented, Cobbett idealized a quiet, medieval order of society in which people knew their place in the social hierarchy. Writing as "Peter Porcupine," Cobbett displayed all of his irascibility with what he perceived to be the democratic disorder of the late eighteenth century. He blamed Franklin and Jefferson for promoting French radicalism in America, but saved his choicest invective for Bache, an editor he said was the tool of the "execrable cause." Bache was described as blackhearted, seditious, sleepy-eyed, vile, and perverted. Addressing "Young Lightening Rod" on one occasion, he remarked that only a weak government would fear "such an animal" and that he should be left to live the life and die the death of the wicked.[50]

Too vitriolic even for many Federalists, Cobbett failed to provoke Bache into pitched battle. Admitting his "inferiority in the arts of scurrility and defamation," the editor of the *Aurora* said he would never engage in newspaper controversy with Porcupine and only asked "to have any thing but his praise." Still, Bache was far from timid. Elizabeth Hewson thought that he was "going fast to destruction" and said that she was afraid some people would take violent action against him if he did not change. "I am afraid very fatal consequences will attend his publishing the pieces he does," she wrote to her brother, adding that he was in an embarrassing financial situation. Cobbett helped spread the news of Bache's troubles by saying that he had failed to pay a five dollar fine in the mayor's court. "Suppose, in these difficult times, you and I were to join hands, and endeavour to raise the ghost of your abominable old grandfather?" Porcupine said to Bache in his *Gazette*. "He would teach us a trick or two, that could baffle all the damned harpies: and I dare to say it would be much easier for you to raise him, flesh, blood and bones, than for you to raise a hundred dollars."[51]

Bache found Cobbett's charges that the few printers supporting France were receiving French gold inconsistent with his gloating descriptions of their destitution but the *Aurora* was in financial trouble. Federalists avoided doing business with Bache, and many customers were in arrears. William Duane, a writer employed by the *Aurora* in 1798, observed in October of that year that the paper had picked up two hundred additional subscribers since July, but that many bills had not been paid to Bache and that there was between fifteen and twenty thousand dollars "due south of the Delaware." Jefferson and Madison may have been responsible for the gains in circulation, but they could not collect the multitude of small amounts owed to the paper. Duane told Tench Coxe, a Republican theorist who was a regular contributor to the paper, that he knew "from experience *Newspaper debts are the worst of all others!*" Four years later, Duane recalled that Bache had had trouble paying him his salary of ten dollars a week for part-time work and that the editor had to go out and raise the money "by a contribution of a number of republicans living in Philadelphia." Bache's income from the *Aurora* did not cover "the expenses of a frugal establishment—nor of a family managed with exemplary economy," Duane said, and the editor himself "had expended a fortune of more than 20,000 dollars."[52]

Cobbett and money were not Bache's only problems in 1797 and 1798. In the charged atmosphere of the conflict with France, the violence Abigail Adams and Elizabeth Hewson predicted did occur. In April 1797, while Bache was inspecting the frigate *United States*, one of three ships Congress was having built at Philadelphia in response to French actions, he was attacked by Clement Humphreys, son of the ship's architect, Joshua Humphreys. Humphreys delivered several hard blows to Bache's face as the ship's carpenters looked on. Before he could leave with the aid of friends, Bache heard voices in the crowd saying he deserved the beating for treating Washington as he had in his paper and for accusing the carpenters of taking bribes. Humphreys, who pleaded guilty to assault and battery, was soon given a diplomatic appointment in Europe by Adams.[53]

In the spring of 1798, someone smashed the glass in the door to Bache's office, and, in the wake of the XYZ disclosures, a number of tense partisan confrontations took place in Philadelphia at the theater and other public places. A large crowd of young men marched through the streets of the city on May 7, stopping at the president's home to make known their willingness to fight France. Adams, wearing a full military uniform, came out to address them. Some of the young men drank heavily at a dinner that followed, then walked to Bache's house where they began yelling threats. Bache, who was not at home, told his readers that no damage had been done before the youths were driven off by friends and neighbors, but that his wife and children had been terrified. "It has been wrong, from the beginning, to encourage young men not of age, to meddle in politics, especially at times as critical at these," Bache wrote two days later, the national day of fasting and prayer proclaimed by Adams. "They have not discretion sufficient to ballast their zeal." That evening new disorders broke out and the president's home seemed in danger for a time. Bache collected and armed friends, but a mob that planned to attack and burn his house heard of his preparations and satisfied themselves with raising disturbances in the streets. Governor Thomas Mifflin called out soldiers to restore calm. While urging self-restraint in the following days, Bache blamed Cobbett for inciting the violence with inflammatory editorials.[54]

Fenno's *Gazette of the United States*, however, suggested that Bache was the real incendiary. The paper, which pointed out that the editor of the *Aurora* had been active in political organizing, published an essay by "Americus" who reminded readers that Bache had disseminated Paine's works, published the forged Washington letters, and ridiculed Adams because of his age. The writer also noted that earlier in the year Bache had accused Secretary of State Timothy Pickering of accepting an improper gratuity for issuing a passport, a charge Pickering was able to deny, but which led to the dismissal of two of his clerks. "Americus" said of Bache:

> He has founded the lowest depths of human depravity, and now exhibits to the world an example of wickedness that no man of his years ever

arrived at before. Let none attempt to describe him—language is too weak—no combination of words will come so near to expressing every thing that is monstrous in human nature as BENJAMIN FRANKLIN BACHE. Let him sink into contempt, and let oblivion cover him.[55]

Three months later, angry that his father had been called a mercenary scoundrel in the *Aurora*, John Ward Fenno appeared at Bache's office seeking a published apology. After Bache refused, Fenno's son assaulted him on Fourth Street. Bache struck him with his cane and pinned him to a wall before the two were separated by a crowd of about three dozen people who had gathered to watch. "He deserves a reward for the exploit better than his worthy predecessor Humphries, as he was not a little mauled in the combat," Bache reported. "He scratched the nose of his antagonist and his teeth took off the skin of the editor's knuckles; for which he got in return a sound rap or two across the head and face."[56]

In each encounter with his enemies, Bache asserted in the *Aurora* that he would remain steadfast in his cause. In June 1798, he wrote to his childhood friend from Switzerland, Gabriel Cramer, that he had worked for eight years for the good of his country and expected to triumph over his persecutors. He told Cramer that he had three sons and that even if he could not give them a fortune, he could give them an education that would make them useful to themselves and their country. Later in the summer, responding to one of the frequent accusations that he was a "French hireling," Bache gave a summary of his upbringing and career to show the "uniformity of his conduct" and adherence to principle. "The editor of the Aurora was educated in the lap of republicanism," he wrote, "ever since he has thought and acted for himself, his thoughts and actions have been those of a democratic republican." Bache said he was taught to wish France a republic before its revolution and had opposed the administrations' attempts "to infringe the constitution, and sap the liberty of the citizen."[57]

Bache could afford to make enemies like Cobbett and the Fennos. He said that his "persecution" only helped circulation. The editor had more formidable opponents, however. One was Alexander Hamilton, the subject of much sarcasm and many references to his confessed adultery, a fact that was brought to public attention through a pamphlet written by one of Bache's associates, James Thomson Callender. Other antagonists were the Federalist members of Congress who found themselves and their decisions maligned in the *Aurora*. The paper's general desire was that the representatives of the people "would as a faithful mirror reflect the sentiments of their constituents." Specific complaints about Congress ranged from a need for better winter heating in the House to high salaries, an expense the paper did not think would be necessary if the representatives were genuine patriots. One contributor, noting Franklin's adage that "Time is money," provided a table with minute-by-minute calculations of the costs of Congress being in session. Early in 1798, in a battle over the privileges of reporters, Speaker of the House Jonathan Dayton returned Bache's favors by excluding him from the floor where he and other journalists took notes.[58]

Congress became more serious about dealing with difficulties like Bache when, in the summer, it passed the Sedition Act of 1798. The law was signed by Adams on July 14, making "false, scandalous and malicious writing or writings against the government of the United States, or either house of the Congress of the United States, or the President of the United States" illegal. A partisan measure justified as necessary in time of national crisis, the act was passed despite the Republicans' strenuous objections shortly after Bache infuriated war-minded Federalists by printing a conciliatory letter from Talleyrand to the American peace envoys. Federalists, already angry that Bache had been promoting good relations with France, took the publication of the letter, which had not been released to the public, as evidence that Bache was a French agent in treasonous correspondence with the Directory. Bache was able to explain satisfactorily the circumstances of his receiving the document, but calls were being made for action. As early as April, Jefferson informed Madison that the Federalists wanted a sedition bill. "The object of that, is the suppression of the whig presses," he wrote. "Bache's has been particularly named."[59]

The Federalists, however, did not wait to use the Sedition Act against the editor. Ten days after he published the Talleyrand letter, Bache was arrested under a federal common law charge of seditious libel for "sundry" publications. He appeared in court and posted bail, but spent most of the summer denouncing the Sedition Act as a violation of the First Amendment's guarantee that Congress shall make "no law" abridging freedom of the press.[60]

Bache did not come to trial. Yellow fever returned to Philadelphia in August. The *Aurora* blamed "the unbounded and unfeeling rapaciousness of *some* merchants" for their not having taken better quarantine precautions with shipments from the West Indies. Their "only god is money," the paper said, and they left "the honest and industrious poor" to suffer in the epidemic while they retired to their country estates. As other papers began shutting down, Bache thought of leaving the city, but he wrote his father on September 2 that his finances would not allow him to discontinue the *Aurora*. "Is it not heartrending," he added, "that the laboring poor should almost exclusively be the victims of the disease introduced by that commerce, which, in prosperous times, is a source of misery to them, by the inequality of wealth which it introduces." Margaret Bache went into labor before the letter was sent and in the early morning hours of September 3 delivered a baby boy. "There is everything provided for him but a name," Bache told his father, "it will puzzle us our wits for a month to find one."[61]

Within two days of his son's birth, Bache fell ill with yellow fever. A French doctor ordered frequent bathings, but the tub leaked and spread water through the room. Margaret attended her husband. On September 7, Bache wrote a will leaving his property to his wife, "firmly confiding from the tenderness and love which I have in every shape experienced from her uniformly, that she will bestow on our dear Children a suitable and enlightened Education, such as shall be worthy of us, and advantageous to themselves and render them virtuous, generous, and attached to the immutable principles of Civil Liberty." Three days later, Bache was dead. "He settled all his affairs," Elizabeth Hewson noted, "and died with the greatest composure."[62]

CHAPTER

8

Conclusion: Finding the Future

Benjamin Franklin Bache died a month after reaching twenty-nine years of age. His arch-rival in the journalistic debate over the future of the United States, John Fenno, succumbed to yellow fever four days later. Fenno had served Hamilton and the Federalist program for national stability and prosperity. Bache, like his grandfather, was among those Enlightenment egalitarians who promoted the idea of a magnanimous moral core for the American republic which associated virtue with utility and reason with a passion for justice. This new age of public and private probity was not to be realized suddenly, by overturning what existed, but gradually, by educating citizens through schools and the press. With a more knowledgeable citizenry and a more equitable economy, the resulting state was intended to be a democracy which would neither sink into disorder nor adopt the advantage-seeking policymaking of the European powers. The future they delineated would depend not only on societal structures, but also on the people's willingness to work both for themselves and for the common good.

The Constitution had provided no more than an outline within which fundamental differences of opinion and emphasis would remain in tension as particular decisions were made. While the Federalists tended to approve of hierarchy and privilege in achieving harmony and well-being, the Republicans generally were striving for more equality and more favorable circumstances for personal advancement.[1] The Franklinian-Jeffersonian ideal offered a model of self-sufficient yet in-

164

terdependent individuals achieving national freedom, security and wealth through hard work and wholesome living. This early version of the American dream, with its hope of retaining a classical republican suspicion of power and enacting enlightened republican reforms, had the appeal of a certain distinctive, self-conceived Americanness. Rather than accept the evils they saw around them, the people at large could become increasingly the masters of their own fate with optimism about opportunities and mutual help in adversity.

I

Those who spoke of progress for the excluded usually did not want to see the inspiring notion of overcoming the barriers of status and wealth become too intoxicating. Yet, in their efforts to point out the reasons for party turmoil, they magnified class frictions and identified political options in ways that resulted in democratic discussion of the directions the nation could take. The country's leaders were, in Bache's metaphor, regularly put on trial in the court of public opinion, sometimes with tactics which exceeded the boundaries of truth and propriety.

The Federalists of the 1790s condemned the journalism of enlightened republicanism as a threat to all that the United States rested upon. When the Sedition Act of 1798 was brought before the House of Representatives, statements from the *Aurora* were repeatedly used as evidence that, as Rep. John Allen put it, "a conspiracy against the Constitution, the Government, the peace and safety of this country, is formed, and is in full operation." In a long speech which the *Aurora* said would have "disgraced a Robespiere," the Connecticut Federalist said Bache's paper was "the great engine of all these treasonable combinations, and must be strongly supported, or it would have fallen long ago." He said that Bache walked on the streets arm-in-arm with Jefferson and met with him at all hours. The danger, Allen told the House, was real and the remedy necessary:

> At the commencement of the Revolution in France those loud and enthusiastic advocates for liberty and equality took special care to occupy and command all the presses in the nation; they well knew the powerful influence to be obtained on the public mind by that engine; its operations are on the poor, the ignorant, the passionate, and the vicious;

over all these classes of men the freedom of the press shed its baleful effects, and they all became tools of faction and ambition, and the virtuous, the pacific, and the rich, were their victims. The Jacobins of our country, too, sir, are determined to preserve in their hands, the same weapon; it is our business to wrest it from them.[2]

Whether out of actual fear of brutal upheaval or only anxiety about losing their political predominance, Federalists issued dire warnings about the need for order and strong, stable government in the young and untested nation. Republican rhetoric, at the same time, was replete with references to social and economic conflicts which suggested that the work of the American revolution remained unfinished. In this, they opened themselves up to being spattered with charges of fanaticism. Bache insisted he was merely carrying out his duty as a journalist in a democratic republic where liberty and justice had not yet been gained for everyone.

Hours after his death, Margaret Bache published a public notice which described her husband as "a man inflexible in virtue, unappalled by power or persecution." Federalists, however, heaped abuse on the deceased editor and even upon "Mother Bache," as Peter Porcupine called the widow. Her handbill announcing the death, Cobbett said, was "struck off before his corps was cold!" An approving reference to the abolition of castration in Italy in the first issue of the *Aurora* published under her name inspired one of Porcupine's correspondents to say that her concern was quite natural considering the loss she had recently suffered.[3]

One Federalist in particular, Alexander Hamilton, no doubt thought Bache lived eight years too long. The *Aurora* had continued to raise doubts about his actions even after he had left office. Among other suspicions, the paper speculated that Hamilton and other principal Federalists, through their friendship with Talleyrand, might have created the conditions for the XYZ Affair to occur. After Bache's death, reports circulated in the press that the former treasury secretary, although he professed to have little money of his own, had attempted to buy the *Aurora*, perhaps with British gold, in order to suppress it. In a letter to New York's attorney general which was published in New York newspapers, Hamilton said the story had no foundation and that he could no longer ignore the "malignant calumnies" directed at him by the Republican press:

The design of that faction to overturn our government, and with great pillars of social security and happiness, in this country, bec every day more manifest, and have of late acquired a degree of syste which renders them formidable. One principal Engine for effecting the scheme is by audacious falsehoods to destroy the confidence of the people in all those who are in any degree conspicuous among the supporters of the Government: an Engine which has been employed in time past with too much success, and which unless counteracted in future is likely to be attended with very fatal consequences. To counter act it is therefore a duty to the community.

Hamilton told the attorney general that "public motives" compelled him to seek legal action against the New York *Argus*, a Republican paper that had reprinted the allegations. In a state case tried two weeks after the letter appeared, David Frothingham, the foreman of the *Argus*, was found guilty of libeling Hamilton and was sentenced to four months in jail.[4]

In all, about two dozen persons, mostly Republican journalists, faced state or federal charges which Federalists brought between 1798 and 1800 to curtail their political opponents' expression. The number included some of the approximately eighteen British and Irish "Jacobins" who, fleeing from England's suppression of radicalism in the 1790s, became stalwarts of the Republican press in the administrations of Adams and Jefferson. Two of the émigrés, James Thomson Callender and William Duane, assisted Bache in 1798 and were, after their employer, the writers the Federalists most despised. Callender and Duane were among the five "foreign liars" Adams blamed for his being "overthrown" as he left the presidency in 1801. "No party, that ever existed," Adams wrote at the time, "knew itself so little, or so vainly overrated its own influence and popularity, as ours."[5]

Before taking a position at the *Aurora*, according to an account Duane later gave, Callender was about to sell his talents to the British minister, Robert Liston. Bache intervened and hired him to take Duane's place, with Duane agreeing to relinquish his salary for the good of the cause. The editor, who had a policy of approving whatever appeared in his newspaper, was soon rejecting some of Callender's more scurrilous pieces, and the Republicans who had been contributing to Duane's salary demanded that the new employee be dismissed. Out of a job and bitter at Bache, Callender left Philadelphia for Virginia in July 1798, hoping to evade enforcement of the _on Act. Callender industriously contributed to five publications _e in Virginia and wrote an election pamphlet for Jefferson's can- _dacy in 1800, a pamphlet which led to his being sentenced under _he Sedition Act to nine months in prison. When Jefferson took of- fice and issued him a pardon, Callender, who had received funds from Jefferson at various times, was not satisfied and demanded to be ap- pointed postmaster at Richmond. Considering him unfit for the job, Jefferson refused. Callender then switched sides and began writing personal attacks on the president.[6]

William Duane was more interested in advancing principles than his own career. Deported from India for angering officials of the East India Company while editor of a Calcutta newspaper, Duane joined in the journalistic efforts of London radicals before seeking safety in the United States in 1796. He then compiled a history of the French Revolution which lauded the new French government and accused the Washington administration of siding with Britain. Poor enough to have difficulty paying his rent for rooms off an alley, Duane, with uncropped hair, a long beard, and Irish parentage, appeared to be the very incarnation of the French-spirited radicalism Federalists loathed. Bache published his 1796 pamphlet, *A Letter to George Washington*, in which Duane brought up the usual Republican complaints about the president, from the funding system to slaveholding, and stated that as chief executive he had done nothing to secure the foundations of freedom—education and equality.[7]

Duane was employed at the *Aurora* when its editor contracted yellow fever in September 1798. Bache, when he was close to death, wrote a confidential note to Tench Coxe asking that the paper be continued for the good of his "family, his country and mankind." Acting for Bache's heirs, Coxe and a group of other Philadelphia Re- publicans offered the editorship to Duane. When the paper re- appeared on November 1, Bache's obituary mentioned unspecified "intrigues" against the *Aurora* which had attempted "either to sup- press it for ever, or convert it into a vehicle of atrocious delusion." The enemies of republicanism and "equal freedom" could not have known, the piece maintained, that it was the editor's dying wish "that his paper should be continued with inflexible fidelity to the principles upon which it was founded and reared up." Bache was a man of "tran- scendant genius and talents," the obituary said, and his principles were the same simple, virtuous ones of loving liberty which had inspired the revolution "and the sacrifice of near 100,000 American lives, of both sexes."[8]

For his own part, Duane promised to conduct the *Aurora* with "an unwearied watchfulness against those eternal foes of republics, avarice, ambition, and corruption." In the next two years, he managed to overcome indictments for sedition, but was mobbed and beaten by federal troops he had criticized, was menaced with deportation by Secretary of State Timothy Pickering, and was forced into hiding for a time after being found guilty of contempt of the Senate. In the midst of his troubles he and Margaret decided to marry. Jefferson found some of Duane's behavior more passionate than prudent in the years before the editor retired from the *Aurora* in 1822. Duane was able to get an appointment as a lieutenant-colonel in the army, and he received a considerable amount of government stationery and printing business during the Jefferson administration, but the apparent favorite in patronage was the more refined Samuel Harrison Smith, editor of the *National Intelligencer*. Still, after leaving the presidency, Jefferson credited the *Aurora*, which continued to be financially shaky and occasionally offended even faithful supporters, with "incalculable services" to republicanism and with being "the rallying point" for the struggles of political "orthodoxy" against the Federalists. "It was our comfort in the gloomiest days," Jefferson wrote in 1811, "and is still performing the office of a watchful sentinel."[9]

II

The expectation of patronage and the praise of prominent men may have been some inducement for journalists to follow a particular party line in the early republic, but it was indoctrination and experience that were crucial to their commitment. The editors of the nation's preeminent Republican newspaper were committed to their cause to the point of recklessness at times, even to facing financial ruin and threats to their personal safety and freedom. Although the *Aurora* often reflected a party's opinions and sometimes received its aid, the newspaper was not run by the Republicans so much as it was conducted by two editors who were Republicans. William Duane, who lived with poverty and suppression, came by his politics largely through what he read and the harsh realities he experienced. Benjamin Franklin Bache, on the other hand, was the product of an educational regimen carefully calculated by his grandfather to impart the humanitarian values he and others of his persuasion hoped to see perpetuated in succeeding generations.

Whatever their shortcomings, some American journalists had assumed a role their successors would profess to be carrying on, that of tribune of the people and sentinel of republican virtue.[10] The opposition writers during the Washington and Adams administrations thus did more than convey information. They presented news and opinion in ways that animated readers and politicians. The stirring of popular passions outraged Federalists like Hamilton who, with inflated, inflammatory rhetoric, emphasized the need for order and for consolidating the power of the government. Jefferson and his partisans spoke of empowering the governed and having the people look to themselves for solutions. The Republican success in the elections of 1800 was due in part to the ability of Jeffersonian journalists to involve voters emotionally by appealing to their pride in liberty and aspirations for better lives. They proffered the simple, but profoundly revolutionary message that the majority of people could rule themselves wisely, in peace and common prosperity.

By the end of the century, after uncounted attempts to envision an exemplary society for America, new, wavering images of human emancipation and progress had begun emitting from the United States. Readers were being told that the fate of the republic was at stake in the partisan disputes of the moment, but what they were witnessing was a democratic culture being introduced to the world with all its inherent uncertainty and contention over matters of freedom and social justice. The fears of the time, including those of the menace of stronger nations and the dangers of ignorance and misery, were rational responses to immediate realities, even if they led to exaggeration and extreme behavior. The risk of failing to resolve the issues appeared serious enough to threaten all the varying vistas of the future. The Jeffersonian journalism of early America applied the standards of enlightened republicanism to personal, societal, and international relations and encouraged the public to believe and act upon the idea that an egalitarian political economy could be a proper and practical goal of the new nation.

The objective of the Jeffersonians was a system that would operate on natural principles and provide widespread material comfort. For some, like Benjamin Franklin Bache, the yearning for righteousness may have outpaced decorum at times. Indeed, the tenor of debate became acerbic and apocalyptic on all sides in the years following the French Revolution. Yet, for those Americans who foresaw greater happiness and harmony in a future where one person was supposed to count as much as another, the ultimate necessity was not merely feeling good, but being good. Lives would be good, they thought, if people were able and willing to work diligently for themselves and for their communities. Such moral aspirations were not out of place in a country where republican ethics and religious scruples still were being given avowals of allegiance. With leaders like Franklin and Jefferson and journalists like Paine and Bache, the American Revolution made a reasonable turn toward equality and cooperation, not an unrealistically radical change with a totalitarian outcome.

Notes

Abbreviations

A   [Philadelphia] *Aurora*

APS   Franklin and Bache collections, American Philosophical Society, Philadelphia

Autobiography   *The Autobiography of Benjamin Franklin, A Genetic Text*, ed. J. A. Leo Lemay and P. M. Zall (Knoxville: University of Tennessee Press, 1981)

GA   [Philadelphia] *General Advertiser*

HSP   Historical Society of Pennsylvania, Philadelphia

NEC   [Boston] *New-England Courant*

PBF   *The Papers of Benjamin Franklin*, ed. Leonard W. Labaree et al. (New Haven: Yale University Press, 1959—   )

PG   [Philadelphia] *Pennsylvania Gazette*

PMHB   *Pennsylvania Magazine of History and Biography*

WBF   *The Writings of Benjamin Franklin*, ed. Albert H. Smyth, 10 vols. (New York: Macmillan Co., 1905–1907).

Yale   Franklin Collection, Yale University Library, New Haven, Connecticut

Introduction

1. For summaries of the scholarship on republicanism, see Robert E. Shalhope, "Toward a Republican Synthesis: The Emergence of an Understanding of Republicanism in American Historiography," *William and Mary Quarterly*, 3rd ser., 29 (January 1972): 49–80; Robert E. Shalhope, "Republicanism and Early Amer-

ican Historiography," ibid., 39 (April 1982): 334–56; Joyce Appleby, "Introduction: Republicanism and Ideology," *American Quarterly* 37 (Fall 1985): 461–73.

2. See Jeffery A. Smith, *Printers and Press Freedom: The Ideology of Early American Journalism* (New York: Oxford University Press, 1988), p. 24; Lance Banning, *The Jeffersonian Persuasion, Evolution of a Party Ideology* (Ithaca, N.Y.: Cornell University Press, 1978), pp. 62–69; Linda Kerber, *Federalists in Dissent, Imagery and Ideology in Jeffersonian America* (Ithaca, N.Y.: Cornell University Press, 1970), pp. 192–215.

3. Smith, *Printers and Press Freedom*, pp. 17–30, 57–92.

4. One form of evidence of public enthusiasm for a new age of politics is the way in which illustrators and artists depicted leaders as triumphant figures of the Enlightenment. See, e.g., Garry Wills, *Cincinnatus, George Washington and the Enlightenment* (Garden City, N.Y.: Doubleday, 1984); Noble E. Cunningham, Jr., *The Image of Thomas Jefferson in the Public Eye, Portraits for the People, 1800–1809* (Charlottesville: University Press of Virginia, 1981).

5. Joyce Appleby, "The Social Origins of American Revolutionary Ideology," *Journal of American History* 64 (March 1978): 935–58; Joyce Appleby, "What Is Still American in the Political Philosophy of Thomas Jefferson?" *William and Mary Quarterly*, 3rd ser., 39 (April 1982): 287–309.

6. James T. Kloppenburg, "The Virtues of Liberalism: Christianity, Republicanism, and Ethics in Early American Political Discourse," *Journal of American History* 74 (June 1987): 9–33.

7. Gary B. Nash, "The Social Evolution of Preindustrial American Cities, 1700–1820, Reflections and New Directions," *Journal of Urban History* 13 (February 1987): 115–45.

8. Linda K. Kerber, "The Republican Ideology of the Revolutionary Generation," *American Quarterly* 37 (Fall 1985): 495.

9. See Lester H. Cohen, *The Revolutionary Histories, Contemporary Narratives of the American Revolution* (Ithaca, N.Y.: Cornell University Press, 1980).

10. Circular to the States, June 8, 1783, in *The Writings of George Washington*, ed. John C. Fitzpatrick, 39 vols. (Washington: Government Printing Office, 1931–1944), 26: 484–85.

11. Douglass C. Adair, "Experience Must Be Our Only Guide: History, Democratic Theory, and the United States Constitution," in Jack P. Greene, ed., *The Reinterpretation of the American Revolution, 1763–1789* (New York: Harper & Row, 1968), pp. 397–416; Douglass C. Adair, "That Politics May Be Reduced to a Science: David Hume, James Madison, and the Tenth *Federalist*," in Greene, ed., *The Reinterpretation of the American Revolution*, pp. 487–503. See also, Garry Wills, "A More Perfect Union," *Proceedings of the American Philosophical Society* 131 (September 1987): 289–97; Jack P. Greene, " 'An Instructive Monitor': Experience and the Fabrication of the Federal Constitution," *Proceedings of the American Philosophical Society* 131 (September 1987): 298–307.

12. The pattern was set by Bernard Bailyn, who detected "real fears" in the rhetoric of revolutionary America. Bernard Bailyn, *The Ideological Origins of the American Revolution* (Cambridge: Belknap Press of Harvard University Press, 1967), p. ix.

13. After noting that some major figures of "Enlightenment" thought would

be excluded if it were defined as optimism about human nature, rationalism, or empiricism, Henry F. May has suggested that the term should be understood to mean the belief that the present was more enlightened than the past and that humans and nature were best understood through natural faculties. Henry F. May, *The Enlightenment in America* (New York: Oxford University Press, 1976), pp. xiii–xiv.

14. See, e.g., the thirteen essays in *"The Creation of the American Republic, 1776–1787,* A Symposium of Views and Reviews," *William and Mary Quarterly,* 3rd ser., 44 (July 1987): 549–640.

15. Sir Lewis Namier, *Personalities and Powers* (New York: Macmillan, 1955), p. 4. In discounting the notion that political ideas spring from pure reason, Namier wrote, "What matters most is the underlying emotions, the music, to which ideas are a mere libretto, often of a very inferior quality; and once the emotions have ebbed, the ideas, established high and dry, become doctrine, or at best innocuous clichés" (pp. 4–5).

16. Nash, "The Social Evolution of Preindustrial American Cities," pp. 126–33.

17. Smith, *Printers and Press Freedom,* pp. 42–53.

18. In contrast to pamphlets, newspapers had the advantage of being circulated widely, constantly, and rapidly. Jeffery A. Smith, "Impartiality and Revolutionary Ideology: Editorial Policies of the *South-Carolina Gazette,* 1732–1775," *Journal of Southern History* 49 (November 1983): 511.

19. For examples, see Paul M. Spurlin, *Montesquieu in America, 1760–1801* (Baton Rouge: Louisiana State University Press, 1940); Paul M. Spurlin, *Rousseau in America, 1760–1809* (University, Ala.: University of Alabama Press, 1969).

20. Adrienne Koch, "Pragmatic Wisdom and the American Enlightenment," *William and Mary Quarterly,* 3rd ser., 17 (July 1961): 313–29.

Chapter 1

1. Edwin J. Perkins, *The Economy of Colonial America* (New York: Columbia University Press, 1980), p. 164.

2. Gary B. Nash, "Urban Wealth and Poverty in Prerevolutionary America," *Journal of Interdisciplinary History* 6 (Spring 1976): 549–51. See also Jackson Turner Main, *The Social Structure of Revolutionary America* (Princeton, N.J.: Princeton University Press, 1965), pp. 286–87; Jack P. Greene, "The Social Origins of the American Revolution: An Evaluation and Interpretation," *Political Science Quarterly* 88 (March 1973): 1–22; Kenneth A. Lockridge, "Social Change and the Meaning of the American Revolution," *Journal of Social History* 6 (Summer 1973): 403–39.

3. See Gary B. Nash, "The Social Evolution of Preindustrial American Cities, 1700–1820, Reflections and New Directions," *Journal of Urban History* 13 (February 1987): 134–36.

4. Gary B. Nash, "The Transformation of Urban Politics, 1700–1765," *Journal of American History* 60 (December 1973): 605–32.

5. Gary B. Nash, "Social Change and the Growth of Prerevolutionary Urban Radicalism," in Alfred F. Young, ed., *The American Revolution,* (DeKalb:

Northern Illinois University Press, 1976), pp. 3–36. Economic complaints were particularly evident during the often overlooked period of the French and Indian War. For examples of charges that taxation was not reasonable or equitable, see *Boston Gazette*, June 9, July 7, 14, 21, August 4, 11, 18, 1755; [New Haven] *Connecticut Gazette*, March 20, April 10, May 15, July 24, August 7, 1756.

6. See Pauline Maier, *From Resistance to Revolution, Colonial Radicals and the Development of American Opposition to Britain, 1765–1776* (New York: Alfred A. Knopf, 1972).

7. James Madison, *The Federalist No. 10*, in Jacob E. Cooke, ed., *The Federalist* (Middletown, Conn.: Wesleyan University Press, 1961), pp. 56–59.

8. See Jeffery A. Smith, *Printers and Press Freedom: The Ideology of Early American Journalism* (New York: Oxford University Press, 1988), pp. 95–167.

9. "Of publick Spirit," "Of the Equality and Inequality of Men," and "Of Charity, and Charity-Schools," in [John Trenchard and Thomas Gordon], *Cato's Letters*, 6th ed., 4 vols. (London: Printed for J. Walthoe and others, 1755), 2: 11–17, 85–90, 4: 236–46.

10. Immanuel Kant, *Critique of Pure Reason*, trans. Norman K. Smith (London: Macmillan and Co., 1929), p. 9.

11. *Autobiography*, p. 164.

12. See, in general, Jeffery A. Smith, "The Enticements of Change and America's Enlightenment Journalism," paper presented at the Publishing and Readership in Revolutionary France and America symposium, Library of Congress, May 2, 1989. For examples, see [Boston] *Weekly Rehearsal*, September 27, 1731; [Philadelphia] *American Weekly Mercury*, April 6, 1732; *New-York Mercury*, January 27, 1755; [Portsmouth] *New-Hampshire Gazette*, October 7, 1756; [Burlington] *New-Jersey Gazette*, December 5, 1777; [Philadelphia] *Freeman's Journal*, April 25, 1781; *Carlisle Gazette, and the Western Repository of Knowledge*, August 10, 1785; *Concord Herald, and Newhampshire Intelligencer*, January 6, 1790; *Newport Mercury*, March 1, 1790. See also Smith, *Printers and Press Freedom*, pp. 37, 99, 145; Thomas C. Leonard, *The Power of the Press, The Birth of American Political Reporting* (New York: Oxford University Press, 1986), pp. 35–36; Arthur M. Schlesinger, *Prelude to Independence, The Newspaper War on Britain, 1764–1776* (New York: Alfred A. Knopf, 1958), p. 214. On the marketplace of ideas concept in the seventeenth and eighteenth centuries, see Smith, *Printers and Press Freedom*, pp. 31–41.

13. [Salem, Massachusetts] *Essex Gazette*, August 2, 1768.

14. For discussions of some of the better-known instances, see Cathy Covert, " 'Passion Is Ye Prevailing Motive': The Feud Behind the Zenger Case," *Journalism Quarterly* 50 (Spring 1973): 3–10; *The Independent Reflector*, ed. Milton M. Klein (Cambridge: Harvard University Press, 1963), pp. 1–48; Paul Boyer, "Borrowed Rhetoric: The Massachusetts Excise Controversy of 1754," *William and Mary Quarterly*, 3rd ser., 21 (July 1964): 328–51; Dwight L. Teeter, " 'King' Sears, the Mob, and Freedom of the Press in New York, 1765–76," *Journalism Quarterly* 41 (Autumn 1964): 539–44.

15. [Baltimore] *American and Daily Advertiser*, May 16, 1799.

16. John Adams to Benjamin Rush, August 28, 1811, in *The Works of John Adams*, ed. Charles F. Adams, 10 vols. (Boston: Little, Brown, and Co., 1850–1856), 9: 636. On the virtues of endurance, sacrifice, and renunciation in the

Washington legend, see Barry Schwartz, *George Washington: The Making of an American Symbol* (New York: The Free Press, 1987).

17. Gary B. Nash, "Up from the Bottom in Franklin's Philadelphia," *Past & Present* 77 (November 1977): 57–83; Nash, "Social Change and the Growth of Prerevolutionary Urban Radicalism," p. 10.

18. See Pauline Maier, "Coming to Terms with Samuel Adams," *American Historical Review* 81 (February 1976): 12–37; Eric Foner, *Tom Paine and Revolutionary America* (New York: Oxford University Press, 1976); Aleine Austin, *Matthew Lyon: "New Man" of the Democratic Revolution, 1749–1822* (University Park: Pennsylvania State University Press, 1981). One of the periodicals Lyon started was titled *The Scourge of Aristocracy (and Repository of Important Political Truths)*.

19. *Autobiography*, pp. 11, 78–80.

20. Ibid., pp. 88–89.

21. Ibid., p. 76.

22. Ibid., p. 1.

23. See William Pencak, "Benjamin Franklin's *Autobiography*, Cotton Mather, and a Puritan God," *Pennsylvania History* (January 1986): 1–25. Pencak notes, "Significantly, there is not one character in the entire book (the young Franklin included) who behaves admirably without being animated by religious faith" (p. 12).

24. *Autobiography*, p. 9.

25. Ibid., p. 2.

26. "Motion for Prayers in the Convention," June 28, 1787, in *WBF*, 9: 600–601.

27. Ibid., p. 601. Franklin repeated his belief in providence in a letter written shortly before his death. Benjamin Franklin to Ezra Stiles, March 9, 1790, in *WBF*, 10: 84.

28. "Motion for Prayers in the Convention," June 28, 1787, in *WBF*, 9: 600.

29. "Speech in the Convention, at the Conclusion of its Deliberations," September 17, 1787, in *WBF*, 9: 607–8.

30. Benjamin Franklin to Joseph Priestly, June 7, 1782, in *WBF*, 8: 451–53. Franklin's remark on pride in making war and shame in making love is one of his apparent borrowings from Montaigne. Robert Newcomb, "Franklin and Montaigne," *Modern Language Notes* 72 (November 1957): 489–91.

31. Benjamin Franklin to Sir Joseph Banks, July 27, 1783, in *WBF*, 9: 74.

32. *Autobiography*, p. 127.

33. Ibid., p. 116.

34. *Ben Franklin Laughing, Anecdotes from Original Sources by and about Benjamin Franklin*, ed. P. M. Zall (Berkeley: University of California Press, 1980), pp. 86, 91, 102.

35. *Autobiography*, p. 105.

36. Ibid., p. 35. For a similar discounting of human reason, see "An Arabian Tale," in *WBF*, 10: 124.

37. *Poor Richard*, 1747, in *PBF*, 3: 102.

38. Zall, ed., *Ben Franklin Laughing*, p. 147.

39. *Autobiography*, pp. 76–78. See, in particular, "Articles of Belief and Acts

of Religion," November 20, 1728, in PBF, 1: 101–9. Franklin did write or revise some works for others, including Abridgment of the Book of Common Prayer (1773). Benjamin Franklin to Granville Sharp, July 5, 1785, in WBF, 9: 358–59.

40. Benjamin Franklin to Jonathan Shipley, March 17, 1783, in WBF, 9: 23; "Speech in the Convention; on the Subject of Salaries," June 2, 1787, in WBF, 9: 591.

41. Benjamin Franklin to Messrs. The Abbés Chalut and Arnaud, April 17, 1787, in WBF, 9: 569.

42. "Observations on my Reading History in Library," May 9, 1731, in PBF, 1: 193.

43. "Speech in the Convention; on the Subject of Salaries," June 2, 1787, in WBF, 9: 591; "Speech in the Convention, at the Conclusion of its Deliberations," September 17, 1787, in WBF, 9: 607–8.

44. "Speech in the Convention; on the Subject of Salaries," June 2, 1787, in WBF, 9: 591, 594.

45. The Records of the Federal Convention of 1787, ed. Max Farrand, 4 vols. (New Haven: Yale University Press, 1911–1937), 2: 248, 249. Franklin's egalitarianism was here clashing with a classical republican view of political leadership, that poor men were more likely to succumb to the lures of corruption.

46. See Carl Van Doren, The Great Rehearsal, The Story of the Making and Ratifying of the Constitution of the United States (New York: Viking Press, 1948), pp. 141–43.

47. On the status of those lacking property and autonomy in the eighteenth century, see Edmund S. Morgan, "Slavery and Freedom: The American Paradox," Journal of American History 59 (June 1972): 5–29.

48. "Queries and Remarks Respecting Alterations in the Constitution of Pennsylvania," 1789, in WBF, 10:54.

49. Zall, ed., Ben Franklin Laughing, p. 163.

50. "Speech in the Convention, at the Conclusion of its Deliberations," September 17, 1787, in WBF, 9: 607–9.

51. Gordon S. Wood, The Creation of the American Republic, 1776–1787 (Chapel Hill: University of North Carolina Press for the Institute of Early American History and Culture, 1969), pp. 65–70; Lance Banning, The Jeffersonian Persuasion, Evolution of a Party Ideology (Ithaca, N.Y.: Cornell University Press, 1978), pp. 42–77.

52. James Madison, The Federalist No. 10, in Cooke, ed., The Federalist, p. 60.

53. Ibid. In the Federalist No. 57, Madison observed: "The aim of every political Constitution is or ought to be first to obtain for rulers, men who possess most wisdom to discern, and most virtue to pursue the common good of society; and in the next place, to take the most effectual precautions for keeping them virtuous, whilst they continue to hold their public trust" (p. 384).

54. On Madison's chilly worldview, see Kenneth A. Lockridge, Settlement and Unsettlement in Early America, The Crisis of Political Legitimacy before the Revolution (Cambridge: Cambridge University Press, 1981), pp. 112–21; Neal Riemer, "James Madison's Theory of the Self-Destructive Features of Republican Government," Ethics 65 (October 1954): 34–43.

55. James Madison, *The Federalist No. 10*, in Cooke, ed., *The Federalist*, p. 65.

56. On Pennsylvania's 1776 constitution, see Wood, *Creation of the American Republic*, pp. 226–37.

57. "Speech in the Convention, at the Conclusion of its Deliberations," September 17, 1787, in *WBF*, 9: 608–9.

58. Speech of June 20, 1788, in *The Papers of James Madison*, ed. Robert A. Rutland and Charles F. Hobson (Charlottesville: University Press of Virginia, 1977—), 11: 163. "PUBLIC opinion sets bounds to every government," Madison said in a newspaper essay, "and is the real sovereign in every free one" [Philadelphia] *National Gazette*, December 19, 1791.

59. James Madison to W. T. Barry, August 4, 1822, in *The Writings of James Madison*, ed. Gaillard Hunt, 9 vols. (New York: G. P. Putnam's Sons, 1900–1910), 9: 103.

60. See Adrienne Koch, *Jefferson & Madison, The Great Collaboration* (New York: Alfred A. Knopf, 1950). In addition to their services to the University of Virginia, both Madison and Jefferson proposed the creation of a national university, ibid., p. 257. Franklin, Madison, and Jefferson promoted freedom of the press, but maintained that personal libel was not necessarily protected. See Smith, *Printers and Press Freedom*, pp. 11–12, 84–86, 88–90, 163–67, and passim.

61. *Autobiography*, p. 72.

62. Stow Persons, "The Cyclical Theory of History in Eighteenth Century America," *American Quarterly* 6 (Summer 1954): 147–63; Peter Gay, *The Enlightenment: An Interpretation*, 2 vols. (New York: Alfred A. Knopf, 1966–1969), 2: 98–108; Banning, *The Jeffersonian Persuasion*, pp. 19–69.

63. Thomas Jefferson to James Madison, January 30, 1787, in *The Papers of Thomas Jefferson*, ed. Julian P. Boyd et al. (Princeton: Princeton University Press, 1950—   ), 11: 93.

64. Wood, *The Creation of the American Republic*, pp. 28–65.

65. The variety of secondary perspectives includes those of Ralph Ketcham, *Presidents Above Party, The First American Presidency, 1789–1829* (Chapel Hill: University of North Carolina Press for the Institute of Early American History and Culture, 1984); John P. Diggins, *The Lost Soul of American Politics, Virtue, Self-Interest, and the Foundations of Liberalism* (New York: Basic Books, 1984); John Ashworth, "The Jeffersonians: Classical Republicans or Liberal Capitalists," *Journal of American Studies* 18 (August 1984): 425–35; Drew McCoy, *The Elusive Republic, Political Economy in Jeffersonian America* (Chapel Hill: University of North Carolina Press for the Institute of Early American History and Culture, 1980), pp. 67–98; J. G. A. Pocock, "Virtue and Commerce in the Eighteenth Century," *Journal of Interdisciplinary History* 3 (Summer 1972): 119–34; Edmund S. Morgan, "The Puritan Ethic and the American Revolution," *William and Mary Quarterly*, 3rd ser., 24 (January 1967): 3–43.

66. See Joyce Appleby, *Capitalism and a New Social Order: The Republican Vision of the 1790s* (New York: New York University Press, 1984).

67. Ibid., pp. 40–50, 86–104. See also Joyce Appleby, "Commercial Farming and the 'Agrarian Myth' in the Early Republic," *Journal of American History* 68 (March 1982): 833–49.

68. Thomas Jefferson to John Adams, October 28, 1813, in *The Writings of Thomas Jefferson*, ed. Albert E. Bergh, 18 vols. (Washington, D. C.: Thomas Jefferson Memorial Association, 1907), 13: 395.

69. Thomas Jefferson to James Madison, December 20, 1787, in Boyd, ed., *The Papers of Thomas Jefferson*, 12: 442; Inaugural Address, March 4, 1801, in *The Works of Thomas Jefferson*, ed. Paul L. Ford, 12 vols. (New York: G. P. Putnam's Sons, 1904–1905), 9: 198.

70. Articles that attempt to resolve the issues of interpretation raised by Banning's idea of a "Jeffersonian persuasion" and Appleby's "liberal hypothesis" include John Ashworth, "The Jeffersonians: Classical Republicans or Liberal Capitalists?" *Journal of American Studies* 18 (August 1984): 425–35; Lance Banning, "Jeffersonian Ideology Revisited: Liberal and Classical Ideas in the New American Republic," *William and Mary Quarterly*, 3rd ser., 43 (January 1986): 3–19; Joyce Appleby, "Republicanism in Old and New Contexts," ibid., pp. 20–34; and James T. Kloppenberg, "The Virtues of Liberalism: Christianity, Republicanism, and Ethics in Early American Political Discourse," *Journal of American History* 74 (June 1987): 9–33.

71. Thomas Jefferson to Thomas Mann Randolph, Jr., May 30, 1790, in Boyd, ed., *The Papers of Thomas Jefferson*, 16: 449.

72. Thomas Jefferson, *Notes on the State of Virginia*, ed. William Peden (Chapel Hill: University of North Carolina Press for the Institute of Early American History and Culture, 1955), pp. 164–65.

73. Inaugural Address, March 4, 1801, in Ford, ed., *The Works of Thomas Jefferson*, 9: 195–98.

74. Charles O. Lerche, Jr., "Jefferson and the Election of 1800: A Case Study in the Political Smear," *William and Mary Quarterly*, 3rd ser., 5 (October 1948): 467–91.

75. See Banning, *The Jeffersonian Persuasion*, pp. 13–14, 273–74; Thomas Jefferson to Spencer Roane, September 6, 1819, in Ford, ed., *The Works of Thomas Jefferson*, 12: 136.

76. Inaugural Address, March 4, 1801, in Ford, ed., *The Works of Thomas Jefferson*, 9: 195.

77. Thomas Jefferson to James Madison, December 20, 1787, in Boyd, ed., *The Papers of Thomas Jefferson*, 12: 442.

78. Jefferson, *Notes on the State of Virginia*, pp. 148, 149, 165.

79. Thomas Jefferson to John Adams, October 28, 1813, in Bergh, ed., *The Writings of Thomas Jefferson*, 13: 396–97, 399, 402.

80. Jefferson, *Notes on the State of Virginia*, p. 165.

81. For somewhat differing assessments, see Appleby, *Capitalism and a New Social Order*, pp. 103–4, and Banning, *The Jeffersonian Persuasion*, pp. 273–302.

82. Thomas Jefferson to Jean Baptiste Say, February 1, 1804, in Bergh, ed., *The Writings of Thomas Jefferson*, 11: 3.

83. For an excellent review of Franklin's assumptions, see Drew McCoy, "Benjamin Franklin's Vision of a Republican Political Economy for America," *William and Mary Quarterly*, 3rd ser., 35 (October 1978): 605–28.

84. On the importance of using the press to recapture the "egalitarian polit-

ical idiom," see Gary B. Nash, "Also There at the Creation: Going beyond Gordon S. Wood," *William and Mary Quarterly*, 3rd ser., 44 (July 1987): 603, 607.

85. Inaugural Address, March 4, 1801, in Ford, ed., *The Works of Thomas Jefferson*, 9: 198.

Chapter 2

1. *Autobiography*, pp. 10–11; Benjamin Franklin to Samuel Mather, May 12, 1784, in WBF, 9: 208.

2. On Franklin's reading, see Arthur B. Tourtellot, *Benjamin Franklin, The Shaping of Genius, The Boston Years* (Garden City, N.Y.: Doubleday, 1977).

3. *Autobiography*, pp. 68, 89, 91.

4. *Diary and Autobiography of John Adams*, ed. L. H. Butterfield, 4 vols. (Cambridge: Belknap Press of Harvard University Press, 1961–1962), 2: 367. For recollections by Jefferson and Madison, see *Ben Franklin Laughing, Anecdotes from Original Sources by and about Benjamin Franklin*, ed. P. M. Zall (Berkeley: University of California Press, 1980), pp. 68, 76, 104, 122–23, 135–42, 274.

5. Butterfield, ed., *Diary and Autobiography of John Adams*, 2: 391.

6. Ibid., 4: 118–19. For a sketch of Adams as a classical republican, see Lance Banning, *The Jeffersonian Persuasion, Evolution of a Party Ideology* (Ithaca, N.Y.: Cornell University Press, 1978), pp. 94–100.

7. On the leveling effect in one state, see Edmund S. Morgan, *American Slavery, American Freedom, The Ordeal of Colonial Virginia* (New York: W. W. Norton, 1975), pp. 378–81.

8. James Madison, *The Federalist No. 52*, in Jacob E. Cooke, ed., *The Federalist* (Middletown, Conn.: Wesleyan University Press, 1961), pp. 352–53.

9. *Autobiography*, pp. 2, 74–75, 90–91, 117.

10. Gordon S. Wood, *The Creation of the American Republic, 1776–1787* (Chapel Hill: University of North Carolina Press for the Institute of Early American History and Culture, 1969), pp. 107–18, 413–25. Commenting on bribery and corruption in British politics while in England, for example, Franklin wrote, "Luxury introduces Necessity even among those that make the most splendid Figures here; this brings most of the Commons as well as Lords to Market; and if America would save for 3 or 4 Years the Money she spends in the Fashions and Fineries and Fopperies of this Country, she might buy the whole Parliament, Minister and all." Benjamin Franklin to Thomas Cushing, October 10, 1774, in PBF, 21: 329. See also, Benjamin Franklin to Joseph Galloway, March 21, 1770, in PBF, 17: 115–19.

11. *Autobiography*, p. 76; Benjamin Franklin to Benjamin Vaughan, July 26, 1784, in WBF, 9: 243–44, 246–47.

12. David Hume, "Of Refinement in the Arts," and "Of Commerce," in *David Hume's Political Essays*, ed. Charles W. Hendel (Indianapolis: Bobbs-Merrill, 1953), pp. 123–41; Alexander Hamilton, *The Federalist No. 11*, in Cooke, ed., *The Federalist*, pp. 65–73.

13. Joyce Appleby, *Capitalism and a New Social Order: The Republican Vision of the 1790s* (New York: New York University Press, 1984), pp. 79–105; Drew

McCoy, *The Elusive Republic, Political Economy in Jeffersonian America* (Chapel Hill: University of North Carolina Press for the Institute of Early American History and Culture, 1980), pp. 62–66, 80–83, 107–13, 132–35, 176–78.

14. Benjamin Franklin to Joshua Babcock, January 13, 1772, in *PBF*, 19: 7. See also Benjamin Franklin to Thomas Cushing, January 13, 1772, in *PBF*, 19: 22–23.

15. Alexis de Tocqueville, *Democracy in America*, trans. Henry Reeve and ed. Henry Steele Commager (New York: Oxford University Press, 1947), pp. 319–32.

16. *Autobiography*, pp. 7, 62–63, 65–66.

17. "Standing Queries for the Junto" [1732], in *PBF*, 1: 255–58; "Proposals and Queries to be Asked the Junto" [1732], in *PBF*, 1: 262.

18. "Standing Queries for the Junto" [1732], in *PBF*, 1: 255–59; *Autobiography*, pp. 61–63, 71–72, 101–3, 117; "On the Providence of God in the Government of the World" [1732], in *PBF*, 1: 264–69.

19. *Autobiography*, pp. 60, 61, 91–93.

20. Ibid., p. 93. On the role of virtue and on Franklin's leadership in diverse areas, see ibid., pp. 59, 63, 88–89, 101, 109–10, 129–30, 144–51.

21. Ibid., p. 14; *Poor Richard Improved*, 1750, in *PBF*, 3: 437.

22. *Autobiography*, p. 12; "On Literary Style," *PG*, August 2, 1733, in *PBF*, 1: 331. On Franklin's journalism as literature with a purpose, see James A. Sappenfield, *A Sweet Instruction, Franklin's Journalism as a Literary Apprenticeship* (Carbondale: Southern Illinois University Press, 1973); David M. Larson, "Benevolent Persuasion: The Art of Benjamin Franklin's Philanthropic Papers," *PMHB* 110 (April 1986): 195–217.

23. *Autobiography*, pp. 16–17; *NEC*, February 11, 1723, in *PBF*, 1: 49. On the troubles of James Franklin and other journalists with legislatures, see Jeffery A. Smith, "A Reappraisal of Legislative Privilege and American Colonial Journalism," *Journalism Quarterly* 61 (Spring 1984): 97–103, 141.

24. The Silence Dogood essays are reprinted in *PBF*, 1: 8–45. Passages quoted here are on pp. 10, 12, 13, and 23.

25. *Autobiography*, pp. 13–14; *The Spectator*, ed. Donald F. Bond, 5 vols. (Oxford: Oxford University Press, 1965), 1: 5, 44, 395.

26. *Autobiography*, p. 19; *NEC*, July 9, 1722, in *PBF*, 1:28, September 17, 1722.

27. *NEC*, February 11, 1723; *Autobiography*, pp. 17, 18–20. On the *Courant*, see Jeffery A. Smith, *Printers and Press Freedom: The Ideology of Early American Journalism* (New York: Oxford University Press, 1988), pp. 97–106.

28. *Autobiography*, pp. 19–21; *NEC*, April 16, 1722, in *PBF*, 1:13. See Bruce Granger, "The Addisonian Essay in the American Revolution," *Studies in the Literary Imagination* 9 (Fall 1976): 43–52; Bruce Granger, *Benjamin Franklin, An American Man of Letters*, new ed. (Norman: University of Oklahoma Press, 1976).

29. *American Weekly Mercury*, February 4, 1729, in *PBF*, 1: 115, 116; *American Weekly Mercury*, February 25, 1729, in *PBF*, 1: 122; J. A. Leo Lemay, "Franklin's Suppressed 'Busy-Body,' " *American Literature* 37 (November 1965): 307–11; *A Modest Enquiry into the Nature and Necessity of a Paper-Currency*, in *PBF*, 1: 139–57; *Autobiography*, p. 67.

30. John R. Aiken, "Benjamin Franklin, Karl Marx, and the Labor Theory of Value," *PMHB* 110 (July 1966): 378–84.

31. A *Modest Enquiry*, in *PBF*, 1: 148–50.

32. *Autobiography*, p. 66; Thomas Wendel, "The Keith–Lloyd Alliance: Factional and Coalition Politics in Colonial Pennsylvania," *PMHB* 92 (July 1968): 289–305; *Votes and Proceedings of the House of Representatives of the Province of Pennsylvania*, 6 vols. (Philadelphia: Franklin and Hall, 1752–1776), 2: 335.

33. Wendel, "The Keith–Lloyd Alliance," pp. 295–304; *Autobiography*, pp. 28, 34, 39, 42. For background, see Gary B. Nash, *The Urban Crucible, Social Change, Political Consciousness, and the Origins of the American Revolution* (Cambridge: Harvard University Press, 1979), pp. 148–56.

34. *Autobiography*, pp. 63–64; *American Weekly Mercury*, February 18, 1729, in *PBF*, 1: 121.

35. *Autobiography*, p. 64; *PG*, October 2, 1729, in *PBF*, 1: 158–59; *PG*, October 9, 1729, in *PBF*, 1: 160.

36. *Autobiography*, pp. 64–68; *PG*, August 2, 1736, in *PBF*, 2: 159; "Articles of Agreement with Thomas Whitmarsh," September 13, 1731, in *PBF*, 1: 205–8; "Advice to a Young Tradesman," July 21, 1748, in *PBF*, 3: 306, 308.

37. *Autobiography*, p. 94; *PG*, February 11, 1735, in *PBF*, 2: 15–19; *PG*, February 18, 1735, *PBF*, 2: 19–21.

38. *Autobiography*, pp. 94, 122; *PG*, October 22, 1730, in *PBF*, 1: 182–83; *PG*, June 10, 1731, in *PBF*, 1: 195, 196, 197. On the content of the paper, see Charles E. Clark and Charles Wetherell, "The Measure of Maturity: The *Pennsylvania Gazette*, 1728–1765," *William and Mary Quarterly*, 3rd ser., 46 (April 1989): 279–303. Franklin may well have inspired later journalists with the idea of using the press to exert influence for the good. Among them was Henry Luce, founder of *Time* and *Life* and an admirer of Franklin's autobiography. See James L. Baughman, *Henry Luce and the Rise of the American News Media* (Boston: Twayne, 1987), pp. 14, 22.

39. *Autobiography*, p. 95; *American Weekly Mercury*, February 25, 1729, in *PBF*, 1: 122; *American Weekly Mercury*, February 18, 1729, in *PBF*, 1: 121; *Poor Richard*, 1733, in *PBF*, 1: 311; *Poor Richard*, 1734, in *PBF*, 1: 350–51; *Poor Richard*, 1733, in *PBF*, 1: 313; *PG*, November 13, 1740, in *PBF*, 2: 264.

40. *PG*, November 16, 1733, in *PBF*, 1: 333–38; *PG*, August 6, 1741, in *PBF*, 2: 327.

41. *PG*, November 17, 24, December 1, 8, 1737.

42. *PG*, April 1, 8, 15, 22, 1736.

43. *Autobiography*, pp. 21, 32–33, 45–46, 53, 56, 64, 65, 101–2, 120–21; *PG*, December 7, 1732, in *PBF*, 1: 278; *NEC*, September 10, 1722, in *PBF*, 1: 39–41; *PG*, January 13, 1737, in *PBF*, 2: 173–78; *Poor Richard*, 1733, in *PBF*, 1: 317.

44. *Autobiography*, pp. 93, 94.

45. Ibid., p. 95; Merton A. Christensen, "Franklin on the Hemphill Trial: Deism Versus Presbyterian Orthodoxy," *William and Mary Quarterly*, 3rd ser., 10 (July 1953): 422–40; *Plain Truth*, 1747, in *PBF*, 3: 180–204; Smith, *Printers and Press Freedom*, pp. 129–36.

46. *PG*, April 1, 1736. On Franklin's partners, see Smith, *Printers and Press Freedom*, pp. 124–41.

Chapter 3

1. *Autobiography*, p. 119.
2. Ibid., p. 120; Benjamin Franklin to Cadwallader Colden, September 29, 1748, in *PBF*, 3: 318; Benjamin Franklin to Cadwallader Colden, October 11, 1750, in *PBF*, 4: 68.
3. See Russell F. Weigley, ed., *Philadelphia, A 300-Year History* (New York: W. W. Norton, 1982), pp. 1–2, 43, 47, 100, 108; Frederick B. Tolles, *Meeting House and Counting House, The Quaker Merchants of Colonial Philadelphia, 1682–1763* (Chapel Hill: University of North Carolina Press for the Institute of Early American History and Culture, 1948).
4. Jeffery A. Smith, *Printers and Press Freedom: The Ideology of Early American Journalism* (New York: Oxford University Press, 1988), pp. 108–41.
5. *Autobiography*, pp. 134, 167.
6. Ibid., pp. 133, 156–57; Benjamin Franklin to Peter Collinson, November 5, 1756, in *PBF*, 7: 14.
7. *Autobiography*, pp. 156–57.
8. Ibid., p. 132.
9. "The Morals of Chess," 1779, in *WBF*, 7: 357–62.
10. Claude-Anne Lopez and Eugenia W. Herbert, *The Private Franklin, The Man and His Family* (New York: W. W. Norton, 1975), pp. 133–46. On Bache and his business affairs, see Eugenia W. Herbert, "A Note on Richard Bache (1737–1811)," *PMHB* 100 (January 1976): 97–103.
11. Deborah Franklin to Benjamin Franklin, October 4, 1769, in *PBF*, 16: 213; Deborah Franklin to Benjamin Franklin, August 16, 1770, in *PBF*, 17: 205–7; Benjamin Franklin to Deborah Franklin, June 10, 1770, in *PBF*, 17: 166; Benjamin Franklin to Jane Mecom, January 13, 1772, in *PBF*, 19: 29.
12. Deborah Franklin to Benjamin Franklin, December 13, 1769, in *PBF*, 16: 262; Deborah Franklin to Benjamin Franklin, June 13, 1770, in *PBF*, 17: 175; Deborah Franklin to Benjamin Franklin, March 30, 1771, in *PBF*, 18: 63.
13. Deborah Franklin to Benjamin Franklin, August 16, 1770, in *PBF*, 17: 205–7; Sarah Bache to Benjamin Franklin, January 2, 1774, in *PBF*, 21: 5.
14. Deborah Franklin to Benjamin Franklin, October 14, 1770, in *PBF*, 17: 252, 254; Deborah Franklin to Benjamin Franklin, June 30, 1772, in *PBF*, 19: 193; Deborah Franklin to Benjamin Franklin, October 29, 1773, in *PBF*, 20: 450.
15. Benjamin Franklin to Deborah Franklin, September 1, 1773, in *PBF*, 20: 383.
16. "Reply to Coffee-House Orators," April 9, 1767, in *Benjamin Franklin's Letters to the Press, 1758–1775*, ed. Verner W. Crane (Chapel Hill: University of North Carolina Press for the Institute of Early American History and Culture, 1950), p. 83.
17. Benjamin Franklin to Deborah Franklin, August 14, 1771, in *PBF*, 18: 204–5.

18. See Eugene F. Miller, "On the American Founders' Defense of Liberal Education in a Republic," *Review of Politics* 46 (January 1984): 65–90.

19. Benjamin Rush, *A Plan for the Establishment of Public Schools and the Diffusion of Knowledge in Pennsylvania; To Which Are Added Thoughts upon the Mode of Education, Proper in a Republic* (Philadelphia: Printed for Thomas Dobson, 1786), pp. 20–21, 27.

20. *Poor Richard,* 1752, in *PBF,* 4: 247; *Poor Richard,* 1739, in *PBF,* 2: 221.

21. Benjamin Franklin to Deborah Franklin, October 3, 1770, in *PBF,* 17: 239; Sarah Bache to Benjamin Franklin, October 30, 1773, in *PBF,* 20: 453.

22. Benjamin Franklin to Deborah Franklin, February 2, 1773, in *PBF,* 20: 34.

23. Benjamin Franklin to Deborah Franklin, July 4, 1771, in *PBF,* 18: 162; Benjamin Franklin to Richard Bache, October 7, 1772, in *PBF,* 19: 314.

24. Benjamin Franklin to Deborah Franklin, August 17, 1771, in *PBF,* 18: 208.

25. Benjamin Franklin to Sarah Bache, April 6, 1773, in *PBF,* 20: 142.

26. Benjamin Franklin to Deborah Franklin, August 22, 1772, in *PBF,* 19: 274.

27. Benjamin Franklin to William Franklin, August 16, 1784, in *WBF,* 9: 252.

28. Franklin's Last Will and Testament, 1788, in *WBF,* 10: 494.

29. Codicil, 1789, in *WBF,* 10: 503–7. On the use of the money, see Carl Van Doren, *Benjamin Franklin* (New York: Viking Press, 1938), pp. 763–64.

30. Benjamin Franklin to Sarah Bache, January 26, 1784, in *WBF,* 9: 161. On the public reaction to the Cincinnati, see Merrill Jensen, *The New Nation, A History of the United States During the Confederation, 1781–1789* (New York: Vintage Books, 1950), pp. 260–65.

31. *The Diary and Letters of His Excellency Thomas Hutchinson, Esq.,* ed. Peter O. Hutchinson, 2 vols. (London: Low, Marston, Searle, and Rivington, 1883–1886), 2: 237; Franklin's Last Will and Testament, 1788, in *WBF,* 10: 496; Lopez and Herbert, *The Private Franklin,* pp. 306–7.

32. See, e.g., Benjamin Franklin to Deborah Franklin, February 2, 1773, April 6, 1773, in *PBF,* 20: 34, 145.

33. Benjamin Franklin to Richard Bache, December 1, 1772, in *PBF,* 19: 394.

34. Benjamin Franklin to Sarah Bache, January 26, 1784, in *WBF,* 9: 166–67.

35. See Peter Gay, *The Enlightenment: An Interpretation,* 2 vols. (New York: Alfred A. Knopf, 1966–1969), 2: 501–522.

36. For discussions of changes in educational philosophy, see J. H. Plumb, "The New World of Children in Eighteenth-Century England," *Past and Present* No. 67 (May 1975): 64–95; Jacqueline S. Reinier, "Rearing the Republican Child: Attitudes and Practices in Post-Revolutionary Philadelphia," *William and Mary Quarterly,* 3rd ser., 39 (January 1982): 150–63.

37. Benjamin Rush, *A Plan for the Establishment of Public Schools and Diffusion of Knowledge in Pennsylvania,* 1786, in Wilson Smith, ed., *Theories of Education in Early America, 1655–1819* (Indianapolis: Bobbs-Merrill, 1973), pp. 248, 249. Rush's

statement on subordination echoes the sentiments of Lord Kames, *Loose Hints Upon Education, Chiefly Concerning the Culture of the Heart,* 1781, ibid., p. 135.

38. See David M. Post, "Jeffersonian Revisions of Locke: Education, Property Rights, and Liberty," *Journal of the History of Ideas* 47 (January-March 1986): 147–57.

39. Benjamin Franklin to Samuel Johnson, August 23, 1750, in *PBF,* 4: 41.

40. Benjamin Franklin to Samuel Johnson, August 23, 1750, in *PBF,* 4: 41.

41. Kames, *Loose Hints Upon Education,* in Smith, ed., *Theories of Education in Early America,* pp. 133, 137–39.

42. Locke wrote: "A Sound Mind in a sound Body, is a short, but full Description of a happy State in this World." John Locke, *Some Thoughts Concerning Education,* ed. R. H. Quick (Cambridge: The University Press, 1913), p. 1.

43. *Proposals Relating to the Education of Youth in Pennsylvania,* 1749, in *PBF,* 3: 399–419.

44. *Autobiography,* p. 119; *Paper on the Academy,* in *PBF,* 4: 35; *Observations Relative to the Intentions of the Original Founders of the Academy in Philadelphia,* June 1789, in *WBF,* 10: 29. See Jurgen Herbst, *From Crisis to Crisis, American College Government, 1636–1819* (Cambridge: Harvard University Press, 1982), pp. 88–96, 176–83.

45. Benjamin Franklin to William Franklin, July 14, 1773, in *PBF,* 20: 311–12.

46. On Temple's early life and education, see Lopez and Herbert, *The Private Franklin,* pp. 93, 98, 151–53; Willard S. Randall, *A Little Revenge, Benjamin Franklin and his Son* (Boston: Little, Brown, and Co., 1984), pp. 169–70, 315–17.

47. Benjamin Franklin to William Temple Franklin, June 13, 1775, in *PBF,* 22: 65.

48. Benjamin Franklin to Richard Bache, September 30, 1774, in *PBF,* 21: 325–26. Paine's intention was to begin an academy in Philadelphia.

49. Benjamin Franklin to Thomas Paine, September 27, 1785, in *WBF,* 9: 467–68.

50. See J. A. Leo Lemay, "The American Aesthetic of Franklin's Visual Creations," *PMHB* 111 (October 1987): 465–99.

51. "Report of the Committee," in *The Papers of Thomas Jefferson,* ed. Julian P. Boyd et al. (Princeton: Princeton University Press, 1950—   ), 1: 496.

52. Benjamin Franklin to Joseph Priestly, July 7, 1775, in *PBF,* 22: 92–93.

53. Benjamin Franklin to Lord Howe, July 20, 1776, in *PBF,* 22: 520.

54. Both Benjamin and William agreed that Temple should be trained in the law, but the grandfather was in the habit of making decisions for the boy. Benjamin Franklin to William Franklin, August 1, 1774, in *PBF,* 21: 266; William Franklin to Benjamin Franklin, December 24, 1774, in *PBF,* 21: 404; Benjamin Franklin to William Temple Franklin, June 13, 1775, in *PBF,* 22: 64.

55. Benjamin Franklin to William Temple Franklin, September 19, 1776, in *PBF,* 22: 612–13.

56. Benjamin Franklin to William Franklin, August 16, 1784, in *WBF,* 9: 252.

57. Benjamin Franklin to William Temple Franklin, September 19, 1776, in *PBF,* 22: 612–13; William Temple Franklin to Benjamin Franklin, September 21,

1776, in *PBF*, 22: 620–21; Benjamin Franklin to William Temple Franklin, September 22, 1776, in *PBF*, 22: 622; Benjamin Franklin to William Temple Franklin, September 28, 1776, in *PBF*, 22: 634. On the military situation, see Robert Middlekauf, *The Glorious Cause, The American Revolution, 1763–1789* (New York: Oxford University Press, 1982), pp. 336–49.

58. "Sketch of the Services of B. Franklin to the United States of America," in *WBF*, 9: 696; Benjamin Franklin to Silas Deane, December 7, 1776, in *PBF*, 23: 30; Benjamin Franklin to Mary Hewson, January 12, 1777, in *PBF*, 23: 156; Benjamin Franklin to Mary Hewson, July 8, 1775, in *PBF*, 22: 100.

59. Benjamin Franklin to Mr. and Mrs. Richard Bache, May 10, 1785, in *WBF*, 9: 327; "Sketch of the Services of B. Franklin to the United States of America," in *WBF*, 9: 696; "From the Little Journal," in *Benjamin Franklin's Autobiographical Writings*, ed. Carl Van Doren (New York: Viking Press, 1948), p. 422.

60. Benjamin Franklin to Jane Mecom, December 8, 1776, in *The Letters of Benjamin Franklin & Jane Mecom*, ed. Carl Van Doren (Princeton: Princeton University Press for the American Philosophical Society, 1950), p. 168.

61. Jane Mecom to Benjamin Franklin, December 15, 1776, in Van Doren, ed., *The Letters of Benjamin Franklin & Jane Mecom*, p. 169.

62. Benjamin Franklin to Jane Mecom, October 5, 1777, in Van Doren, ed., *The Letters of Benjamin Franklin & Jane Mecom*, pp. 171–72. On Franklin's accommodations, which were provided by the merchant Jacques-Donatien Le Ray de Chaumont, see John Bigelow, "Franklin's Home and Host in France," *Century Magazine* 35 (March 1888): 741–54.

63. A. Owen Aldridge, *Voltaire and the Century of Light* (Princeton: Princeton University Press, 1975), pp. 399–400. Various accounts of this meeting exist, some of which suggest that Voltaire blessed Franklin's other grandson, but the versions seem to agree that it was a young child rather than the fully grown Temple. Prof. Aldridge's opinion that it was Benny Bache appears to be the most authoritative. See Alfred O. Aldridge, "Benjamin Franklin and the Philosophes," *Studies on Voltaire and the Eighteenth Century* 24 (1963): 46–48. He had concluded earlier that the grandson involved was Temple. Alfred O. Aldridge, *Franklin and his French Contemporaries* (New York: New York University Press, 1957), pp. 9–10. The boy is identified as Benny in Claude-Anne Lopez, *Mon Cher Papa, Franklin and the Ladies of Paris* (New Haven: Yale University Press, 1966), p. 15. An alternate explanation is that both grandsons received Voltaire's blessing, but at different times, and that Voltaire said to Bache, "Liberty and Equality." Willis Steell, *Benjamin Franklin of Paris, 1776–1785* (New York: Minton, Balch & Co., 1928), pp. 123–24.

64. Hutchinson, ed., *The Diary and Letters of His Excellency Thomas Hutchinson, Esq.*, 2: 276.

65. Sarah Bache to Benjamin Franklin, February 23, 1777, in *PBF*, 23: 362.

66. Richard Bache to Benjamin Franklin, November 5, 1783, APS.

67. Benjamin Franklin to Richard Bache, May 22, 1777, in *PBF*, 24: 63.

68. Richard Bache to Benjamin Franklin, January 31, 1778, in *PBF*, 25: 553.

69. *Diary and Autobiography of John Adams*, ed. L. H. Butterfield, 4 vols. (Cambridge: Belknap Press of Harvard University Press, 1961–1962), 4: 58.

70. Butterfield, ed., *Diary and Autobiography of John Adams*, 4: 118–19, 120. See also p. 59. On Franklin's friends, see Lopez, *Mon Cher Papa*; Bruce Gustafson, "The Music of Madame Brillon," *MLA Notes* 43 (March 1987): 522–43. On Helvétius, see D. W. Smith, *Helvétius, A Study in Persecution* (London: Oxford University Press, 1965). On the lack of evidence that Franklin had sexual encounters with French women, see Lopez and Herbert, *The Private Franklin*, pp. 274–75.

71. Benjamin Franklin to Robert R. Livingston, July 22, 1783, in *WBF*, 9: 62.

72. Benjamin Franklin to William Carmichael, April 12, 1781, in *WBF*, 8: 237. On the relationship of Adams and Franklin, see William B. Evans, "John Adams' Opinion of Benjamin Franklin," *Pennsylvania Magazine of History and Biography* 92 (April 1968): 220–38. On their diplomacy, see Jonathan R. Dull, *A Diplomatic History of the American Revolution* (New Haven: Yale University Press, 1985); James H. Hutson, *John Adams and the Diplomacy of the American Revolution* (Lexington: The University Press of Kentucky, 1980). On the repercussions of Franklin's relations with American diplomats, see H. James Henderson, "Congressional Factionalism and the Attempt to Recall Benjamin Franklin," *William and Mary Quarterly*, 3rd ser., 27 (April 1970): 246–67.

73. See "Dialogue Between the Gout and Mr. Franklin," 1780, in Richard E. Amacher, *Franklin's Wit & Folly, The Bagatelles* (New Brunswick: Rutgers University Press, 1953), pp. 32–41.

74. For differing assessments of the captain's involvement, see Samuel Eliot Morison, *John Paul Jones, A Sailor's Biography* (Boston: Little, Brown and Co., 1959), pp. 123, 174, 185–86; Lopez, *Mon Cher Papa*, p. 129.

75. Benjamin Franklin to John Quincy Adams, April 21, 1779, in *WBF*, 7: 289. See also, Benjamin Franklin to Jane Mecom, April 22, 1779, in Van Doren, ed., *The Letters of Benjamin Franklin & Jane Mecom*, p. 191.

76. Benjamin Franklin to Richard Bache, June 2, 1779, in *WBF*, 7: 346; Benjamin Franklin to Sally Bache, March 16, 1780, APS; Benjamin Franklin to Samuel Cooper, December 9, 1780, Yale.

Chapter 4

1. James Madison, *The Federalist No. 10*, in Jacob E. Cooke ed., *The Federalist* (Middletown, Conn.: Wesleyan University Press, 1961), p. 62; see also *The Federalist No. 39*, p. 251.

2. James Madison, *The Federalist No. 10*, in Cooke, ed., *The Federalist*, p. 58.

3. *The Complete Writings of Thomas Paine*, ed. Philip S. Foner, 2 vols. (New York: The Citadel Press, 1945), 1: 370.

4. See Isaac Kramnick, "The 'Great National Discussion': The Discourse of Politics in 1787," *William and Mary Quarterly*, 3rd ser., 45 (January 1988): 3–32.

5. "Petition from Inhabitants of Kentucky" [January 2, 1784], in *The Papers of Thomas Jefferson*, ed. Julian P. Boyd et al. (Princeton: Princeton University Press, 1950–   ), 6: 553.

6. Thomas Jefferson to James Madison, October 20, 1785, in Boyd, ed., *The Papers of Thomas Jefferson*, 8: 681–82.

7. James Madison to Thomas Jefferson, June 19, 1786, in Boyd, ed., *The Papers of Thomas Jefferson*, 9: 659–60.

8. Drew McCoy, *The Elusive Republic, Political Economy in Jeffersonian America* (Chapel Hill: University of North Carolina Press for the Institute of Early American History and Culture, 1980), pp. 121–32.

9. *The Records of the Federal Convention of 1787*, ed. Max Farrand, 4 vols. (New Haven: Yale University Press, 1911–1937), 1: 422–23.

10. Farrand, ed., *Records of the Federal Convention of 1787*, 1: 410, 424, 431, 432.

11. See David D. Raphael, *Adam Smith* (Oxford: Oxford University Press, 1985), pp. 3, 20–21, 81–83; Ronald L. Meek, *The Economics of Physiocracy, Essays and Translations* (Cambridge: Harvard University Press, 1963); Martin Albaum, "The Moral Defense of the Physiocrats' Laissez-Faire," *Journal of the History of Ideas* 16 (April 1955): 170–97.

12. Alfred O. Aldridge, *Franklin and his French Contemporaries* (New York: New York University Press, 1957), pp. 23–31; Thomas D. Eliot, "The Relations Between Adam Smith and Benjamin Franklin Before 1776," *Political Science Quarterly* 39 (1924): 67–96.

13. Benjamin Franklin to Cadwallader Evans, February 20, 1768, in *PBF*, 15: 52. See also "Remarks on Agriculture and Manufacturing" [late 1771?], in *PBF*, 18: 273–74.

14. Benjamin Franklin to Jean-Baptiste LeRoy, January 31, 1769, in *PBF*, 16: 34. See also Benjamin Franklin to George Whatley, May 18, 1787, in *WBF*, 9: 588.

15. Benjamin Franklin to Robert Livingston, July 22, 1783, in *WBF*, 9: 63. See also Benjamin Franklin to John Adams, May 19, 1781, in *WBF*, 8: 261.

16. McCoy, *The Elusive Republic*, p. 186.

17. E. P. Thompson, "The Moral Economy of the English Crowd in the Eighteenth Century," *Past & Present*, No. 50 (February 1971): 76–136.

18. *Common Sense*, in P. Foner, ed., *The Complete Writings of Thomas Paine*, 1: 18, 20–21.

19. Merrill D. Peterson, "Thomas Jefferson and Commercial Policy, 1783–1793," *William and Mary Quarterly*, 3rd ser., 22 (October 1965): 584–610.

20. See, e.g., Benjamin Franklin to Jared Eliot, December 24, 1751, in *PBF*, 4: 221–22. On the basis of a letter mistakenly attributed to Franklin, some historians have assumed that he had a farm in New Jersey. See [to Jared Eliot, c. 1749], in *PBF*, 3: 436.

21. Thomas Jefferson, *Notes on the State of Virginia*, ed. William Peden (Chapel Hill: University of North Carolina Press for the Institute of Early American History and Culture, 1955), p. 165. A similar point about Franklin's seeing the possibility of morality in nonagricultural workers is made in Ralph Ketcham, *Presidents Above Party, The First American Presidency, 1789–1829* (Chapel Hill: University of North Carolina Press for the Institute of Early American History and Culture, 1984), pp. 180–81.

190

22. Benjamin Franklin to Richard Bache, June 2, 1779, in *WBF*, 7: 345.
23. On Temple's activities, see Claude-Anne Lopez and Eugenia W. Herbert, *The Private Franklin, The Man and His Family* (New York: W. W. Norton, 1975), pp. 213–14, 233–48, 272–73, 307–10.
24. Thomas Jefferson to James Monroe, July 5, 1785, in Boyd ed., *The Papers of Thomas Jefferson*, 8: 262.
25. Benjamin Franklin to Richard Bache, June 2, 1779, in *WBF*, 7: 345–46.
26. Lucien Cramer, *Une Famille Genevoise, Les Cramer* (Geneva: Librairie E. Droz, 1952), p. 60; Benjamin Franklin to Philibert Cramer, August 19, 1779, in *WBF*, 7: 369–70. For a former student's detailed description of the school and city at this time, see Albert Gallatin to Eben Dodge, January 21, 1847, in *The Writings of Albert Gallatin*, ed. Henry Adams, 3 vols. (New York: J. B. Lippincott, 1879; reprint ed., New York: Antiquarian Press, 1960), 2: 638–50.
27. Benjamin Franklin to Benjamin Franklin Bache, May 3, 1779, Yale; Benjamin Franklin to Benjamin Franklin Bache, August 19, 1779, in *WBF*, 7: 368.
28. Benjamin Franklin Bache to Benjamin Franklin, May 30, 1779, APS.
29. Benjamin Franklin to Benjamin Franklin Bache, August 19, 1779, in *WBF*, 7: 369.
30. Gabriel Louis de Marignac to Benjamin Franklin, November 20, 1781, Yale.
31. Franklin's use of reward psychology extended beyond his family, as he demonstrated in listing contributors in his pamphlet on the Philadelphia Hospital. *Some Account of the Pennsylvania Hospital*, in *PBF*, 5: 327–30. See also, Terry J. Knapp and Susan A. Shodahl, "Ben Franklin as a Behavior Modifier: A Note," *Behavior Therapy* 5 (1974): 656–60.
32. John Locke, *Some Thoughts Concerning Education*, ed R. H. Quick (Cambridge: The University Press, 1913), p. 133.
33. See, e.g., Bache's letters of December 21, 1779, March 25, May 6, May 30, 1780, APS.
34. Benjamin Franklin Bache to Benjamin Franklin, June 5, 1780, APS.
35. Benjamin Franklin Bache to Benjamin Franklin, July 18, 1780, APS.
36. Benjamin Franklin to Benjamin Franklin Bache, January 25, 1782, in *WBF*, 8: 372.
37. Benjamin Franklin to Benjamin Franklin Bache, April 16, 1781, APS.
38. Benjamin Franklin to Benjamin Franklin Bache, September 25, 1780, as quoted in Lopez and Herbert, *The Private Franklin*, p. 228.
39. Benjamin Franklin to Benjamin Franklin Bache, January 25, 1782, in *WBF*, 8: 372–73.
40. William Temple Franklin to Benjamin Franklin Bache, January 24, 1782, Society Collection, HSP.
41. Benjamin Franklin to Sarah Bache, June 3, 1779, in *WBF*, 7: 347, 349.
42. Benjamin Franklin Bache to Benjamin Franklin, January 30, 1783, Franklin Papers, HSP; Benjamin Franklin to Benjamin Franklin Bache, May 2, 1783, APS.
43. See, e.g., the Bache to Franklin letters of March 25, May 6, May 30, July 18, September 20, October 17, November 26, 1780, APS.

44. Madame Cramer to Benjamin Franklin, January 10, 1780, in Cramer, *Une Famille Genevoise, Les Cramer,* p. 61. On Bache's relationship with Marignac, see Samuel Powel Griffitts to Benjamin Franklin, October 6, 1782, Franklin Papers, HSP.

45. Madame Cramer to Benjamin Franklin, May 15, 1781, APS. See also, Madame Cramer to Benjamin Franklin, December 10, 1781, Franklin Papers, University of Pennsylvania.

46. On the daily routine at the school, see Cramer, *Une Famille Genevoise, Les Cramer,* p. 61.

47. Benjamin Franklin Bache to Benjamin Franklin, September 20, 1780, APS.

48. *Autobiography,* pp. 1, 87.

49. Benjamin Franklin to James Hutton, February 1, 12, 1778, in WBF, 7: 98–99, 101.

50. For the "erratum" metaphor, see *Autobiography,* pp. 20, 34, 43, 45, 65, 71.

51. Benjamin Franklin to Sarah Bache, June 3, 1779, in WBF, 7: 347.

52. Studies include John Brewer, *Party Ideology and Popular Politics at the Accession of George III* (Cambridge: Cambridge University Press, 1976); Nicholas Hans, "Franklin, Jefferson, and the English Radicals at the End of the Eighteenth Century," *Proceedings of the American Philosophical Society* 98 (December 1954): 406–21; Robert Darnton, *The Literary Underground of the Old Regime* (Cambridge: Harvard University Press, 1982); Claude Manceron, *The Wind from America, 1778–1781,* trans. Nancy Amphoux (New York: Alfred A. Knopf, 1978); Claude Manceron, *Their Gracious Pleasure, 1782–1785,* trans. Nancy Amphoux (New York: Alfred A. Knopf, 1980).

53. *Ben Franklin Laughing, Anecdotes from Original Sources by and about Benjamin Franklin,* ed. P. M. Zall (Berkeley: University of California Press, 1980), pp. 142–43.

54. Benjamin Franklin to Lord Howe, July 20, 1776, in PBF, 22: 520, 521.

55. *A Modest Enquiry into the Nature and Necessity of a Paper-Currency,* April 3, 1729, in PBF, 1: 155.

56. *Observations Concerning the Increase of Mankind,* 1751, in PBF, 4: 225–34.

57. *The Interest of Great Britain Considered,* 1760, in PBF, 9: 73. Here, as he did in his *Observations* and elsewhere, Franklin accepted the observation made by Hume and others, that sparsely populated places relied on hunting, moderately populated places on pasturing and farming, and heavily populated places on manufacturing. PBF, 9: 73–74.

58. Benjamin Franklin to Joseph Galloway, February 25, 1775, in PBF, 21: 509–10.

59. See, e.g., "On the Price of Corn, and Management of the Poor," November 29, 1766, in PBF, 13: 512–16; Benjamin Franklin to Joshua Babcock, January 13, 1772, in PBF, 19: 7; Benjamin Franklin to Thomas Cushing, January 13, 1772, in PBF, 19: 22–23.

60. See, e.g., Benjamin Franklin to Timothy Folger, September 29, 1769,

in *PBF*, 16: 208–10; Benjamin Franklin to Joseph Galloway, March 21, 1770, in *PBF*, 17: 118.

61. "Note Respecting Trade and Manufactures," July 7, 1767, in *PBF*, 14: 212.

62. For an example of Franklin's vision of the country's expansion into new agricultural regions, see "A Plan for Settling Two Western Colonies," 1754, in *PBF*, 5: 457, 462. For Franklin's view that Americans would thrive from the use of the land and sea, "the true Sources of Wealth and Plenty," if they did not waste money on British "Gewgaws," see Benjamin Franklin to Timothy Folger, September 29, 1769, in *PBF*, 16: 209.

63. Benjamin Franklin to Thomas Percival, October 15, 1773, in *PBF*, 20: 443.

64. "Positions to be Examined," April 4, 1769, in *PBF*, 16: 109. On the publication history of this essay, see Aldridge, *Franklin and his French Contemporaries*, pp. 27–28.

65. "On the Price of Corn, and Management of the Poor," in *PBF*, 13: 512–15.

66. *Advice to a Young Tradesman*, July 21, 1748, in *PBF*, 3: 306–7.

67. *Poor Richard*, 1736, in *PBF*, 2: 140.

68. *Poor Richard Improved*, 1758, in *PBF*, 7: 326–50.

69. *Comparison of Great Britain and America as to Credit, in 1777*, in *PBF*, 24: 508–14.

70. *Information to Those Who Would Remove to America*, in *WBF*, 8: 603–14.

71. Benjamin Franklin to Richard Oswald, January 14, 1783, in *WBF*, 9: 3–7; Benjamin Franklin to David Hartley, May 8, 1783, in *WBF*, 9: 40–41.

72. "Recommendation of a Galley Slave," May 22, 1783, in *WBF*, 9: 46; Pierre-André Gargaz, *A Project of Universal and Perpetual Peace* (New York: George Simpson Eddy, 1922), pp. 8, 11–12. In a somewhat similar vein, one of Franklin's friends proposed an office of peace. See Sidney Kaplan, ed., "A Plan of a Peace Office for the United States by Benjamin Rush," *Massachusetts Review* 25 (Summer 1984): 269–84.

73. Benjamin Franklin to Mary Hewson, September 7, 1783, in *WBF*, 9: 91.

74. Benjamin Franklin to Robert R. Livingston, April 15, 1783, in *WBF*, 9: 34; Benjamin Franklin to the Earl of Buchan, March 17, 1783, in *WBF*, 9: 21. For a similar recital of advantages, see Benjamin Franklin to [?], n.d., in *WBF*, 9: 150.

75. Benjamin Franklin to the Marquis de Lafayette, April 17, 1787, in *WBF*, 9: 571. On Temple's brief career in agriculture and later life, see Lopez and Herbert, *The Private Franklin*, pp. 286–87, 308–10.

76. Benjamin Franklin Bache to Benjamin Franklin, June 30, September 12, 1781, APS.

77. Benjamin Franklin Bache to Benjamin Franklin, May 26, 1781, July 27, 1782, APS. Franklin, in turn, gave assurances to Benny's parents. Franklin to Richard and Sarah Bache, June 26, 1782, APS.

78. Benjamin Franklin to Samuel Cooper, December 2, 1780, in *WBF*, 8: 183.

79. Benjamin Franklin to Samuel Cooper Johonnot, January 25, 1782, in *WBF*, 8: 372. For accounts of the events in Geneva and of Sammy's behavior, see Lopez and Herbert, *The Private Franklin*, pp. 228–31; Claude-Anne Lopez, "A Story of Grandfathers, Fathers, and Sons," *Yale University Library Gazette* 53 (April 1979): 177–95.

80. Benjamin Franklin to Samuel Cooper Johonnot, January 7, 1782, in *WBF*, 10: 363.

81. Samuel Cooper Johonnot to Benjamin Franklin, January 1, 1783, Yale.

82. Benjamin Franklin Bache to Benjamin Franklin, July 27, 1782, APS.

83. Benjamin Franklin Bache, Diary, August 1, 1782 to September 14, 1785, manuscript translation, APS. On the Johonnot journal, now among the Adams papers, see Lopez, "A Story of Grandfathers, Fathers, and Sons," pp. 179, 191.

84. Benjamin Franklin Bache to Sarah Bache, Richard Bache, September 15, 1782, APS; Sarah Bache to Benjamin Franklin Bache, October 1, 1782, APS; Benjamin Franklin to Polly Hewson, January 8, 1783, APS; Samuel Cooper to Samuel Cooper Johonnot, December 26, 1782, Beinecke Library, Yale University; Benjamin Franklin to Benjamin Franklin Bache, June 23, 1783, Franklin Papers, University of Pennsylvania. See Lopez, "A Story of Grandfathers, Fathers, and Sons," pp. 187–88. On Gallatin, see John A. Stevens, *Albert Gallatin* (Boston: Houghton, Mifflin and Co., 1898), p. 17; Raymond Walters, Jr., *Albert Gallatin, Jeffersonian Financier and Diplomat* (New York: Macmillan, 1957), p. 14. Franklin's explanation for bringing Bache back because of his ill health and loneliness is given in a letter to Richard and Sarah Bache, July 27, 1783 (misdated 1782), Yale.

85. Robert Pigott to Benjamin Franklin, November 26, 1782, APS. Similar encouraging reports were issued by Dorcas Montgomery, a widowed American who, following Franklin's advice, placed her son Robert under Marignac's supervision. Dorcas Montgomery to Benjamin Franklin, November 17, 1781, APS; Dorcas Montgomery to Benjamin Franklin, January 25, 1782, Yale. See also Samuel Powel Griffitts to Benjamin Franklin, October 6, 1782, Franklin Papers, HSP.

86. Robert Pigott to Benjamin Franklin, June 27, 1783, Yale.

87. Benjamin Franklin to Samuel Cooper Johonnot, August 19, 1783, Beinecke Library, Yale University; Samuel Cooper Johonnot to Benjamin Franklin, April 21, 1784, Yale. See Lopez, "A Story of Grandfathers, Fathers, and Sons," pp. 189–95.

88. Benjamin Webb to Benjamin Franklin, July 7, 1783, Yale; Benjamin Franklin to Richard and Sarah Bache, July 27, 1783 (misdated 1782), Yale; Dorcas Montgomery to Sarah Bache, July 26, 1783, APS, Benjamin Franklin Bache to Richard and Sarah Bache, October 30, 1783, Yale.

89. Benjamin Franklin Bache to Richard and Sarah Bache, October 30, 1783, Yale.

90. Benjamin Franklin to Mary Hewson, September 7, 1783, in *WBF*, 9: 89–90.

91. Mary Stevenson Hewson to Benjamin Franklin, September 28, 1783, APS.

92. Benjamin Franklin to William Strahan, December 4, 1781, in *WBF*, 8: 336.

93. Benjamin Franklin to Richard Bache, November 11, 1784, in *WBF*, 9: 279. On Bache's difficulties with the Post Office, see Wesley E. Rich, *The History of the United States Post Office to the Year 1829* (Cambridge: Harvard University Press, 1924), pp. 48–67.

94. Mary Stevenson Hewson to Barbara Hewson, January 25, 1785, Miscellaneous Manuscripts, APS.

Chapter 5

1. *Poor Richard Improved*, 1750, in *PBF*, 3: 448–49; *Poor Richard Improved*, 1757, in *PBF*, 7: 84.

2. Benjamin Franklin to Richard Price, June 13, 1782, in *WBF*, 8: 457; Benjamin Franklin to Sir Edward Newenham, October 2, 1783, in *WBF*, 9: 102; Benjamin Franklin to Thomas Brand Hollis, October 5, 1783, in *WBF*, 9: 104.

3. Benjamin Franklin to Francis Hopkinson, December 24, 1782, in *WBF*, 8: 647–48.

4. Benjamin Franklin to David Hartley, September 6, 1783, in *WBF*, 9: 87–88.

5. Thomas Jefferson to Maria Cosway, October 12, 1786, in *The Papers of Thomas Jefferson*, ed. Julian P. Boyd et al. (Princeton: Princeton University Press, 1950–   ), 10: 447. For other examples from this time of Jefferson's opinion that the British press was inaccurate in its reports of America, see "Jefferson's Observations on Démeunier's Manuscript," 1786, ibid., 10: 55; Thomas Jefferson to Jean Chas, December 7, 1786, ibid., 10: 580.

6. Thomas Jefferson to Edward Carrington, January 16, 1787, in Boyd, ed., *The Papers of Thomas Jefferson*, 11: 49.

7. The printed ode is reproduced in Luther S. Livingston, *Franklin and his Press at Passy* (New York: Grolier Club, 1914), between pp. 72 and 73. On Jones, see p. 75. Bache sent his printing of the ode to his parents. Benjamin Franklin Bache to Sarah Bache, December 27, 1783, APS; Benjamin Franklin Bache to Richard Bache, December 27, 1783, APS.

8. Benjamin Franklin Bache to Richard and Sarah Bache, May 11, 1785, Society Collection, HSP; Benjamin Franklin Bache to Sarah Bache, February 9, 1785, APS. The Didot son was presumably Firmin (1764–1836) who distinguished himself in the operation of his family's type foundry.

9. Benjamin Franklin to Richard and Sarah Bache, May 10, 1785, in *WBF*, 9: 328; Benjamin Franklin to Mary Hewson, May 5, 1785, in *WBF*, 9: 323; William Franklin to Sarah Bache, August 1, 1785, Yale; Jonathan Shipley to Benjamin Franklin, November 27, 1785, Yale. On Bache and the departure, see Livingston, *Franklin and his Press at Passy*, pp. 74–75, 125–28.

10. "Dr. Franklin's Answer," in *WBF*, 10: 476.

11. Bache, Diary, September 13, 14, 1785; Tuition Money book, October 1, 1782 to October 8, 1788, University of the State of Pennsylvania, Archives of the University of Pennsylvania, p. 77; Mark Frazier Lloyd, "The University of Pennsylvania and the Creation of the Constitution," unpublished exhibit catalog, 1987, Archives of the University of Pennsylvania; Benjamin Franklin Bache to [Robert Alexander], October 30, 1785, APS; Benjamin Franklin Bache to Robert

Alexander, October 16, 1786, APS; Benjamin Franklin to Jane Mecom, June 3, 1786, in *WBF*, 9: 515. On the instruction in moral philosophy, see David W. Robson, *Educating Republicans, The College in the Era of the American Revolution, 1750–1800* (Westport, Conn.: Greenwood Press, 1985), pp. 162–63.

12. Mark Frazier Lloyd, "Historical Notes," in the commencement program, University of Pennsylvania, May 18, 1987, Archives of the University of Pennsylvania, pp. 6–7; Benjamin Franklin to Madame Brillon, April 19, 1788, Yale; Benjamin Franklin to Catherine Greene, March 2, 1789, in *WBF*, 10: 4. In addition to the Bachelors of Arts, the 1787 graduation included four Masters of Arts, five Bachelors of Medicine, and three honorary degrees, one of which was awarded to the Marquis de la Fayette in absentia. For the full list, see [Philadelphia] *Pennsylvania Herald and General Advertiser*, November 28, 1787. On Bache's printing office, see John D. R. Platt, *The Home and Office of Benjamin Franklin Bache* (Washington: U.S. Department of the Interior, 1970).

13. Benjamin Franklin to George Washington, March 5, 1780, in *WBF*, 8: 29.

14. Benjamin Franklin to William Hunter, November 24, 1786, in *WBF*, 9: 548.

15. "The Internal State of America," May 17, 1786, in *WBF*, 10: 116–22.

16. Benjamin Franklin to Jonathan Shipley, March 17, 1783, in *WBF*, 9: 23; "Speech in the Convention on the Subject of Salaries," in *WBF*, 9: 590–95; "Proposal for Consideration," in *WBF*, 9: 602–4. See Carl Van Doren, *Benjamin Franklin* (New York: Viking Press, 1938), pp. 744–50.

17. On Franklin's pleasure at being reelected president without opposition despite the party divisions in the state, see Benjamin Franklin to William Hunter, November 24, 1786, in *WBF*, 9: 547. On the support for Franklin, see Van Doren, *Benjamin Franklin*, pp. 731–34.

18. "The Internal State of America," May 17, 1786, in *WBF*, 10: 120–21; Benjamin Franklin to Thomas Jefferson, April 19, 1787, in *WBF*, 9: 573–74.

19. *The Complete Writings of Thomas Paine*, ed. Philip S. Foner, 2 vols. (New York: The Citadel Press, 1945), 2: 41–42. For a slightly different contemporary version, see *Rules and Regulations of the Society for Political Enquiries. Established at Philadelphia, 9th February, 1787* (Philadelphia: Printed by Robert Aitken, 1787). For background, see Michael Vinson, "The Society for Political Inquiries: The Limits of Republican Discourse in Philadelphia on the Eve of the Constitutional Convention," *PMHB* 113 (April 1989): 185–205.

20. Benjamin Franklin to Samuel Mather, May 12, 1784, in *WBF*, 9: 210; *Autobiography*, p. 95.

21. Benjamin Franklin to Jean Baptiste Le Roy, November 13, 1789, in *WBF*, 10: 68, 69; Benjamin Franklin to David Hartley, December 4, 1789, in *WBF*, 10: 72. See also Benjamin Franklin to Samuel Moore, November 5, 1789, in *WBF*, 10: 63.

22. "Queries and Remarks," 1789, in *WBF*, 10: 54–60; Benjamin Franklin to Charles Carroll, May 25, 1789, in *WBF*, 10: 7. For Franklin's concern about obedience in the context of the opposition to the Constitution, see Benjamin Franklin to Charles Vaughan, February 12, 1788, APS.

23. For examples of Franklin's bitter reactions to attacks on his character,

see Benjamin Franklin to Robert Morris, July 26, 1781, in *WBF*, 8: 288; Benjamin Franklin to Caleb Whitefoord, July 27, 1787, in *WBF*, 9: 605–6. He nevertheless told his sister that he ignored attempts to disgrace him in the press. "My friends defend me," he wrote. "I have long been accustomed to receive more blame, as well as more praise, than I have deserved." Benjamin Franklin to Jane Mecom, November 26, 1788, in *WBF*, 9: 685.

24. *Autobiography*, pp. 94, 95. See also, Benjamin Franklin to ————, November 25, 1786, in *WBF*, 9: 549; "To the Editors of the *Pennsylvania Gazette*, 1788, in *WBF*, 9: 639. On Jefferson's anger, see Frank Luther Mott, *Jefferson and the Press* (Baton Rouge: Louisiana University Press, 1943).

25. Jeffery A. Smith, *Printers and Press Freedom: The Ideology of Early American Journalism* (New York: Oxford University Press, 1988), pp. 151–53; Elizabeth Holt Oswald to Benjamin Franklin, August 3, 1788, APS; Benjamin Franklin to Elizabeth Oswald, n.d., APS; "An Account of the Supremest Court of Judicature in Pennsylvania, viz. The Court of the Press," September 12, 1789, in *WBF*, 10: 36–40.

26. Benjamin Franklin to Thomas Jefferson, April 19, 1787, in *WBF*, 9: 573.

27. "Speech in the Convention, at the Close of its Deliberations," September 17, 1787, in *WBF*, 9: 607–9; Benjamin Franklin to William Cocke, August 12, 1786, in *WBF*, 9: 535.

28. [Advertisement], *Pennsylvania Gazette*, December 22, 1730, in *PBF*, 1: 189; Benjamin Franklin to John Waring, December 17, 1763, in *PBF*, 10: 395–96. On Franklin and slavery, see Claude-Anne Lopez and Eugenia W. Herbert, *The Private Franklin, The Man and His Family* (New York: W. W. Norton, 1975), pp. 291–302.

29. Van Doren, *Benjamin Franklin*, pp. 742, 774–75; "Plan for Improving the Condition of the Free Blacks," in *WBF*, 10: 127–29; "Address to the Public," November 9, 1789, in *WBF*, 10: 66–68; "On the Slave Trade," March 23, 1790, in *WBF*, 10: 86–91.

30. Alfred F. Young, "English Plebian Culture and Eighteenth-Century American Radicalism," in Margaret Jacob and James Jacob, eds., *The Origins of Anglo-American Radicalism* (London: George Allen & Unwin, 1984), pp. 200–203.

31. *Order of Procession* (Philadelphia: Hall and Sellers, 1788).

32. See Ruth Bogin, "Petitioning and the New Moral Economy of Post-Revolutionary America," *William and Mary Quarterly*, 3rd ser., 45 (July 1988): 391–425.

33. See Gary B. Nash, "The Social Evolution of Preindustrial American Cities, 1700–1820, Reflections and New Directions," *Journal of Urban History* 13 (February 1987): 115–45; Sharon V. Salinger, "Artisans, Journeymen, and the Transformation of Labor in Late Eighteenth-Century Philadelphia," *William and Mary Quarterly*, 3rd ser., 40 (January 1983): 62–84; Billy G. Smith, "Inequality in Late Colonial Philadelphia: A Note on Its Nature and Growth," *William and Mary Quarterly*, 3rd ser., 41 (October 1984): 629–45; Billy G. Smith, "The Material Lives of Laboring Philadelphians, 1750 to 1800," *William and Mary Quarterly*, 3rd ser., 38 (April 1981): 163–202; John K. Alexander, "The Fort Wilson

Incident of 1779: A Case Study of the Revolutionary Crowd," *William and Mary Quarterly*, 3rd ser., 31 (October 1974): 589–612; Gary B. Nash, "Artisans and Politics in Eighteenth-Century Philadelphia," in Jacob and Jacob, eds., *Anglo-American Radicalism*, pp. 162–82; Steven Rosswurm, " 'As a Lyen out of His Den': Philadelphia's Popular Movement, 1776–80," in Jacob and Jacob, eds., *Anglo-American Radicalism*, pp. 300–23; Eric Foner, *Tom Paine and Revolutionary America* (New York; Oxford University Press, 1976), pp. 145–82; Ronald Douglas Schultz, "Thoughts Among the People: Popular Thought, Radical Politics, and the Making of Philadelphia's Working Class, 1765–1828" (Ph.D. dissertation, University of California, Los Angeles, 1985), pp. 82–134.

34. *To the Several Battalions of Military Associatiors in the Province of Pennsylvania* [Philadelphia, 1776].

35. *The Federal and State Constitutions, Colonial Chapters, and Other Organic Laws of the States, Territories, and Colonies*, ed. Francis N. Thorpe, 7 vols. (Washington, D.C.: Government Printing Office, 1909), 5: 3082–83; "Revisions of the Pennsylvania Declaration of Rights," in *PBF*, 22: 529–33.

36. "A Serious Address to the People of Pennsylvania on the Present Situation of their Affairs," in P. Foner, ed., *The Complete Writings of Thomas Paine*, 2: 282–83.

37. Dixon Wecter, "Thomas Paine and the Franklins," *American Literature* 12 (November 1940): 306–17; Eric Foner, "Tom Paine's Republic: Radical Ideology and Social Change," in Alfred F. Young, ed., *The American Revolution* (DeKalb: Northern Illinois University Press, 1976), pp. 189–232; E. Foner, *Tom Paine and Revolutionary America*, pp. 145–82. For Bache's support of the federal Constitution, see Benjamin Franklin Bache to Robert Alexander, October 21, 1787, APS.

38. *Information to Those Who Would Remove to America*, 1782, in *WBF*, 8: 613; Thomas Jefferson to James Madison, October 20, 1785, in Boyd, ed., *The Papers of Thomas Jefferson*, 8: 682; Benjamin Franklin to Robert Morris, December 25, 1783, in *WBF*, 9: 138. For Franklin's support of taxing wealth proportionally, see Benjamin Franklin to Samuel Cooper, April 22, 1779, in *WBF*, 7: 293–94; Benjamin Franklin to Thomas Ruston, October 9, 1780, in *WBF*, 8: 151–52.

39. Adam Smith, *An Inquiry into the Nature and Causes of the Wealth of Nations*, ed. Edwin Cannan (New York: Modern Library, 1937), pp. 66, 79, 565–66; *Autobiography*, pp. 55–56.

40. [Philadelphia] *Independent Gazetteer*, January 21, 1786.

41. *Constitution of the Franklin Society* ([Philadelphia]: Stewart and Cochran, 1792); Henry P. Rosemont, "Benjamin Franklin and the Philadelphia Typographical Strikers of 1786," *Labor History* 22 (Summer 1981): 398–429; Isaiah Thomas, *The History of Printing in America*, ed. Marcus A. McCorison (New York: Weathervane Books, 1970), p. 371.

42. Benjamin Franklin to Jonathan Williams, Sr., November 26, 1788, Yale; Benjamin Franklin to Jane Mecom, February 22, 1789, in *The Letters of Benjamin Franklin & Jane Mecom*, ed. Carl Van Doren (Princeton: Princeton University Press for the American Philosophical Society, 1950), p. 321. On Barbauld, see Jacqueline S. Reinier, "Rearing the Republican Child: Attitudes and Practices in Post-Revolutionary Philadelphia," *William and Mary Quarterly*, 3rd ser., 39 (January 1982): 153.

43. [Anna Letitia Barbauld], Lessons for Children, From Two to Four Years Old (Philadelphia: Printed by B. F. Bache, 1788), pp. 11, 87; [Anna Letitia Barbauld], Lessons for Children of Four Years Old. Part 1 (Philadelphia: Printed by B. F. Bache, 1788), pp. 32, 78–83; [Anna Letitia Barbauld], Lessons for Children from Four to Five Years Old (Philadelphia: Printed by B. F. Bache, 1788), pp. 13–30.

44. Jane Mecom to Benjamin Franklin, April 2, 1789, in Van Doren, ed., The Letters of Benjamin Franklin & Jane Mecom, p. 322; Jonathan Williams, Sr., to Benjamin Franklin, September 6, 1789, ibid., pp. 320–21; Autobiography, pp. xxii, xl, xlii-xliv, xlvi. For an example of Franklin's frustrations in the typefounding business, see Benjamin Franklin to Francis Childs, May 8, 1787, in WBF, 9: 580–81.

45. Benjamin Franklin to M. Le Veillard, September 5, 1789, in WBF 10: 35; Benjamin Franklin to Mary Hewson, May 6, 1786, in WBF, 9: 511–12; Benjamin Franklin to Jane Mecom, April 12, 1788, in Van Doren, ed., The Letters of Benjamin Franklin & Jane Mecom, p. 308; Benjamin Franklin to George Washington, September 16, 1789, in WBF, 10: 41.

46. [Benjamin Franklin Bache] to [Margaret H. Markoe], May 2, 1790, APS; Benjamin Franklin to Thomas Jefferson, April 8, 1790, in WBF, 10: 92–93. On Franklin's last days and the lives of family members after his death, see Lopez and Herbert, The Private Franklin, pp. 303–14.

47. [Benjamin Franklin Bache] to [Margaret H. Markoe], May 2, 1790, APS; "Franklin's Last Will and Testament," July 17, 1788, in WBF, 10: 493–501.

48. "Franklin's Last Will and Testament," July 17, 1788, in WBF, 10: 493; Benjamin Franklin Bache, Proposals for Publishing a News-paper, to be Entitled The Daily Advertiser [Philadelphia, 1790].

49. Smith, Printers and Press Freedom, pp. 124–41; Alfred O. Aldridge, "Benjamin Franklin and the Philosophes," Studies on Voltaire and the Eighteenth Century 24 (1963): 54; Richard B. Kielbowicz, "The Press, Post Office, and Flow of News in the Early Republic," Journal of the Early Republic 3 (Fall 1983): 255–80.

50. GA, October 1, 1790.

51. Smith, Printers and Press Freedom, pp. 42–53, 114; David Paul Nord, "A Republican Literature: A Study of Magazine Reading and Readers in Late Eighteenth-Century New York," American Quarterly 40 (March 1988): 42–64. When Mathew Carey, a Philadelphia printer Franklin had employed in France, asked him to sign an endorsement of his new American Museum magazine in 1788, Franklin refused, saying "it might appear to the Public impertinent." The endorsement said the magazine was "a very useful work, calculated to disseminate agricultural, political, and other valuable information." Franklin may have actually been anticipating that Carey would one day be Bache's competitor. Benjamin Franklin to Mathew Carey, June 10, 1788, in WBF, 9: 660; Mathew Carey to Benjamin Franklin, June 10, 1788, in WBF, 9: 661.

52. GA, October 1, 1790; William Duane, Circular, November 1834, in Worthington C. Ford, ed., "The Letters of William Duane," Proceedings of the Massachusetts Historical Society, 2nd ser., 20 (May 1906): 392; Jane Mecom to Sarah Bache, December 2, 1790, in Van Doren, ed., The Letters of Benjamin Franklin & Jane Mecom, p. 344.

53. GA, October 1, 1790.

54. Benjamin Franklin Bache to Thomas Jefferson, August 20, 1790, in Boyd, ed., *The Papers of Thomas Jefferson*, 17: 397; Thomas Jefferson to Francis Hopkinson, July 6, 1788, ibid., 13: 309; Benjamin Franklin to Thomas Jefferson, October 24, 1788, ibid., 14: 36; William Temple Franklin to Thomas Jefferson, October 13, 1790, ibid., 17: 591; Thomas Jefferson to William Temple Franklin, November 27, 1790, ibid., 18: 86–97; *The Autobiography of Thomas Jefferson* (New York: Capricorn Books, 1959), pp. 117–19.

55. For a description of these dealings, see Editorial Note, "Jefferson's Alliance in 1790 with Fenno's *Gazette of the United States*," in Boyd, ed., *The Papers of Thomas Jefferson*, 19: 237–47. On the Leyden paper, see Jeremy Popkin, "International Gazettes and Politics of Europe in the Revolutionary Period," *Journalism Quarterly* 62 (Autumn 1985): 482–88.

56. Benjamin Rush to Thomas Jefferson, August 15, 1790, in Boyd, ed., *The Papers of Thomas Jefferson*, 17: 391–92; Henry Remsen, Jr., to Benjamin Russell and Others, November 23, 1790, ibid., 18: 65–66; Thomas Jefferson, *Report on the Memorial of Andrew Brown*, February 5, 1791, ibid., 19: 251–52; Thomas Jefferson to Benjamin Franklin Bache, April 22, 1791, ibid., 20: 246.

57. Thomas Jefferson to Thomas Mann Randolph, Jr., May 15, 1791, in Boyd, ed., *The Papers of Thomas Jefferson*, 20: 416.

58. GA, January 1, 1791; Thomas Jefferson to George Washington, September 9, 1792, in *The Writings of Thomas Jefferson*, ed. Paul L. Ford, 10 vols. (New York: G. P. Putnam's Sons, 1892–1899), 6: 106.

59. Editorial Note, "Jefferson, Freneau, and the Founding of the *National Gazette*," in Boyd ed., *The Papers of Thomas Jefferson*, 20: 718–53; [Philadelphia] *National Gazette*, December 19, 1791. Jefferson told his family that Freneau put as much good material in two issues a week as Bache did in six. Thomas Jefferson to Martha Jefferson Randolph, November 13, 1791, in Boyd, ed., *The Papers of Thomas Jefferson*, 22: 294; Thomas Jefferson to Thomas Mann Randolph, Jr., November 20, 1791, ibid., 22: 310.

60. Donald H. Stewart, *The Opposition Press of the Federalist Period* (Albany: State University of New York Press, 1969), pp. 622–24; Editorial Note, "Jefferson, Freneau, and the Founding of the *National Gazette*," in Boyd, ed., *The Papers of Thomas Jefferson*, 20: 734–36, 747. On Logan, see Lance Banning, *The Jeffersonian Persuasion, Evolution of a Party Ideology* (Ithaca, N.Y.: Cornell University Press, 1978), pp. 186–92.

61. Editorial Note, "Jefferson, Freneau, and the Founding of the *National Gazette*," in Boyd, ed., *The Papers of Thomas Jefferson*, 20: 747–53; Thomas Jefferson to George Washington, September 9, 1792, in Ford, ed., *The Writings of Thomas Jefferson*, 6: 101–9; Stewart, *The Opposition Press of the Federalist Period*, pp. 609–10.

62. GA, January 1, 1791; November 25, 1793; Benjamin Franklin Bache to Richard Bache, January 10, 1793, as quoted in James D. Tagg, "Benjamin Franklin Bache and the Philadelphia *Aurora*" (Ph.D. dissertation, Wayne State University, 1973), p. 128.

63. Editorial Note, "Death of Franklin, The Politics of Mourning in France and the United States," in Boyd, ed., *The Papers of Thomas Jefferson*, 19: 78–106;

The President of the National Assembly of France to "The President of Congress," June 20, 1790, ibid., 19: 109; The President to the President of the National Assembly of France, January 27, 1791, ibid., 19: 110–11; The Secretary of State to the President of the National Assembly, March 8, 1791, ibid., 19: 114–15. On the eulogies Franklin received in France, see Alfred O. Aldridge, *Franklin and his French Contemporaries* (New York: New York University Press, 1957), pp. 212–34.

64. Lawrence S. Kaplan, *Entangling Alliances with None: American Foreign Policy in the Age of Jefferson* (Kent, Ohio: Kent State University Press, 1987), pp. 16–27.

65. Thomas Jefferson to Rev. William Smith, February 19, 1791, in Boyd, ed., *The Papers of Thomas Jefferson*, 19: 113.

Chapter 6

1. GA, October 1, 2, 23, 1790.

2. GA, January 1, August 16, 1791.

3. On the exchanges and how the system was altered in the nineteenth century, see Richard B. Kielbowicz, "News Gathering by Mail in the Age of the Telegraph: Adapting to a New Technology," *Technology and Culture* 28 (January 1987): 26–41.

4. GA, November 10, 11, 15, 1790; June 18, 1791. See also GA, September 19, 1792; July 23, 1793; July 16, 1794.

5. GA, July 4, 27, August 16, 1793. On the influence of American ideas—particularly unicameralism—in France, see Joyce Appleby, "America as a Model for the Radical French Reformers of 1789," *William and Mary Quarterly*, 3rd ser., 28 (April 1971): 267–86.

6. GA, October 30, 1790.

7. GA, April 12, December 24, 1792. See also GA, September 22, 1791.

8. GA, July 19, 1792; December 31, 1793.

9. GA, June 22, July 23, 1792. See also GA, November 26, 1791; October 26, 1792.

10. GA, July 17, August 18, 1792; July 3, August 27, 1793. On the potential economic links, see GA, December 16, 1793. For examples of demonstrations of support for the French Revolution, see GA, August 1, 1792, March 15, 1793.

11. Elisabeth and Robert Badinter, *Condorcet, Un Intellectuel en Politique* (Paris: Fayard, 1988), pp. 217, 607, 619–21. The Badinters and other historians have accepted the notion that Bache was among those who frequented Sophie's salon in Paris before the downfall of her husband, but the young man left France before she began entertaining such luminaries as Jefferson and Paine. Her philosopher-politician husband did share many of Franklin's beliefs, ranging from the adages of Poor Richard to the advantages of unicameral legislatures. See Alfred O. Aldridge, *Franklin and his French Contemporaries* (New York: New York University Press, 1957), pp. 49–50, 87–88, 223–32. Sophie survived and reentered French intellectual life after the death of Robespierre.

12. GA, November 6, 1790; July 31, 1794; Benjamin Franklin Bache to

Richard Bache, August 22, 1793, as quoted in Tagg, "Benjamin Franklin Bache and the Philadelphia *Aurora,*" p. 329. See also GA, July 17, 1794.

13. GA, July 12, 1793; "No Jacobin No. 1," in *The Papers of Alexander Hamilton,* ed. Harold C. Syrett, 27 vols. (New York: Columbia University Press, 1961–1987), 15: 145. For an example of pro-French war coverage, see "Good News From France," in GA, July 11, 1793.

14. GA, July 11, 15, December 23, 27, 1793. For criticisms of Washington, see, e.g., GA, July 12, 1793; February 10, 1794.

15. GA, July 25, 1793.

16. GA, September 22, 1791; May 24, 1793.

17. GA, October 10, 17, 20, 1794. For examples of Federalist hostility toward France and Bache, see [Philadelphia] *Gazette of the United States,* December 8, 1792; February 9, March 16, April 6, 1793; May 2, 5, 6, 8, 9, 16, 30, 1794; for an example of the principles vs. person distinction being made, see February 9, 1793, "A Republican." On the suppression of publications, see Hugh Gough, *The Newspaper Press in the French Revolution* (London: Routledge, 1988); Jeremy D. Popkin, *The Right-Wing Press in France, 1792–1800* (Chapel Hill: University of North Carolina Press, 1980).

18. GA, May 19, October 7, 23, 1794; John Fenno to Alexander Hamilton, November 9, 1793, in Syrett, ed., *The Papers of Alexander Hamilton,* 15: 393–94; Alexander Hamilton to John Kean, November 29, 1793, ibid., p. 418. On Federalist papers being assisted by postal appointments, see Carl E. Prince, "The Federalist Party and Creation of a Court Press, 1789–1801," *Journalism Quarterly* 53 (Summer 1976): 238–41. On Fenno's finances, see Culver H. Smith, *The Press, Politics, and Patronage, The American Government's Use of Newspapers, 1789–1875* (Athens: University of Georgia Press, 1977), pp. 13–19. For examples of the accusations made against Bache, see *Gazette of the United States,* June 3, 1796; [Philadelphia] *Porcupine's Gazette,* November 16, 1797. For examples of Bache's denials, see A, November 27, 1795; September 27, 1797. For complaints about Fenno's patronage, see, in particular, GA, May 8, June 18, 1794; A, November 8, 1794; January 15, 1795; June 6, November 3, 1796. For the charge that Fenno received money from private benefactors, see A, April 4, May 12, July 3, 1798.

19. GA, June 21, 1792; January 25, March 15, 1793; May 19, 1794. See also GA, October 29, 1791; November 1, December 12, 1792; March 22, 26, May 31, 1793; July 15, 1794.

20. John R. Nelson, Jr., *Liberty and Property: Political Economy and Policymaking in the New Nation, 1789–1812* (Baltimore: The Johns Hopkins University Press, 1987), pp. 22–79, 165; *Report on the Subject of Manufactures* in Syrett, ed., *The Papers of Alexander Hamilton,* 10: 230–71. For a brief account of physiocratic thought, see John Kenneth Galbraith, *Economics in Perspective: A Critical History* (Boston: Houghton Mifflin, 1987), pp. 46–56.

21. Lance Banning, *The Jeffersonian Persuasion, Evolution of a Party Ideology* (Ithaca, N.Y.: Cornell University Press, 1978), pp. 126–60; "Republican Distribution of Citizens," in *The Writings of James Madison,* ed. Gaillard Hunt, 9 vols. (New York: G. P. Putnam's Sons, 1900–1910), 6: 96–99; "The Union," ibid., 6: 104, 105; "A Candid State of Parties," ibid., 6: 115, 116.

22. GA, September 23, 1791; January 7, 23, May 1, 30, 1792. For examples

of the paper's essays on economics, see GA, June 28, October 6, 27, November 19, December 5, 1791; January 7, 9, 16, 23, 1792; A, June 20, 1795.

23. GA, August 12, 1791; March 1, 1792. See also GA, July 11, 14, 1791; February 15, 1793.

24. GA, October 12, 1790; June 15, 1791. See also, GA, November 8, 28, 1790; January 16, 1792. Bache advised a friend from his school days in Geneva that investing in land offered an independent life to a person of industry and know-how but would not make a fortune. Benjamin Franklin Bache to Gabriel Cramer, December 20, 1794, in Lucien Cramer, Une Famille Genevoise, Les Cramer (Geneva: Librairie E. Droz, 1952), pp. 66–67.

25. GA, January 12, 19, 1792. On Jefferson's commitment to agriculture, see Edwin M. Betts, ed., Thomas Jefferson's Farm Book (Princeton: Princeton University Press for the American Philosophical Society, 1953). On Franklin's place in Americans' belief in the virtue of industry, see J. E. Crowley, This Sheba, Self: The Conceptualization of Economic Life in Eighteenth-Century America (Baltimore: The Johns Hopkins University Press, 1974), pp. 82–92, 122.

26. GA, March 19, May 17, 1791; see also October 17, 1791; May 2, 1792. On the need for brotherhood, see GA, December 26, 1791.

27. GA, July 4, 1791; May 2, 29, 1792; A, October 9, 1797.

28. GA, January 27, 1794. For definitions and discussions of "classical republicanism," see Banning, The Jeffersonian Persuasion, pp. 21–41; Jonathan Scott, Algernon Sidney and the English Republic, 1623–1677 (Cambridge: Cambridge University Press, 1988), pp. 14–17, 28–30.

29. GA, May 24, 1791; August 16, 1793. On the operation of the three branches of government, see, e.g., GA, January 16, February 7, 1792. On popular sovereignty, see, e.g., GA, May 18, 22, 1792.

30. A, January 29, 1795.

31. Remarks Occasioned by the Late Conduct of Mr. Washington as President of the United States (Philadelphia: Printed for Benjamin Franklin Bache, 1797), pp. 3, 35–39. For the newspaper's charge that Washington acted against the will of the majority, see A, August 21, September 7, 8, 21, 1795; January 13, 1796.

32. Remarks, pp. 34, 39. On unicameral legislatures, see GA, March 12, 1791; A, April 14, 1795; Ben Franklin Laughing, Anecdotes from Original Sources by and about Benjamin Franklin, ed. P. M. Zall (Berkeley: University of California Press, 1980), pp. 57, 92.

33. Gazette of the United States, September 16, 18, 1795. On the rise and fall of the Democratic-Republican societies, see Philip S. Foner, ed., The Democratic-Republican Societies, 1790–1800, A Documentary Sourcebook of Constitutions, Declarations, Addresses, Resolutions, and Toasts (Westport, Conn.: Greenwood Press, 1976).

34. Thomas Jefferson to John Adams, February 28, 1796, in The Adams–Jefferson Letters, The Complete Correspondence Between Thomas Jefferson and Abigail and John Adams, ed. Lester J. Cappon, 2 vols. (Chapel Hill: University of North Carolina Press for the Institute of Early American History and Culture, 1959), 1: 259–60; John Adams to Thomas Jefferson, April 6, 1796, ibid., 1: 261–62.

35. Remarks, p. 32. On Freneau's efforts, see Gerald L. Grotta, "Philip Freneau's Crusade for Open Sessions of the U.S. Senate," Journalism Quarterly 48

(Winter 1971): 667–71. Bache's newspaper had dozens of commentaries on Congressional secrecy. See, e.g., GA, February 15, November 16, 17, 20, 28, December 15, 19, 1792; February 7, 28, December 13, 24, 28, 30, 31, 1793; February 24, March 5, 6, April 16, July 22, September 8, 1794; A, April 30, June 16, 17, 22, 1795; April 30, 1796.

36. A, May 5, 8, 1797.

37. GA, January 20, May 15, 1792; August 21, 1794.

38. GA, February 8, 1792; A, May 21, July 22, 1796. For examples of classical republican rhetoric, see GA, August 20, November 21, 1791; July 6, October 19, December 15, 1792.

39. GA, July 7, 1791; October 19, 1792; February 9, 1793.

40. GA, December 7, 1792.

41. GA, April 4, 1794; A, February 8, 1796; October 27, November 21, 1797.

42. Thomas Paine, *Agrarian Justice* (Philadelphia: Printed by R. Folwell for B. F. Bache, 1797), pp. iv, 11. On the pamphlet, see Eric Foner, *Tom Paine and Revolutionary America* (New York: Oxford University Press, 1976), pp. 249–51. On English radicalism at this time, see Iain McCalman, *Radical Underworld: Prophets, Revolutionaries and Pornographers in London, 1795–1840* (Cambridge: Cambridge University Press, 1988); H. T. Dickinson, *British Radicalism and the French Revolution, 1789–1815* (New York: Basil Blackwell, 1985).

43. GA, March 8, 1792; July 25, 1793; May 6, August 9, 1794; A, July 12, 1796; December 18, 1797.

44. GA, November 1, 1790; January 15, 17, 18, 24, 27, February 4, 12, March 5, May 4, August 19, November 24, 1791; January 10, 1792; February 13, 1794; A, July 28, 1796.

45. GA, March 17, April 21, 27, August 19, 1791; January 9, June 29, 1792. See also GA, January 28, February 5, June 14, August 15, 1791. On the conditions for blacks, see Gary B. Nash, *Forging Freedom: The Formation of Philadelphia's Black Community, 1720–1840* (Cambridge: Harvard University Press, 1988). For Franklin's views, see Benjamin Franklin to John Waring, December 17, 1763, in *PBF*, 10: 395–96; "A Conversation on Slavery," *Public Advertiser*, January 30, 1770, in *PBF*, 17: 37–44; "The Sommersett Case and the Slave Trade," *London Chronicle*, June 18–20, 1772, in *PBF*, 19: 187–88; Benjamin Franklin to Anthony Benezet, February 10, 1773, in *PBF*, 20: 40–41; Benjamin Franklin to Anthony Benezet, July 14, 1773, in *PBF*, 20: 296; Benjamin Franklin to the Marquis de Condorcet, March 20, 1774, in *PBF*, 21: 151.

46. GA, June 29, 1792; October 18, 1794; A, October 20, 1797. On Indians, see also, GA, May 14, 1791; February 7, 20, 21, 1792; July 24, 1794. On women's participation, see also GA, January 20, 24, 1791; December 26, 1792. For a summary of the attitudes of Americans, particularly Jefferson, toward slaves, Indians, and women, see Richard B. Morris, *The Forging of the Union, 1781–89* (New York: Harper & Row, 1987), pp. 179–93. On the image of women, see Karen K. List, "The Post-Revolutionary Woman Idealized: Philadelphia Media's 'Republican Mother'," *Journalism Quarterly* 66 (Spring 1989): 65–75.

47. GA, October 9, 1790; March 1, July 8, August 5, 1791; June 12, 1792. See also, GA, January 14, April 14, 15, June 9, July 22, 1791; January 14, 1792.

For a study of the city's efforts to deal with the poor and with criminals, see John K. Alexander, *Render Them Submissive: Responses to Poverty in Philadelphia, 1760–1800* (Amherst: The University of Massachusetts Press, 1980). On the scale of poverty in Philadelphia and other cities, see Billy G. Smith, "Poverty and Economic Marginality in Eighteenth-Century America," *Proceedings of the American Philosophical Society* 132 (March 1988): 85–118. For background, see Bradley Chapin, "Felony Law Reform in the Early Republic," *PMHB* 113 (April 1989): 163–83.

    48. GA, August 4, 1791; A, September 8, 1797.

Chapter 7

    1. GA, May 3, 4, 1792.

    2. GA, August 6, 1791; February 1, November 3, 1793. On the importance of education, see also GA, July 7, 11, November 10, December 8, 1791; March 1, 8, 15, August 18, 1792; A, August 24, 1795; February 5, August 1, 6, 11, September 5, 1796. On the role of newspapers, see, e.g., GA, October 1, November 16, 1790; February 12, 14, 21, August 1, November 14, December 1, 1791; July 28, 1792.

    3. GA, January 1, 1794; A, November 8, 1794; November 27, 1795.

    4. GA, June 12, 1794; A, November 8, 1794; November 27, 1795.

    5. A, November 8, 1794; James Monroe to [?], April 23, 1794, Simon Gratz Collection, HSP. For Franklin's comment on the chair, see *Ben Franklin Laughing, Anecdotes from Original Sources by and about Benjamin Franklin*, ed. P. M. Zall (Berkeley: University of California Press, 1980), pp. 96, 148. For his scientific paper and an illustration of the northern lights which resembled Bache's nameplate, see "Aurora Borealis," 1778, in *WBF*, 7: 209–15.

    6. GA, April 19, June 7, 1791; A, December 11, 1795. For examples of the praise and tributes Franklin received after his death, see GA, November 1, 4, 12, 1790; May 14, 1791; February 24, March 6, April 9, 14, 20, September 20, November 23, 1792. For instances of Franklin being cited on the legitimacy of parties and the need to oppose the British, see GA, April 12, 1794; A, January 23, April 13, 1795; May 4, 1796. For an example of Bache defending Franklin against Federalist writers, see A, June 9, 1796.

    7. GA, January 28, July 11, 1791; January 2, 1792; August 12, 28, September 5, 6, 22, October 13, 1794; Philip S. Foner, ed., *The Democratic-Republican Societies, 1790–1800, A Documentary Sourcebook of Constitutions, Declarations, Addresses, Resolutions, and Toasts* (Westport, Conn.: Greenwood Press, 1976), p. 30. See, in general, Roland M. Baumann, "Philadelphia's Manufacturers and the Excise Taxes of 1794: The Forging of the Jeffersonian Coalition," *PMHB* 106 (January 1982): 3–39.

    8. Jeremiah Wadsworth to Alexander Hamilton, [July 11–12, 1795], in *The Papers of Alexander Hamilton*, ed. Harold C. Syrett, 27 vols. (New York: Columbia University Press, 1961–1987), 18: 459–60; Jerald A. Combs, *The Jay Treaty, Political Battleground of the Founding Fathers* (Berkeley: University of California Press, 1970), pp. 161–63. See also Joseph Charles, "The Jay Treaty: The Origins of the American Party System," *William and Mary Quarterly*, 3rd ser., 12 (October 1955):

581–630; Everette E. Dennis, "Stolen Peace Treaties and the Press: Two Case Studies," *Journalism History* 2 (Spring 1975): 6–14.

9. A, July 25, 26, August 15, September 7, 8, 1795.

10. GA, January 1, 1794; *Remarks Occasioned by the Late Conduct of Mr. Washington as President of the United States* (Philadelphia: Printed for Benjamin Franklin Bache, 1797), pp. 31, 34. Franklin's "The Court of the Press" essay appeared in the *Federal Gazette* on September 12, 1789.

11. GA, August 1, December 1, 1791; July 28, 1792; A, November 27, 1795. For condemnations of personal libel, see GA, March 5, December 1, 1791; October 2, 1792. On the lack of clarity in the law, see GA, March 12, April 23, 1791, and Jeffery A. Smith, *Printers and Press Freedom: The Ideology of Early American Journalism* (New York: Oxford University Press, 1988), pp. 74–92, 164–65.

12. *Remarks*, pp. 3, 34; Thomas Paine, *Letters to George Washington* (Philadelphia: Benjamin Franklin Bache, 1796); *Letters from General Washington to Several of His Friends, In June and July, 1776* (Philadelphia: Federal Press [Benjamin Franklin Bache], 1795). On the forged correspondence, see Worthington C. Ford, ed., *The Spurious Letters Attributed to Washington* (Brooklyn, N.Y.: Privately Printed, 1889). Paine's pamphlet said, "Monopolies of every kind marked your administration almost in the moment of its commencement. The lands obtained by the revolution were lavished upon partizans; the interest of the disbanded soldier was sold to the speculator; injustice was acted under the pretence of faith; and the chief of the army became the patron of the fraud." Paine, *Letters to George Washington*, p. 7.

13. George Washington to Rev. William Gordon, October 15, 1797, in *The Writings of George Washington*, ed. John C. Fitzpatrick, 39 vols. (Washington: Government Printing Office, 1931–1944), 36:50; George Washington to Jeremiah Wadsworth, March 6, 1797, ibid., 35: 421; George Washington to Benjamin Walker, January 12, 1797, ibid., 35: 364; George Washington to the Secretary of State, March 3, 1797, ibid., 35: 414–15; A, March 3, 6 (as quoted in Ford, ed., *The Spurious Letters Attributed to Washington*, p. 158), 1797.

14. GA, April 23, June 18, October 27, 1791; February 22, 1792. For an early example of a correspondent criticizing the attention given to Washington as monarchical, see GA, March 4, 1791. For Washington's visits to Franklin Court, see *The Diaries of George Washington*, ed. Donald Jackson and Dorothy Twohig, 6 vols. (Charlottesville: University Press of Virginia, 1976–1979), 5: 155, 157, 166, 181, 183, 184, 237, 239, 245, 246. Richard Bache met with Washington in 1789 in the hope of being nominated to serve again as postmaster general. Richard Bache to Sally Bache, September 18, 1789, Yale. His formal petition to the president stated that there were no charges against him and that he never knew why he was replaced by one of his deputies, who was given "additional emoluments of office." This, he said, caused him "no small mortification." Richard Bache to George Washington, April 21, 1789, George Washington Papers, Library of Congress, microfilm, series 7, reel 119, vol. 2, p. 1. A decade later a visitor to the Bache home found the family still "very embittered against Gl. Washington." Julian Ursyn Niemcewicz, *Under Their Vine and Fig Tree, Travels through America in 1797–1799, 1805, With Some Further Account of Life in New Jersey*, trans. and

ed. Metchie J. E. Budka (Elizabeth, N. J.: Grassman Publishing Co., 1965), p. 61.

15. GA, January 2, 29, 1793. See also January 23, 24, 25, 26, 28, 31, February 4, 5, 18, 1793.

16. GA, January 21, 31, February 16, 1793. Besieged by callers, Washington instituted Tuesday afternoon levees and Friday evening soirees to handle visitors. He made it known in a newspaper announcement that he did not wish to receive casual callers at other times and that he would not return visits or accept invitations. Meryle Evans, "Washington's Days as a Host in New York," *New York Times*, April 26, 1989, p. 21.

17. GA, February 5, 1793.

18. *The Anas of Thomas Jefferson*, ed. Franklin B. Sawvel (New York: Da Capo Press, 1970), pp. 111–12. On Washington's approach to Jefferson and the lack of help, see James Thomas Flexner, *George Washington and the New Nation (1783–1793)* (Boston: Little, Brown and Co., 1969), pp. 392–93. Jefferson asserted in 1800 that he had never written a sentence for a newspaper, ibid., p. 202.

19. Benjamin Franklin to George Washington, March 5, 1780, in WBF, 8: 28–29; George Washington to Sarah Bache, January 15, 1781, in Fitzpatrick, ed., *The Writings of George Washington*, 21: 102; Codicil, 1789, in WBF, 10: 508.

20. George Washington to Henry Lee, July 21, 1793, in Fitzpatrick, ed., *The Writings of George Washington*, 33: 24; GA, June 25, 26, 1794.

21. A, October 16, November 23, 1795.

22. A, October 23, 24, 26, November 2, 18, 19, 20, 21, 26, 1795.

23. George Washington to the Secretary of State, July 18, 1796, in Fitzpatrick, ed., *The Writings of George Washington*, 35: 144; George Washington to Thomas Jefferson, July 6, 1796, ibid., 35: 119, 120; George Washington to the Secretary of the Treasury, July 6, 1796, ibid., 35: 126. On Washington as a slaveholder, see, e.g., A, October 21, December 29, 1795; April 12, 16, 1796; January 23, 1797. On Washington's foreign policy, see, e.g., A, December 10, 1795; January 1, March 3, April 4, December 17, 1796; March 3, 1797.

24. Farewell Address [First Draft], [May 15, 1796], in Fitzpatrick, ed., *The Writings of George Washington*, 35: 59; George Washington to Alexander Hamilton, August 25, 1796, ibid., 35: 190, 191; Farewell Address, September 19, 1796, ibid., 35: 230.

25. Alexander Hamilton to George Washington, July 30, 1796, in Victor H. Paltsits, ed., *Washington's Farewell Address* (New York: New York Public Library, 1935), p. 249; George Washington to Alexander Hamilton, August 10, 1796, ibid., p. 250; A, December 17, 23, 1796.

26. George Washington to Alexander Hamilton, August 25, 1796, in Paltsits, ed., *Washington's Farewell Address*, p. 252; Remarks on Monroe's "View of the Conduct of the Executive of the United States," [March 1798], in Fitzpatrick, ed., *The Writings of George Washington*, 36: 195; James Monroe to Benjamin Franklin Bache, January 28, 1798, Etting Papers, HSP; James Monroe to Benjamin Franklin Bache, March 26, 1798, APS; Thomas Jefferson to James Monroe, October 25, 1797, in *The Writings of Thomas Jefferson*, ed. Paul L. Ford, 10 vols. (New York: G. P. Putnam's Sons, 1892–1899), 7: 177–78; Thomas Jefferson to James

Monroe, February 8, 1798, ibid., 7: 197; George Washington to the Secretary of War, July 27, 1798, in Fitzpatrick, ed., *The Writings of George Washington*, 36: 368.

27. Mathew Carey, *Autobiography* (Brooklyn, N. Y.: Eugene L. Schwab, 1942), p. 39; Elizabeth Hewson to Thomas Hewson, November 30, 1795, Hewson Family Papers, APS; Elizabeth Hewson to Thomas Hewson, October 24, 1796, ibid.; Elizabeth Hewson to Thomas Hewson, June 5, 1797, ibid.

28. A, September 15, November 27, 1795.

29. GA, January 5, 1793; January 6, 1794; A, November 11, 1795. For an example of Jefferson's correspondence with Bache, see Thomas Jefferson to Benjamin Franklin Bache, December 26, 1795, Jefferson Papers, APS. "Casca" later accused Washington of forcing out the "philosophic patriot." A, October 16, 1795. For examples of Jefferson's politics being described favorably, see A, April 24, June 20, 1795.

30. GA, October 20, 1792. On the use of the slavery issue against Jefferson, see Donald H. Stewart, *The Opposition Press of the Federalist Period* (Albany: State University of New York Press, 1969), pp. 550–51. Jefferson doubted that blacks were inherently equal to whites and that the two races could ever live together in harmony. See Robert McColley, *Slavery and Jeffersonian Virginia*, 2nd ed. (Urbana: University of Illinois Press, 1973), pp. 124–32; William Cohen, "Thomas Jefferson and the Problem of Slavery," *Journal of American History* 56 (June 1969): 503–26; John P. Diggins, "Slavery, Race, and Equality: Jefferson and the Pathos of the Enlightenment," *American Quarterly* 28 (Spring 1976): 206–28.

31. A, February 10, 1796. On Jefferson as a reformer, see Richard B. Morris, *The Forging of the Union, 1781–89* (New York: Harper & Row, 1987), pp. 166–93.

32. GA, December 1, 1792; A, September 13, October 25, November 9, 11, 1796. See also A, June 24, October 6, 12, 21, 29, November 1, 18, 1796. For examples of the paper's early treatment of Adams in which the vice-president was sometimes defended, see GA, June 21, 27, July 13, 22, 30, 1791; November 8, December 4, 5, 21, 1792.

33. A, October 4, 7, 8, 11, 14, 28, 1796; October 12, 1797.

34. A, December 21, 1796; March 11, 18, 20, 1797; James Thomson Callender, *Sketches of the History of America* (Philadelphia: Snowden & McCorkle, 1798), pp. 232–33.

35. John Adams to Abigail Adams, April 24, 1797, in *Letters of John Adams to His Wife*, ed. Charles F. Adams, 2 vols. (Boston: Little and Brown, 1841), 2: 254; A, May 19, 22, June 8, July 20, November 28, 1797; March 21, 1798.

36. *Gazette of the United States*, April 18, 1798; A, April 19, 1798; Thomas Jefferson to Samuel Smith, August 22, 1798, in *The Works of Thomas Jefferson*, ed. Paul L. Ford, 12 vols. (New York: G. P. Putnam's Sons, 1904–1905), 8: 443. On the reaction to the events in France, see Thomas M. Ray, " 'Not One Cent for Tribute': The Public Addresses and American Popular Reaction to the XYZ Affair, 1798–1799," *Journal of the Early Republic* 3 (Winter 1983): 389–412.

37. Thomas Jefferson to James Madison, April 26, 1798, in Ford, ed., *The Works of Thomas Jefferson*, 8: 412; *Gazette of the United States*, June 4, 1798; A, June 5, 1798. In 1797, a Washington, D. C., newspaper described the contents

of a "confidential" Jefferson letter recommending the *Aurora* "as the best paper printed on the Continent." The story was accompanied by a comment that Jefferson would earn the contempt of every American for supporting Bache's libels. *Washington Gazette*, July 22, 1797.

38. Thomas Jefferson to Elbridge Gerry, January 26, 1799, in Ford, ed., *The Works of Thomas Jefferson*, 9: 16; Thomas Jefferson to James Madison, February 5, 1799, ibid., 9: 34. On Jefferson's strategies, see Noble E. Cunningham, Jr., *The Jeffersonian Republicans, The Formation of a Party Organization, 1789–1801* (Chapel Hill: University of North Carolina Press for the Institute of Early American History and Culture, 1957), pp. 128–43.

39. Thomas Jefferson to George Washington, September 9, 1792, in Ford, ed., *The Works of Thomas Jefferson*, 7: 145, 146–47. On the fight over Freneau, see Cunningham, *The Jeffersonian Republicans*, pp. 24–27. On Freneau's career, see Lewis Leary, *That Rascal Freneau: A Study in Literary Failure* (New Brunswick: Rutgers University Press, 1941).

40. Editorial Note, *Rights of Man*, in *The Papers of Thomas Jefferson*, ed. Julian P. Boyd et al. (Princeton: Princeton University Press, 1950—   ), 20: 268–90; Thomas Jefferson to Jonathan B. Smith, April 26, 1791, ibid., 20: 290; William E. Ames, *A History of the National Intelligencer* (Chapel Hill: University of North Carolina Press, 1972); Eric Foner, *Tom Paine and Revolutionary America* (New York: Oxford University Press, 1976), pp. 257–58.

41. *GA*, June 30, 1791. For Bache's belief that the poor should read Paine, see *GA*, June 26, 1792. For examples of praise for Paine, see *GA*, June 4, 14, 20, July 29, 1791; June 12, October 26, 1792; May 8, 1793. On the vice-president's efforts and Jefferson's predictable reaction, see James H. Hutson, "John Adams' Title Campaign," *New England Quarterly* 41 (March 1968): 30–39.

42. *A*, November 4, 1796; March 3, May 11, 1798; Abigail Adams to Mary Cranch, April 28, 1798, in *New Letters of Abigail Adams, 1788–1801*, ed. Stewart Mitchell (Boston: Houghton Mifflin, 1947), p. 167. On the fasts Adams proclaimed, see Charles E. Dickson, "Jeremiads in the New American Republic: The Case of National Fasts in the John Adams Administration," *New England Quarterly* 60 (June 1987): 187–207. The biblical reference was to Elisha cursing children who mocked him for his bald head. The children were then attacked by bears. 2 *Kings*, II, 23–24. In his own peevish way, Adams later attributed Bache's hostility to "an irreconcilable hatred" Franklin had formed for him while they were carrying out their diplomatic duties in France. John Adams to Benjamin Rush, April 12, 1809, *The Works of John Adams*, ed. Charles F. Adams, 10 vols. (Boston: Little, Brown, and Co., 1850–1856), 9: 619.

43. *GA*, March 31, 1791; *A*, April 13, 1795.

44. *GA*, October 11, 1791; June 5, October 9, 1792; *A*, October 9, 1797.

45. *GA*, December 1, 1792, January 17, 1794. For defenses of the Democratic-Republican societies, see *GA*, January 18, 20, 28, April 16, 17, August 9, 12, September 12, 25, 27, *A*, December 22, 1794; February 9, 24, 1795.

46. *GA*, August 4, 1794; *A*, February 27, 1796. On constitutional rights, see also *GA*, January 18, 1794.

47. *A*, May 22, October 1 (2), 9, 10, 1797. For issues being raised about representation and conduct during elections, see, e.g., *GA*, July 30, August 1, 9,

10, 14, September 5, 7, 8, 12, 14, 15, 25, 26, October 8, November 29, December 6, 1792; January 28, August 26, 1793; May 21, June 13, July 21, October 13, 15, 1794; A, February 17, 1796; March 14, 1797; August 29, 1798.

48. A, October 10, 1797; February 28, August 29, 1798.

49. A, February 24, 27, 28, March 7, 1798. For accounts of the elections, see John K. Alexander, *Render Them Submissive: Responses to Poverty in Philadelphia, 1760–1800* (Amherst: The University of Massachusetts Press, 1980), pp. 37–42; Ronald Douglas Schultz, "Thoughts Among the People: Popular Thought, Radical Politics, and the Making of Philadelphia's Working Class, 1765–1828" (Ph.D. dissertation, University of California, Los Angeles, 1985), pp. 279–84.

50. *Porcupine's Gazette*, March 4, June 29, August 4, September 1, 1797; January 12, March 23, 1798. On Cobbett, see George Spater, *William Cobbett, The Poor Man's Friend*, 2 vols. (Cambridge: Cambridge University Press, 1982); Karen K. List, "The Role of William Cobbett in Philadelphia's Party Press, 1794–1799," *Journalism Monographs* No. 82 (May 1983). For the attacks of Cobbett and others on Franklin after his death, see Eugene S. Bodzin, "The American Popular Image of Benjamin Franklin, 1790–1868" (Ph.D. dissertation, University of Wisconsin, 1969).

51. A, March 7, 1797; Elizabeth Hewson to Thomas Hewson, June 20, 1798, Hewson Family Papers, APS; *Porcupine's Gazette*, November 20, 1797. Two weeks later, Cobbett said that Franklin was a plagiarist who ridiculed the Bible and that everything he had a hand in was "contaminated." *Porcupine's Gazette*, December 4, 1797.

52. William Duane to Tench Coxe, October 15, 1798, in Peter J. Parker, ed., "The Revival of the *Aurora*: A Letter to Tench Coxe," *PMHB* 96 (October 1972): 524–25; A, August 11, 1802; Jacob E. Cooke, *Tench Coxe and the Early Republic* (Chapel Hill: University of North Carolina Press for the Institute of Early American History and Culture, 1978), p. 345. According to one-time *Aurora* writer James Thomson Callender, the contributors to the salary were supposed to be Israel Israel, James Reynolds, John Smith, John Beckley, and Mathew Carey, but Beckley was not asked for his portion and Smith did not have money to spare. [Richmond, Virginia] *The Recorder; Or, Lady's and Gentleman's Miscellany*, August 25, 1802.

53. A, April 6, December 9, 1797. Descriptions of this attack and the incidents which followed are in [Benjamin Franklin Bache], *Truth Will Out! The Foul Charges of the Tories Against the Editor of the Aurora Repelled by Positive Proof and Plain Truth and his Base Calumniators Put to Shame* (Philadelphia, 1798).

54. A, March 3, April 27, May 9, 10, 11, 12, 1798; *Porcupine's Gazette*, March 22, May 7, 8, 10, 1798; Dickson, "Jeremiads in the New American Republic," p. 196. For an account of Bache's preparations for an attack and the mob's intentions, see James T. Callender, *The Prospect Before Us* (Richmond: Printed for the Author, 1800), p. 35.

55. *Gazette of the United States*, May 11, 1798. On the Pickering episode, which resulted in a libel suit that was apparently not pursued, see A, January 24, 26, 29, 1798. Pickering had been one of the favorite targets of the *Aurora*. See, e.g., A, July 19, 1797.

56. A, August 9, 10, 1798.

57. Benjamin Franklin Bache to Gabriel Cramer, June 27, 1798, in Lucien Cramer, *Une Famille Genevoise, Les Cramer* (Geneva: Librairie E. Droz, 1952), p. 71; A, August 27, 1798. For examples of Bache's defiance, see A, May 9, July 13, August 23, 1798.

58. GA, December 17, 1793, May 22, 1794; A, December 13, 1797, February 7, 14, 24, August 23, 1798. On Hamilton's adultery, see A, July 28, September 2, 8, October 10, 19, December 1, 1797; September 5, 1798. For a discussion of the Hamilton–Reynolds affair and the role of one of Bache's close associates in the revelations, see Philip M. Marsh, "John Beckley, Mystery Man of the Early Jeffersonians," *PMHB* 72 (January 1948): 54–69.

59. A, June 16, 23, 25, 26, 1798; Bache, *Truth Will Out!*, pp. 1–12; Thomas Jefferson to James Madison, April 26, 1798, in Ford, ed., *The Works of Thomas Jefferson*, 8: 412. On Bache and the Sedition Act, see James Morton Smith, *Freedom's Fetters, The Alien and Sedition Laws and American Civil Liberties* (Ithaca: Cornell University Press, Cornell Paperbacks ed., 1966).

60. A, June 27, 30, 1798. For examples of Bache's reaction to the Sedition Act, see A, June 29, July 3, July 11, 14, 16, 17, 21, 23, August 20, 22, 30, 1798.

61. A, August 28, 1798; Benjamin Franklin Bache to Richard Bache, September 2–3, 1798, Society Collection, HSP.

62. Elizabeth Hewson to Thomas Hewson, May 10, 1799, Hewson Family Papers, APS; Benjamin Franklin Bache, Will, September 7, 1798, APS; Elizabeth Hewson to Thomas Hewson, October 2, 1798, Hewson Family Papers, APS.

Chapter 8

1. On the Republican resentment of privilege, see Michael Durey, "Thomas Paine's Apostles: Radical Emigrés and the Triumph of Jeffersonian Republicanism," *William and Mary Quarterly*, 3rd ser., 44 (October 1987): 661–88.

2. *Annals of Congress*, 5 Cong. 2 sess., pp. 2096–97, 2098, 2100; A, July 13, 1798.

3. *Porcupine's Gazette*, May 1, 3, 1799. The notice was reprinted in the [Boston] *Independent Chronicle*, September 17, 1798. Writing as "Columbus" in the *Aurora*, Tench Coxe took aim at the Federalists' contention that the nation had to take special precautions because it was still in its infancy. They had argued that the United States needed the Jay Treaty in order to avoid war with Britain before the new country reached maturity, he observed, but only a few years later thought that the national honor should be preserved at all costs when insulted by the French. See Jacob E. Cooke, *Tench Coxe and the Early Republic* (Chapel Hill: University of North Carolina Press for the Institute of Early American History and Culture, 1978), p. 341.

4. A, April 7, 1798; Alexander Hamilton to Josiah O. Hoffman, [November 6, 1799], in *The Papers of Alexander Hamilton*, ed. Harold C. Syrett, 27 vols. (New York: Columbia University Press, 1961–1987), 24: 5–8; James Morton Smith, *Freedom's Fetters, The Alien and Sedition Laws and American Civil Liberties* (Ithaca: Cornell University Press, Cornell Paperbacks ed., 1966), pp. 400–414.

5. John Adams to Benjamin Stoddert, March 31, 1801, in *The Works of John Adams*, ed. Charles F. Adams, 10 vols. (Boston: Little, Brown, and Co.,

1850–1856), 9: 582. For a list of the radical émigrés who worked in American journalism, see Durey, "Thomas Paine's Apostles," pp. 687–88. For other accounts of their backgrounds and activities, see Richard J. Twomey, "Jacobins and Jeffersonians: Anglo-American Radical Ideology, 1790–1810," in *The Origins of Anglo-American Radicalism*, ed. Margaret Jacob and James Jacob (London: George Allen & Unwin, 1984), pp. 284–99; Ray Boston, "The Impact of 'Foreign Liars' on the American Press, (1790–1800)," *Journalism Quarterly* 50 (Winter 1973): 722–30.

      6. A, August 11, 1802; Kim Tousley Phillips, "William Duane, Revolutionary Editor" (Ph.D. dissertation, University of California, Berkeley, 1968), pp. 57–58; Smith, *Freedom's Fetters*, pp. 334–58; Thomas Jefferson to James Monroe, July 15, 1802, in *The Writings of Thomas Jefferson*, ed. Paul L. Ford, 10 vols. (G. P. Putnam's Sons, 1892–1899), 8: 164–66. For Callender's denial of various details in Duane's story, see *The Recorder*, August 25, 1802.

      7. Phillips, "William Duane, Revolutionary Editor," pp. 4–54.

      8. Tench Coxe to Margaret Bache, September 13, 1798, as quoted in Cooke, *Tench Coxe and the Early Republic*, p. 346; Phillips, "William Duane, Revolutionary Editor," p. 59; A, November 1, 1798.

      9. A, November 1, 1798; Smith, *Freedom's Fetters*, pp. 173, 277–306; Culver H. Smith, *The Press, Politics, and Patronage, The American Government's Use of Newspapers, 1789–1875* (Athens: University of Georgia Press, 1977), pp. 26–29, 43–44; Thomas Jefferson to William Wirt, March 30, 1811, in Ford, ed., *The Writings of Thomas Jefferson*, 9: 316–17; Thomas Jefferson to William Wirt, May 3, 1811, ibid., 9: 319.

      10. On the development of a professional ideology among early American journalists, see, generally, Jeffery A. Smith, *Printers and Press Freedom: The Ideology of Early American Journalism* (New York: Oxford University Press, 1988).

A Note on Sources

AT LEAST TWO OF THE MANY WORKS CONCERNING BENJAMIN FRANKLIN
examine his political identity. Paul W. Conner's *Poor Richard's Politics, Benjamin Franklin and His New American Order* (New York, 1965)
is an excellent starting point for understanding Franklin's idealism.
Also valuable, especially for seeing Franklin as a proto-Jeffersonian,
are portions of Drew McCoy, *The Elusive Republic, Political Economy
in Jeffersonian America* (Chapel Hill, 1980). Particularly useful on his
personal life is Claude-Anne Lopez and Eugenia Herbert, *The Private
Franklin, The Man and His Family* (New York, 1975).

In contrast to the admiration usually given to Franklin, historians have tended to ignore or denounce the grandson he so assiduously
raised to follow in his footsteps. The most detailed treatment of
Franklin's namesake is James D. Tagg, "Benjamin Franklin Bache and
the Philadelphia *Aurora*" (Ph.D dissertation, Wayne State University,
1973). In his published work on Bache to date, Professor Tagg has
depicted Franklin's grandson as a writer of "glib generalities" and as
an embittered radical whose journalism did not always remain "within
the bounds of political sanity." See James D. Tagg, "The Limits of
Republicanism: The Reverend Charles Nisbet, Benjamin Franklin
Bache, and the French Revolution," *Pennsylvania Magazine of History
and Biography* 112 (October 1988): 503–43, and "Benjamin Franklin
Bache's Attack on George Washington," *Pennsylvania Magazine of
History and Biography* 100 (April 1976): 191–230.

Franklin and Bache are the subjects of Bernard Fay's hagio-

213

graphic *The Two Franklins: Fathers of American Democracy* (Boston: 1933). Fay's book, a work colored by adulation and emotion, relies on historical imagination as much as evidence. Its value today lies mainly in its illustrations, such as documents and caricatures from the late eighteenth century.

In evaluating the career of Benjamin Franklin Bache, some room can be found between the scornful and the worshipful. Like his grandfather, Bache was a skilled and generally consistent advocate of populist Jeffersonian themes. Both Franklin and Bache could be formidable and occasionally merciless adversaries when their fundamental convictions were under attack. See Jeffery A. Smith, *Printers and Press Freedom, The Ideology of Early American Journalism* (New York, 1988), pp. 95–161.

Bache's publications were not uniquely outlandish or dogmatic for their time. Scholarship dealing with the highly vituperative journalism of the 1790s includes Lance Banning, *The Jeffersonian Persuasion, Evolution of a Party Ideology* (Ithaca, N.Y., 1978); Donald H. Stewart, *The Opposition Press of the Federalist Period* (Albany, N.Y., 1969); and James Morton Smith, *Freedom's Fetters: The Alien and Sedition Laws and American Civil Liberties* (Ithaca, N.Y., 1956). An article which indicates the importance of British and Irish journalists in the Republican press of the time, including some of Bache's associates, is Michael Durey, "Thomas Paine's Apostles: Radical Emigrés and the Triumph of Jeffersonian Republicanism," *William and Mary Quarterly*, 3rd ser., 44 (October 1987): 661–88.

Many of the surviving Franklin and Bache manuscripts are among the collections at the American Philosophical Society in Philadelphia. Another principal repository of Franklin's papers is the Yale University Library. Scholars are indebted to *The Papers of Benjamin Franklin* project (New Haven, 1959—   ), a comprehensive edition of his works and correspondence. Some Bache papers, which have been used by past historians and which offer fragmentary details of his personal life as an adult, remain in private hands and currently are not available to researchers.

Index

215